FEB 2003

BAD NEIGHBOR POLICY

BAD NEIGHBOR POLICY

Washington's Futile War
on Drugs in Latin America

Ted Galen Carpenter

A Cato Institute Book

1327341?

BAD NEIGHBOR POLICY

First published 2003 by
PALGRAVE MACMILLAN™
175 Fifth Avenue, New York, N.Y. 10010 and
Houndmills, Basingstoke, Hampshire, England RG21 6XS.
Companies and representatives throughout the world.

PALGRAVE MACMILLAN is the global academic imprint of the Palgrave Macmillan
division of St. Martin's Press, LLC and of Palgrave Macmillan Ltd. Macmillan® is a
registered trademark in the United States, United Kingdom and other countries.
Palgrave is a registered trademark in the European Union and other countries.

ISBN 1-4039-6137-9 hardback

Library of Congress Cataloging-in-Publication Data

Carpenter, Ted Galen.
    Bad neighbor policy: Washington's futile war on drugs in Latin America / Ted Galen
Carpenter.
        p. cm.
    Includes index.
    ISBN 1-4039-6137-9
        1. Narcotics, Control of--United States. 2. Drug traffic--Latin America. 3. Drug
    traffic--United States. 4. Drug abuse--United States. 5. United States--Foreign
    relations--Latin America. 6. Latin America--Foreign relations--United States. I. Title.

HV5825 .C34 2003
363.45'0973--dc21

                                                                    20023032248

A catalogue record for this book is available from the British Library.

Design by planettheo.com

First edition: February 2003
10 9 8 7 6 5 4 3 2 1

Printed in the United States of America.

Contents

ACKNOWLEDGMENTS

I owe a debt of gratitude to numerous people for helping to make this book possible. Edward H. Crane, president of the Cato Institute, has provided sustained backing for my work in foreign policy over a period of nearly two decades and was especially enthusiastic about this project. William A. Niskanen, chairman of the Cato Institute, and other members of the Institute's staff have likewise been consistently supportive of my work on the international drug war and other issues.

My appreciation goes out as well to Michael Flamini, my editor at Palgrave/St. Martin's, and his assistant, Amanda Johnson, for their work on this project. David Boaz, Doug Bandow, and Ian Vasquez all made insightful comments and suggestions on an earlier draft of the book. Alina Stefanescu, Daniya Tamendarova, and Jennifer Savage put in many hours and provided invaluable assistance with the research, including tracking down sometimes elusive sources. Jennifer Assenza, my administrative assistant, did her usual splendid job preparing the manuscript.

Most of all, I want to thank my wife, Barbara, for her patience and unwavering support even when her husband at times seemed a trifle obsessed with his subject.

THIRTY YEARS OF FAILURE

Veronica ("Roni") Bowers had no reason to imagine that she and her family would suddenly become casualties of the war on drugs in April 2001. Bowers, her husband, Jim, their seven-month-old daughter, Charity, and six-year-old son, Cory, were aboard a Cessna 185 floatplane flying over northeastern Peru. Bowers and her husband were Baptist missionaries who had spent much of the previous seven years among the inhabitants of that remote region trying to win converts to their faith. On that pleasant Friday afternoon, they were headed for the airport in the city of Iquitos.

Perhaps unknown to the Bowers, the United States and the Peruvian government had been cooperating for years in a controversial effort to stem the outflow of coca leaf from Peru to the cocaine-processing labs in neighboring Colombia. U.S. surveillance planes provided information to the Peruvian air force on aircraft that were suspected of carrying drug shipments. The Peruvians, in turn, would send up fighter planes to intercept a suspicious aircraft and order the pilot to land at a designated airport. If a plane attempted to take evasive action—or even if the pilot merely failed to respond—the Peruvian policy was to shoot the plane down.

On that fateful April afternoon a surveillance plane operated by Central Intelligence Agency (CIA) contract employees identified the plane carrying the Bowers family as a suspect craft and the

Peruvian air force sent up an A-37B Dragonfly attack plane to intercept. What happened next is still not clear. Peruvian authorities have insisted that the Bowers plane was hailed repeatedly by radio but failed to give any response. The pilot of the Cessna, Kevin Donaldson, and others aboard the plane would later testify that there had been no contact. Perhaps the Peruvian fighter and the missionaries' plane were operating on different radio frequencies.

In any case, Roni Bowers and her infant daughter were killed instantly as machine gun bullets from the Peruvian jet ripped through the fuselage of their small plane. Donaldson, who was so badly wounded that he was unable to walk for months after the incident, miraculously managed to crash-land the plane in the nearby Amazon River. Jim and Cory Bowers survived with minor injuries.

Within hours the blame game began. The U.S. surveillance plane had apparently identified the Cessna as a suspect aircraft because no flight plan had been filed for it. (The missionary organization would later assert vehemently that a flight plan had been filed.)[1] What happened after the Cessna had been marked as a suspect became a topic for intense dispute between Peruvian and U.S. authorities. Washington insisted that the crew on the surveillance plane had urged the Peruvians not to fire on the Cessna without additional evidence that it probably was carrying drugs. U.S. officials further implied that the Peruvian air force had disregarded a number of procedures in handling such cases. Officials in Lima told a very different story, insisting that the air force pilot had followed all procedures "to the letter" and that they had acted in good faith on the information supplied by the CIA aircraft.[2] A subsequent U.S. State Department investigation concluded that both U.S. and Peruvian personnel had become lax over the years in executing the procedures required before an aircraft could be fired on and that both sides therefore bore some responsibility for the incident.[3]

Defenders of the drug war conceded that the episode was a terrible tragedy but insisted that it should not detract from the great successes of the program to that date. Critics, though, suggested that approving and funding a strategy that allowed aircraft merely suspected of carrying drugs to be blown out of the skies made such a tragedy inevitable. Indeed, was it certain that all of the passengers in the more than two dozen planes shot down previously had been drug runners? Could some have been innocent victims? Because the victims in the April incident were Americans with impeccable backgrounds, the tragedy received massive media coverage. But was it reasonable to assume that this was the first such bungled episode, or was it more likely that earlier mistakes had been quietly buried?[4] As those and other questions were asked, the United States decided to suspend the surveillance flights and the shoot-down policy indefinitely. That was, of course, small comfort to the surviving members of the Bowers family and their friends and loved ones.

Roni and Charity Bowers had become the latest innocent fatalities in Washington's three-decade-old war on drugs. But they were hardly the only ones.

Nearly a decade earlier, millionaire rancher and businessman Donald Scott and his wife were victimized by excessive zeal—and perhaps outright greed—on the part of drug warriors. In 1992 Scott and his new wife lived on a 200-acre ranch along the spine of the coastal mountains above Malibu, California. A tragic chain of events began when the local deputy sheriff received a tip that several thousand marijuana plants were growing on the ranch. In the early-morning hours, more than a half-dozen local, state, and federal law enforcement agencies executed a search warrant by smashing in the Scotts' front door. Undoubtedly assuming that criminals were breaking into his home, Donald Scott emerged into the hallway with a gun in his hand and was shot down, dying a short time later.

The various agencies scoured the ranch but failed to find the thousands of marijuana plants—or even evidence of any drug use by the Scotts. During a subsequent independent investigation, evidence emerged that the government agencies may have been overzealous because of the potential value of the ranch. Under state and federal forfeiture laws, property can be seized and retained by the government if it can be shown that the property *may* have been involved in the commission of a crime (especially drug trafficking). One document uncovered in the investigation was a map, with a note the deputy had scrawled: "80 acres sold for $800,000 in the same area." The investigator concluded, "Clearly, one of the primary purposes was a land grab by the Sheriff's Department."[5]

Esequiel Hernández came from a very different background from either Roni Bowers or Donald Scott, but he ended up the same way—a fatality in the war on drugs. Hernández was an 18-year-old goatherder in south Texas near the border with Mexico. One spring day in 1997, he was out herding his goats when he encountered a U.S. Marine antidrug patrol. Members of the patrol spotted Hernández and saw that he was carrying a gun (which is lawful in Texas). He allegedly fired two shots from his .22, vaguely in the direction of the patrol. The marines later testified that they did not return fire at that time but instead shadowed Hernández for more than 20 minutes. What happened next is not clear. According to the marines, Hernández again raised his rifle, at which point a marine corporal opened fire and killed him.

At no point did any evidence emerge that the goatherder was involved in the drug trade. Despite its initial efforts to defend the marine's actions, the government eventually settled a wrongful death lawsuit with the Hernández family for $1.9 million.[6]

But innocent parties mistakenly gunned down by the authorities are not the only victims in the war on drugs. The nonviolent drug offenders who fill America's jails and prisons also are casualties in that conflict. So too are the residents of America's inner cities, who have all too often seen their neighborhoods turned into war zones as rival drug gangs battle to control the vast black market profits from selling illegal drugs. Even when inner-city residents avoid getting caught in the crossfire, they must watch as hardened criminals—and often neighborhood teenagers—make vastly more money from an illegal enterprise than they could ever hope to make from legal jobs. That kind of corruption of a community may be difficult to quantify, but it has a very real deleterious effect on the quality of life.

Washington's war on drugs has amassed victims in other countries as well. The upsurge in violence that has occurred in Colombia, Peru, and other drug-source countries is caused—or at least exacerbated—by America's insistence on a prohibitionist strategy. The level of violence in Colombia now places in jeopardy the continued viability of that country's democratic political system. Tens of thousands of innocent people have been injured or killed in the war between government forces and antigovernment insurgents and their drug-trafficking allies. Ordinary farmers are also victimized by U.S.-sponsored and funded aerial spraying programs to eradicate drug crops. Many times, those eradication campaigns destroy not only drug crops but the food crops that hard-pressed peasants need to avert destitution and famine. Those people are very real casualties in the war on drugs.

The growing roster of drug-war victims is one reason why prominent Americans, even elected officials, are beginning to speak out against the prohibitionist strategy. One recent convert is New Mexico's Republican governor Gary Johnson. His assessment of the drug war is scathing: "We are presently spending $50 billion a year on the war on drugs. . . . For all the money we are putting into the war on drugs, it is an absolute failure."[7] Heracio Serpa, the Liberal Party's candidate in Colombia's 2002 presidential election, reaches a strikingly similar conclusion with respect to his country. "Today, there is more cocaine being produced, more trafficking, more traffickers, and larger areas under cultivation," he charges. There needs to be a recognition "that the counterdrug policies applied to date have been a failure."[8]

The futility of the prohibitionist strategy—and especially that component dedicated to eradicating the supply of drugs—was implicitly conceded by a retired agent of the Drug Enforcement Administration (DEA) in October 2000: "Twenty years ago, I read a study in the DEA—I'll never forget it—done by our Intelligence Division—a very well-documented study that said the average drug-trafficking organization . . . could afford to lose 90 percent of its product and still be profitable."[9] Dennis Jett, a former ambassador to Peru and an ardent drug warrior, nevertheless makes a pithy observation: "When the Bush administration tires of patting itself on the back for the successful war in Afghanistan, it might consider the war it is losing—the one on drugs."[10]

Data confirm such pessimistic assessments. But despite what Jett says, the failure is not a recent one attributable to the administration of George W. Bush. President Richard Nixon proclaimed the initial war on drugs more than three decades ago, and since that time the United States has repeatedly pressured the drug-source countries of Latin America to stem the flow of illegal drugs. In 1986 President Ronald Reagan proclaimed drug trafficking to be a threat to the national security of the United States and escalated the pressure on America's hemispheric neighbors. Reagan's successors have all pursued similar policies.

Despite such efforts, the campaign against the supply of illegal drugs is no closer to success than it was when Nixon first issued his declaration of war. The U.S. State Department's own figures show that a larger quantity of drugs is flowing out of Latin America today than during the mid-1980s (see chapter 4). The increase has occurred despite a concerted effort by the United States and the drug-source countries to eradicate the supply.

There is other evidence that the supply-side campaign is especially futile. The main purpose of efforts to disrupt the supply of illicit drugs is to drive up the retail price and thereby, theoretically at least, to reduce demand. Yet after some three decades of intense efforts, the retail prices of heroin and cocaine in the United States are at or near record lows.[11] Measured in 1998 dollars, a pure gram of heroin sold for approximately $1,000 in 2001. The price in

1981 was $5,000. A gram of cocaine sold for $150 in 2001, just slightly above its record low price of $110 in 1996 and well below its $490 going rate in 1981. The price of marijuana has risen—from $3 a bulk gram in 1981 to $9 in 2001—but that drug too is well off its record high of $14 in 1991. If the supply-side campaign were working, we would see sharp and sustained increases in the street prices of drugs. Instead, we see just a slight upward trend in marijuana prices and sharp downward trends in heroin and cocaine prices.

It is even more sobering to note that the illegal drug trade now has a truly global market. Former DEA administrator Jack Lawn notes, "Cocaine has become a substantial problem in Europe, and they were not ready for it."[12] Former assistant secretary of state for international narcotics matters Mathea Falco suggests that the problem is even more widespread: "Worldwide drug production has geometrically expanded." It has "just become larger than we could have ever dreamed in the late 1970s."[13]

But it is not just the production that has soared. Indeed, drug production would not have increased so dramatically if there had not been an increase in consumer demand, much of it occurring outside the United States. Illegal drug use in the United States has been basically flat for several years, with declines in consumption among casual users being offset by increases among hard-core users. But in Europe, especially in the nations that emerged from the wreckage of the Soviet Union, demand has soared in the past decade.[14] A similar development has occurred in other regions. As Brookings Institution scholar Paul B. Stares notes, "By all indications, the market for illicit drugs is expanding inexorably around the world. Moreover, there are good reasons to fear that the global market for drugs will continue to expand in the foreseeable future."[15]

That development has important implications. Even if demand in the United States could be sharply reduced, there is more than enough potential profit globally to keep the drug cartels in business for many years to come. Moreover, satisfying the demand of the American market does not tax the resources of drug-trafficking organizations. As Falco points out, "Four Boeing 747 cargo planes or thirteen trailer trucks can supply American cocaine consumption for a year."[16] The volume required to satisfy the habits of American heroin users would be far less, and that needed to meet annual marijuana consumption only modestly greater.

Given the realities of global consumption, the only alternative open to the prohibitionists is to try to smash the existing suppliers and to prevent other entrepreneurs from replacing them. But as we shall see, that strategy has been tried for three decades without success. Ultimately, the prohibitionist approach is an attempt to repeal the economic law of supply and demand, and therefore it is doomed to fail. Wrapping the prohibitionist strategy in the trappings of a "war" merely shows that its advocates do not understand the nature of real warfare or what constitutes an attainable objective.[17] In only one respect does the drug war resemble a real war: It causes a stupendous amount of collateral damage.

It is bad enough when U.S. policy inflicts such damage on American society. But not only has Washington's drug war caused severe domestic problems, it has created enormous difficulties for our neighbors in the Western Hemisphere. It has fueled civil wars in both Peru and Colombia, where the black market premium caused by a prohibitionist strategy has enabled the illicit drug trade to provide unparalleled financial resources to insurgent groups. Tactics used in the drug war also are creating a variety of grievances among significant portions of the population, thereby generating additional popular support for antigovernment movements. The war on drugs has exacerbated the problems of corruption and criminal violence in all of the drug-source countries. Especially worrisome is evidence that the horrific violence that has convulsed Colombia since the 1980s is now being replicated in our next-door neighbor, Mexico. And, finally, the drug war is leading to a surge of resentment against the United States throughout the hemisphere, as Washington pursues increasingly uncompromising and abrasive tactics to get Latin American governments to wage a more vigorous drug war against their own citizens.

President Franklin D. Roosevelt championed a Good Neighbor Policy for relations with the rest of the hemisphere in the 1930s. Washington's conduct on the drug issue over the past three decades has been the opposite. U.S. officials have bribed, cajoled, and coerced Latin American governments to try to stem the outflow of illegal drugs. The result has been a rising tide of corruption and violence in those countries and a growing dissatisfaction on the part of affected populations with their own governments—and with the United States. Washington's hemispheric war on drugs is the epitome of a Bad Neighbor Policy.

CHAPTER ONE

FORGING THE BAD NEIGHBOR POLICY:
THE DRUG WAR FROM NIXON TO REAGAN

It was perhaps appropriate, given his image, that Richard Nixon would be the president to explicitly declare a "war" on drugs. Although Nixon's announcement to the press on June 17, 1971, and his subsequent message to Congress on the same day generally are viewed as the key events, his strident policy should have come as no surprise.[1] Nixon's election campaign in 1968 had stressed the need to restore "law and order" in America (an especially ironic promise, given that his administration turned out to be the most lawless in the nation's history), and cracking down on narcotics was an important subtheme of that message. In a September 1968 speech in Anaheim, California, Nixon addressed the issue in emotional and uncompromising terms, describing illegal drugs as "a modern curse of American youth" and promising to "take the executive steps necessary to make our borders more secure against the pestilence of narcotics."[2]

Of course, Nixon did not invent the drug prohibitionist strategy or even the nation's commitment to strike at the source of illegal drugs outside our borders. The domestic prohibitionist strategy received its initial impetus from the passage of the Harrison Act in 1914, and the U.S. involvement in international antidrug efforts dates from its adherence to the Hague Convention for the control of opium sales in 1912. In addition, the United States had pursued a variety of antidrug initiatives throughout the Western Hemisphere during the decades prior to the 1970s.[3] But by proclaiming that the fight against illicit drugs was the functional and moral equivalent of war, Nixon escalated the stakes.

Although the Nixon administration's efforts to curtail the supply of illicit drugs focused on such heroin-source countries as France and Turkey, one of the earliest coercive measures was applied against Mexico. In fact, it predated Nixon's celebrated declaration of a war on drugs. In early 1969 Nixon established the Presidential Task Force Relating to Narcotics, Marijuana and Dangerous Drugs (otherwise known as Task Force One), which attempted to combine the talents of the Justice Department's Bureau of Narcotics and Dangerous Drugs and the Treasury Department's customs bureau for a joint operation against Mexican drug traffickers. (It was also apparently a mechanism to try to end the turf fights between the two departments over which group would have the lead role in efforts to stem the flow of drugs into the United States.) Task Force One's report, submitted in June of 1969, recommended that the highest priority should be "an eradication of the production and refinement in Mexico of opium poppies and marijuana."[4] Not only did the report contend that Mexico was a crucial source of heroin entering the United States, but it asserted that marijuana was a critical "stepping stone" to heroin addiction. As usual, the report cited no evidence to support its assertion that marijuana was a gateway drug leading users to move on to more potent—and addictive—drugs.

The resulting confrontation with Mexico is recounted vividly by Watergate conspirator G. Gordon Liddy, who was at the time a special assistant to the secretary of the treasury. Task Force One, on which Liddy served, wanted to obtain Mexico's consent for U.S.-directed aerial reconnaissance of Mexican drug fields and for "chemical crop destruction" efforts. At a bilateral meeting in June 1969, Washington's "request" was presented to Mexican officials.

Liddy describes Mexico's resistance in his own inimitable style: "When the United States and Mexico met . . . the Mexicans, using diplomatic language, of course, told us to go piss up a rope. The Nixon Administration didn't believe in the United States' taking crap from any foreign government. Its reply was Operation Intercept."[5]

Operation Intercept was the concerted application of a maximum-right-to-search policy. Two thousand customs and border patrol agents were deployed along the Mexican border for what was officially described as the nation's largest peacetime search-and-seizure operation. Technically, both Mexico and the United States have the right to carefully search individuals and vehicles crossing the border, but normally inspections are brief or nonexistent. Given the amount of traffic crossing the U.S.-Mexican border each day, comprehensive inspections would create monumental traffic snarls and create havoc with commerce—as they did in the weeks following the September 11, 2001, terrorist attacks. That is precisely what happened with Operation Intercept. The results, according to Liddy, were "as intended: chaos."[6]

Indeed it was. Automobiles and trucks crossing the border were delayed up to six hours in 100-degree temperatures. Travelers who seemed suspicious—or who dared complain—often were strip-searched. Thousands of Mexican workers lost their jobs in the United States because of the customs delays at the border. Ultimately more than 5 million citizens of the United States and Mexico were caught up in that nightmarish dragnet before it finally ended.[7]

Liddy was quite candid about the administration's motives for Operation Intercept, although he conceded that for "diplomatic reasons" the true purpose was not revealed at the time: "Operation Intercept, with its massive economic and social disruption, could be sustained far longer by the United States than by Mexico. It was an exercise in international extortion, pure and simple and effective, designed to bend Mexico to our will. We figured Mexico would hold out for about a month; in fact they caved in after about two weeks and we got what we wanted."[8]

In the short run, Operation Intercept did attain the desired concessions. Mexican leaders swallowed their pride and acquiesced in the notorious Paraquat marijuana eradication project (spraying plants with the herbicide Paraquat). The long-term repercussions of U.S. intimidation, however, may have been less favorable. Mexican leaders complained heatedly at the time about the operation, with President Gustavo Díaz Ordaz stating bluntly that the episode had created "a wall of suspicion" between the two countries.[9] A Mexican expert on the drug issue concluded more than two decades later that "Operation Intercept entailed high political and diplomatic costs."[10] It was certainly apparent to international observers that relations between the two countries were cool at best throughout the 1970s. While it would be too much to suggest that resentment over Operation Intercept was entirely responsible for that situation, it would be naive to assume that residual anger was not a contributing factor.

Although Richard Nixon officially declared a war on drugs, that "war" was waged only sporadically during his administration. Moreover, most of the administration's efforts focused on disrupting the heroin trade. Despite the impression created in the aftermath of Operation Intercept, marijuana was distinctly a secondary concern, and cocaine was barely on the policy radar screen—a situation that would remain largely true through the administrations of Gerald Ford and Jimmy Carter. The emphasis on fighting heroin received a major boost in the spring of 1971 when evidence emerged about the extent of addiction among U.S. troops stationed in Vietnam. Robert DuPont, director of the Narcotics Treatment Administration from 1970 to 1973, describes the influence of that development: "Two congressmen, [Robert] Steele and [Morgan] Murphy, went off to Vietnam, and they came back with explosive news, and that was that 10 to 15 percent of the servicemen were addicted to heroin and that they were coming back to this country by the thousands." According to DuPont, "that was what moved this issue to the front burner."[11] Indeed, Nixon then ordered his senior staff to make the issue of drug abuse their top priority. That, in turn, led to Nixon's announcement to Congress and the public of the war on drugs. As former Nixon aide Bud Krogh put it, "In terms of the narcotics program, this was really D-Day."[12] Congress passed Nixon's antidrug legislative proposal the following year without a single dissenting vote.

Matters continued to escalate. In March 1973 Nixon authorized the formation of a new law enforcement agency, the Drug Enforcement Administration. The DEA combined the narcotics agents from various departments to make a single federal entity responsible for the enforcement of drug laws.

Despite the "war" metaphor, a surprisingly large part of Nixon's anti-drug measures were devoted to treatment. Throughout his administration more money was spent on demand reduction than on law enforcement. Even the law enforcement component concentrated more on domestic aspects than international interdiction and eradication measures. Although there were efforts to get at the supply of narcotics, and some of those efforts sought to enlist the aid of drug-producing countries, the massive international supply-side offensive against drugs that is now such a major part of U.S. policy was still more than a decade away when Nixon left the presidency in disgrace in August 1974.

THE FORD AND CARTER INTERLUDE

Nixon's successors seemed even less committed to substantive action, especially on the domestic front. Gerald Ford and Jimmy Carter did use perfunctory antidrug rhetoric. Ford even called the abuse of hard drugs "a clear and present threat to the health and future of our nation" and urged Congress to authorize "minimum mandatory prison sentences" for high-level hard-drug traffickers."[13] Yet Ford's chief drug policy adviser, Robert DuPont, openly advocated the decriminalization of marijuana. [14] Even Ford himself made an implicit distinction between the purveyors of "hard" drugs and those who trafficked in marijuana. Moreover, there is little evidence that he regarded the campaign against illicit drugs as a high-priority item.

That lack of emphasis was even more evident during the Carter administration. The *New York Times* noted that law enforcement officials across the nation saw the administration "as being uncommitted to fighting drugs."[15] Criticism on that score even came from Carter's own appointees to the White House Council on Drug Abuse Strategy. David Musto, a research professor of psychiatry at Yale Medical School who had served on the council, admitted: "We were supposed to establish drug abuse policy for the Federal Government, and we did not do it." He added that during this period when drug imports were rising sharply, "the council, which was supposed to devise a strategy to deal with it, did not meet, despite our frequent requests for meetings."[16]

Key members of Carter's White House staff operated under a cloud of suspicion that not only did they regard drug use with indifference but that some of them indulged personally. There were, for example, persistent rumors about White House Chief of Staff Hamilton Jordan.[17] Dr. Peter Bourne, Carter's adviser on drug policy, resigned in July 1978 after admitting that he had written a prescription for Quaalude tablets using a phony name for a White House aide who sought the drug.[18] At the time of his resignation, Bourne alleged that there was "a high incidence" of marijuana use—and even some cocaine use—among White House staffers. President Carter issued a warning to his staff against the use of illegal drugs, yet he himself was quoted saying that he was "sure many people smoke marijuana, but I'm not going to ask about it."[19] Carter earlier had told Congress, "Penalties against possession of a drug should not be more damaging to an individual than the use of the drug itself."[20]

Nearly two decades later, drug warriors still regarded the Carter years with loathing. The late Representative Gerald Solomon (R-NY) asserted that "during the Carter administration, drug policy visibility softened," and he sought to establish a cause-and-effect relationship between that approach and the soaring use of illegal drugs during that period. Solomon noted that marijuana use among high school seniors at the end of the Carter presidency increased to the point that 50 percent of seniors admitted to having used the drug in the previous year and 10.7 percent were daily users.[21]

Government policy (especially at the state and local levels) as well as the trend in public opinion appeared to be moving toward a more tolerant approach to drug use throughout the mid-and late 1970s. That trend was most evident regarding the use of marijuana.[22] Eleven states effectively decriminalized private marijuana use during the decade. For example, California passed legislation providing that anyone caught with one ounce or less of marijuana would merely pay a $100 fine.[23] The Alaska supreme court even ruled that personal use of marijuana in one's own home was protected under privacy rights guaranteed by the state constitution.[24] Other jurisdictions substantially reduced penalties for drug offenses, and the legalization option was increasingly discussed.[25] Contrary to the mythology fostered by drug prohibitionists that decriminalization or legalization would produce an explosive increase in drug use, there were negligible effects on the general level of consumption in the eleven states that pursued the decriminalization option.[26]

Americans, and especially American youth, also appeared to be drifting toward a more tolerant attitude toward drug use and a cautious acceptance of the drug culture. From 1975 to 1979 the number of high school seniors reporting that they did not disapprove of occasional use of marijuana increased from 53.1 percent to 65.8 percent. The number who thought that "using marijuana should be entirely legal" increased from 27.3 percent to 32.1

percent. There was even a softening of attitudes regarding the use of harder drugs; the number of high school seniors expressing no disapproval of occasional use of cocaine rose from 18.7 percent in 1975 to 25.3 percent in 1979.[27]

The Ford and Carter administrations did not deemphasize the international phase of the drug war to the same extent that they let the domestic phase wane, however. During those years, the United States continued to apply significant pressure on Mexico to eradicate its marijuana and opium poppy crops.[28] And efforts to encourage crop eradication and interdiction measures in Colombia, Peru, and Bolivia actually increased.[29] But those efforts paled in comparison to the policies Washington would adopt in the 1980s and 1990s.

THE DRUG WAR RESURGENT UNDER REAGAN

The trend toward a more tolerant domestic attitude on drug use reversed dramatically during the Reagan years, as actions taken by the administration created an unprecedented antidrug hysteria. But there were signs of a backlash even before Reagan took office. During the final two years of the Carter administration, a nationwide network of parents groups, concerned about the rising incidence of casual drug use among minors, began to work with the DEA as well as state and local law enforcement agencies to pass new antidrug measures. That network, the Parents Movement, had more than 1,000 chapters by 1980 and was pushing (with the enthusiastic cooperation of the DEA) for a national law to ban the sale of "drug paraphernalia." Keith Stroup, president of the National Organization for the Reform of Marijuana Laws (NORML), the largest organization lobbying for decriminalization, later recalled ruefully, "We very much underestimated the power of that movement." He noted that the decriminalization movement scored its last victory in 1978, when Nebraska voted to decriminalize possession of small quantities of marijuana. "And for the next 20 years, we didn't win a single significant victory."[30]

Ronald Reagan's attitude on the drug issue became clear early in his tenure as president. His September 1981 speech to the International Association of Chiefs of Police launched a new and decidedly militant phase in both the domestic and international components of the drug war. The president placed illicit drug use and the international drug trade in the context of a larger "crime epidemic" afflicting the United States. Mapping a comprehensive assault on the drug problem, he declared his intention to strengthen domestic law-enforcement and educational efforts to stem consumer demand and stressed the need to discourage international production and distribution. Reagan's proposed "narcotics enforcement strategy" included "a foreign policy that vigorously seeks to interdict and eradicate illicit drugs, wherever cultivated, processed, or transported."[31] The president also announced the formation of the Special Council on Narcotics Control—consisting of the attorney general and secretaries of state, defense, and the treasury as well as other officials—to coordinate efforts to stop the flow of illegal drugs into the United States. In June 1982, the president, speaking from the Rose Garden of the White House, declared, "We're taking down the surrender flag that has flown over so many drug efforts. We're running up a battle flag."[32]

Reagan's militancy increased the breadth and intensity of U.S. antidrug efforts, particularly in the international arena. Secretary of State George Shultz succinctly expressed the administration's perspective in a September 1984 address before the Miami Chamber of Commerce. He stressed that "drug abuse is not only a top priority for this Administration's domestic policy, it is a top priority in our foreign policy as well."[33]

The Reagan administration's enthusiasm for revitalizing the drug war was partly a reaction to the tremendous upsurge in drug use that had taken place during the 1970s. By the early 1980s, there were more than 20 million marijuana smokers and 3 to 5 million cocaine users in the United States. The DEA estimated that the value of illicit drug sales in the United Sates exceeded $80 billion in 1981.[34]

For conservatives of Reagan's stamp, widespread drug use was not merely a public health problem, it offended a wide range of deeply held social views. They blamed drugs for the massive increase in street crimes, noting that compulsive drug users committed a high percentage of robberies, burglaries, and other offenses to support their habits.[35] (As in other periods, the drug warriors of the 1980s were oblivious to the point that prohibitionist drug laws, not the mere existence of drugs, cause such problems.) In addition to assuming links between drug use and crime, many conservatives were alarmed that drugs were corrupting America's youth. The drug culture, in their view, both reflected and contributed to the decline of "traditional morality" and "family values." Shultz typified that assumption when he stated, "Drug abuse is one of the lingering symptoms of a deeper social and cultural phenomenon: the weakening of the traditional values of family and community and religious faith that we have suffered for some time in Western Society."[36] Senator Paula Hawkins (R-FL) was even more alarmist when she asserted that drugs constituted "the single most threatening menace to civilization today."[37] Mounting drug use in the United States threatened core conservative doctrine about the nature of a moral society. In the early 1980s, liberals still generally resisted the crusading mentality against drugs, and some openly lampooned it; by the end of the decade, however, many were echoing the beliefs of their conservative brethren.

It was hardly surprising that people who viewed illegal drug use as conduct that threatened the very foundations of civilization were determined to wage a vigorous drug war. As they viewed the situation in the United States, however, they were uncertain whether they could effectively dampen the burgeoning demand for drugs. Consequently, they increasingly emphasized another option: trying to shut off the supply.

It was not a new idea. The United States had been a major sponsor of the 1912 Hague Convention, which established the foundation of international antinarcotics efforts, and had exerted considerable pressure on Peru, Bolivia, Colombia, and other Latin American drug-source countries to adhere to its provisions. U.S. officials had devoted considerable attention to stemming the flow of marijuana and heroin from Mexico during the 1930s and 1940s.[38] Reagan administration leaders were also aware of initiatives taken during the Nixon—and even the Ford and Carter— years to disrupt the supply of illicit drugs. The difference was primarily one of degree: Reagan and his political allies ratcheted the supply-side campaign up several notches beyond any previous efforts. Between fiscal years 1980 and 1987, U.S. spending on international narcotics efforts more than tripled.[39] Since at least 80 percent of the drugs on the nation's streets in the early 1980s came from outside the United States (primarily from Latin America), it was probably inevitable that antidrug efforts would become a more prominent component of U.S. foreign policy. By 1982 the DEA was significantly expanding its activities in Colombia. Soon other drug-producing countries would become targets of increased attention by U.S. drug warriors.

The Reagan administration's supply-side strategy had three major components: drug-crop eradication projects, the interdiction of drug-trafficking routes, and crop substitution programs. To implement those objectives, Washington concentrated on training, equipping, and advising indigenous antinarcotics forces (police or military units), facilitated the creation of special drug eradication paramilitary organizations in those drug-source countries where such units did not yet exist, and injected financial subsidies to support antidrug efforts when local resources were insufficient. The overall goal was to encourage, persuade, bribe, or coerce foreign governments into joining the U.S.-led drug war.

The administration's crusade ran into an array of difficulties. Despite considerable propaganda to the contrary, U.S. officials encountered indifference, passive obstructionism, and occasional outright defiance from foreign governments, especially in Latin America. The leaders of Bolivia and Peru were particularly adamant about not treating coca farming (as opposed to cocaine trafficking) as a criminal matter. Bolivia especially resisted efforts to "militarize" counternarcotics efforts, instead proposing to buy out coca farmers or promote crop substitution and alternative development schemes.[40] As the Reagan administration's campaign progressed, it also became clear that some foreign leaders were themselves deeply involved in the drug trade, or at least were willing to look the other way as important political and economic constituencies pursued profits in the lucrative black market.

Even when that was not the case, U.S. officials conceded that they had to struggle to overcome a pervasive assumption on the part of governments in drug-source and drug-transiting countries that illegal drugs were a U.S. problem. Francisco Thoumi, director of the Center for International Studies at the Universidad de Los Andes in Bogotá, Colombia, described the prevailing attitude in his country in the 1970s and early 1980s: "Colombians tended to see the drug consumption issue as an 'American problem' that had its roots in the Vietnam War and the rebellion of American youth against the establishment. The drug problem, if there was one, had to be dealt with on the demand side."[41] Although foreign leaders tended to respond to Washington's antidrug programs with apathy, some were hostile. Bolivian Undersecretary of the Interior Gustávo Sanchez epitomized such resentment when he asserted that he and his countrymen were being asked to put their lives in danger merely "to prevent drugs from entering the U.S." A high-level Panamanian official was even more caustic. "The U.S. is to blame for most of this mess," he fumed. "If there weren't the frightening demand in the States, we wouldn't even have to worry about trying to eliminate the supply."[42]

There were several reasons for the resistance to the Reagan administration's demands. At the time, most drug-producing nations did not have serious internal drug abuse problems. Consequently, they saw the U.S. sense of urgency as either overwrought or self-serving. Latin American and other Third World leaders concluded that they were being asked to assume onerous law-enforcement burdens merely to alleviate a social problem in the rich and spoiled United States.

A significant cultural difference strengthened the perception that drug abuse was primarily a "Yankee problem." Many—although assuredly not all—Latin American societies exhibited a more tolerant attitude toward moderate drug use. In the mountainous regions of Peru and Bolivia, for example, people chewed coca leaves and drank coca tea for a variety of purposes, including to alleviate the adverse effects of working in high-altitude conditions. That was a custom that went back to the pre-Columbian era.[43] Similarly, rural Jamaicans often drank tea brewed from marijuana for both social and medicinal reasons. Casual marijuana use in Belize and several other Latin American countries was an accepted part of the culture.

Prior to the Reagan administration's intensification of the international drug war, several countries imposed no legal penalties for possession and/or cultivation of various drugs. Marijuana cultivation was legal in more than a half-dozen nations. Bolivia, Peru, Uruguay, and Paraguay permitted the possession of coca and its derivatives, and Bolivia and seven other countries tolerated coca leaf cultivation as well. Even opium poppy cultivation was legal in several (mostly Southwest Asian) countries.[44] Although the Reagan administration successfully pressured drug-source nations to close most of those loopholes, indigenous populations offered substantial resistance to prohibition. (Resistance among growers was so strong in Bolivia that no government was prepared to outlaw the cultivation of coca leaf entirely. Instead, officials sought to limit the size of the legal crop and prevent its diversion to cocaine production, which proved to be a hopeless task.)

Even more disconcerting to U.S. leaders than the apathy or hostility they encountered from many Latin American governments was the burgeoning evidence of official collusion in the drug trade. Long before the notorious case of Panamanian dictator Manuel Noriega at the end of the 1980s, it was clear that high-level members of Panama's government were involved in trafficking, money laundering, and other phases of the illegal drug business. In 1985 the general secretary of the Panamanian National Defense Forces was convicted of allowing Colombian traffickers to transport drug-processing chemicals through Panamanian territory in exchange for a $2 million bribe. It was also an open secret that Panama's reputation as a leading banking center in Latin America was at least partly a function of the money-laundering services that its major banks performed for drug-trafficking organizations.

Official corruption was hardly confined to Panama. The chief minister and two aides of the tiny Caribbean nation of Turks and Caicos were convicted of attempting to arrange a major drug deal in the United States. A 1985 Royal Commission investigative report portrayed the government of the Bahamas as riddled with corruption. Three ministers in the cabinet of Prime Minister Lynden O. Pindling were pressured to resign and two others were dismissed as a result of the report. Pindling himself was deeply implicated in the scandal, although he was able to survive politically for a time.[45] DEA agents based in Mexico, Colombia, Peru, and Bolivia generally operated under the assumption that a large percentage of police and military personnel were directly involved in the drug trade or at least routinely received bribes from drug-trafficking organizations. Such suspicions were confirmed by the frequency with which those organizations knew in advance of supposedly secret raids on their facilities.

Undoubtedly the most blatant and pervasive case of drug-related corruption took place in Bolivia from 1980 to 1982. In what became known as the cocaine coup, General Luis García Meza seized power and made the Bolivian government an active partner in drug-trafficking activities.[46] He proceeded to release imprisoned drug dealers, destroy incriminating evidence contained in government files, and terminate all cooperation with the United States on narcotics matters. Reputed drug traffickers also held important posts in García Meza's government. Although that episode may have been an especially flagrant case of official collusion in the drug trade, it was by no means an aberration in Bolivian politics. Drug-trafficking elements reportedly figured prominently in an abortive 1984 coup against President Hernán Siles Zauzo.[47] Later in the decade, Washington repeatedly pressured Bolivian regimes to dismiss officials who were implicated in the drug trade.[48]

Even when Latin American governments professed allegiance to Washington's supply-side war on drugs, cooperation was often perfunctory at best.[49] The underlying problem was that the Reagan administration's intensified campaign against drugs placed regimes in drug-source countries in an impossible bind. Given the rising anger about the "drug problem" in U.S. official circles, open resistance to Washington's policy demands was increasingly hazardous. At the same time, the drug trade was becoming ever more lucrative and was playing a larger and larger role in Latin American economies, particularly in the Andean region. Powerful political constituencies also had grown up around the trade—constituencies that had demonstrated they were capable of resorting to violence if their interests were threatened. During a period of just 18 months in 1984-85, drug-trafficking organizations assassinated Colombian justice minister Rodrigo Lara Bonilla, bombed the U.S. embassy in Bogotá, plotted the assassination of the U.S. ambassador to Bolivia, kidnapped and executed DEA agent Enrique Camarena in Mexico, and killed 19 members of a U.S.-sponsored coca-eradication project in Peru. There was also some evidence that the seizure of Colombia's Palace of Justice and the subsequent murder of 12 Supreme Court justices in 1985 by a left-wing guerrilla group was financed by the notorious Medellín drug cartel. The violence that has today become almost routine in Colombia received a major impetus in the mid- and late 1980s.

Given those conflicting pressures, officials in drug-source countries danced an elaborate political minuet with the United States and their own populations. They had to create the impression of cooperating with Washington without taking measures that might truly damage the drug-trafficking organizations. A misstep in one direction risked the loss of the vital U.S. export market through the imposition of trade sanctions and other forms of retaliation. A misstep in the other direction risked internal economic disruption and violent reprisals from angry drug traffickers and their followers. The delicate balancing act proved increasingly difficult for Latin American leaders as the decade progressed.

A few bolder Latin political leaders sought to turn the U.S. obsession with the drug problem to their own advantage, concluding that Washington might be willing to provide generous foreign aid packages to secure cooperation from the governments of drug-producing countries. When Peru's newly elected president Alan García announced a vigorous offensive against the cocaine trade in 1985, his interior minister quickly added that "a lot more help" was needed from the United States beyond the $4.4 million in law-enforcement funding that was then being provided. Other Peruvian officials admitted off the record that the new campaign against drugs was spurred largely by the hope that the Reagan administration would respond with assistance to lift Peru out of its economic crisis.

Bolivian vice president Julio Garrett-Aillon made an even more audacious play for extensive aid during an address before the United Nations General Assembly in September 1985. He proposed that the United States and other drug-consuming countries establish a fund to purchase coca leaves, thereby decreasing illicit supplies without damaging the economies of drug-producing nations. Garrett-Aillon likewise emphasized the impossibility of

Bolivia's devoting its limited resources to a campaign against the drug supply without such incentives.[50]

Such ploys for more aid had only limited effectiveness. Although aid flows from Washington increased throughout the decade, culminating in President George Bush's Andean Initiative—a $2.2 billion five-year program—announced in 1989, they never reached the levels that Latin American political leaders sought or hoped for. Furthermore, from the standpoint of the civilian leadership in drug-source countries, the aid that the United States did provide was a mixed blessing. In the view of hemisphere civilian leaders, too much of it went to the military establishments—an extremely dubious strategy given the long history of military coups throughout the region.

Yet some antidrug efforts did go forward. Both Peru and Bolivia committed themselves to ambitious eradication programs in the early 1980s. The Peruvian effort, though, barely passed the laugh test. At its peak in 1984, the program destroyed less than 4,000 hectares (nearly 10,000 acres) of coca—a quantity that one expert noted "was probably smaller than the acreage annually retired and replaced because it has ceased to be productive."[51] U.S. officials became so discouraged that they ended financial support for the forced eradication of drug crops in 1987, thereafter confining aid to seed-bed eradication programs at the edge of the main coca-growing area in the Upper Huallaga Valley. The Peruvian antidrug effort encountered an especially ominous obstacle in the mid-1980s with the appearance of the Maoist Sendero Luminoso (Shining Path) guerrilla movement in the valley. Shining Path agitators successfully portrayed the eradication program as a U.S.-orchestrated imperialist attack on local interests. As the Peruvian government's grip on the territory weakened, it became apparent that pursuing the offensive against coca could have some extremely unpleasant political side effects.

Antidrug programs fared only a little better in Bolivia. After the Bolivian government committed itself to an eradication program in

1983, Washington conditioned continued development assistance and narcotics control aid on the elimination of at least 4,000 hectares of coca by 1985 and the establishment of effective narcotics police control over the chief coca-growing region, the Chapare. La Paz's eradication efforts were minimal, however, and it was not until 1988 that the government relented to U.S. pressure and passed legislation making most coca farming illegal. That statute, Ley 1008, met with fierce resistance from coca farmers in the Chapare and elsewhere.[52] The United States tried to facilitate matters by paying peasants in the Chapare $2,000 for each hectare removed from production, but there was little evidence that the financial inducement actually caused a decline in coca output.

Despite its intensified supply-side war on drugs, the Reagan administration found itself under mounting criticism from even more hard-line elements in Congress as the campaign failed to produce results. Representative Charles Rangel (D-NY), chairman of the House Select Committee on Narcotics Abuse, asked if the executive branch was waging a serious war against the drug supply, "why has the amount of cocaine entering this country jumped from 25 tons in 1980 to over 125 tons this year [1985]?"[53] Rangel castigated the administration for failing to use some tools that Congress had given it to cut off foreign aid to countries that did not cooperate in America's antidrug effort. He boasted that on a recent 17-day trip to Latin America, his committee found that the leaders of Peru and Bolivia were "aware that Congress—not the administration—voted to cut off all aid other than anti-narcotics and humanitarian aid to them because they have ignored treaties they signed years ago to control coca production." Rangel noted with satisfaction that the presidents of both nations "have vowed to rectify that situation."[54] (Eight years after he made that comment, coca production had nearly tripled.) Rangel's criticism was indicative of an increasingly militant attitude toward drug-source countries in the mid-1980s—a militancy that crossed party lines.

Public and government hysteria about drugs reached record levels in 1986. A major catalyst for the upsurge in demand for a more hard-line policy was the highly publicized death of basketball star Len Bias from an overdose of cocaine. Virtually any congressional committee that even arguably had jurisdiction over some aspect of the drug issue held hearings and pushed through tough legislation. Congress began to rewrite virtually all of the nation's federal drug laws, culminating in the passage of the Anti-Drug Abuse Act that year. (Yet another omnibus drug abuse statute was passed just two years later.)[55] Measures included the death penalty for major traffickers, life in prison for some repeat offenders, and far more severe federal penalties for mere possession. The military was assigned a role (albeit a limited one) in drug interdiction. Federal penalties for money laundering were increased, and a new asset forfeiture law allowed federal agencies to keep the property they seized. The latter measure was an especially dangerous innovation. By 1989 the DEA received more income from asset seizures than it did from the budget appropriated by Congress. As one retired DEA special agent put it, "It was almost like a system of taxation. Here was a multibillion-dollar industry that was thriving, and we were able to tax it by taking assets away from it."[56]

DRUGS BECOME A NATIONAL SECURITY THREAT

The year 1986 was an important one for the escalation of both the international and the domestic drug war. A crucial step in both escalating and militarizing the international side of the antidrug effort came in April 1986, when President Reagan signed National Security Decision Directive (NSDD) 221 declaring drug trafficking to be a threat to the security of the United States.[57] The Decision Directive asserted: "The national security threat posed by the drug trade is particularly serious outside U.S. borders. Of primary concern are those nations with a flourishing narcotics industry, where a combination of international criminal trafficking organizations, rural insurgents, and urban terrorists can undermine the stability of local governments; corrupt efforts to curb drug crop production; and distort public perception of the narcotics issue in such a way that it becomes part of an anti-U.S. or anti-Western debate."[58]

The directive noted further that while such problems "are endemic to most nations plagued by narcotics, their effects are particularly insidious for the democratic states of the Western Hemisphere."[59] The narcotics trade "threatens the integrity of the democratic governments by corrupting political and judicial institutions. The effects on U.S. interests from such a situation can range from a regime unwilling or unable to cooperate with counter-narcotics programs to a government that is unable to control key areas of its territory and elements of its own judiciary, military or economy."[60] The directive also expressed concern that "some insurgent groups finance their activities through taxing drug activities, providing protection to local criminal traffickers, or growing their own drug crops. Access to money available from narcotics can have a major impact on the capability of insurgent forces." In addition to (radical leftist) insurgents, "some terrorist groups have been linked to drug smuggling primarily to finance their activities. The profits from even one consignment of narcotics could provide small terrorist cells with substantial operating capital."[61] For all those reasons, drug trafficking per se was deemed a serious menace to the national security of the United States.

In pursuit of the new strategy, NSDD mandated a number of specific actions by various government agencies:

- Full consideration of drug control activities in U.S. foreign assistance planning
- An expanded role for U.S. military forces in supporting counternarcotics efforts
- Additional emphasis on narcotics as a national security issue in discussions with other nations

- Greater participation by the U.S. intelligence community in supporting efforts to counter drug trafficking
- Improvements in counternarcotics telecommunications capabilities
- More assistance to other nations in establishing and implementing their own drug abuse and education programs.

Although portions of the directive remain classified, it is clear that the military and intelligence portions of the document were deemed the most important. The secretary of defense was directed to "develop and implement any modifications to applicable statutes, regulations, procedures, and guidelines to enable U.S. military forces to support counter-narcotics efforts more actively, consistent with the maintenance of force readiness and training."[62] Likewise, the director of central intelligence was ordered to "ensure that the intelligence community gives special emphasis . . . on all aspects of the international drug trade."[63] Unfortunately, major portions of the document that specify *how* the Department of Defense and the intelligence agencies were to increase their participation in the international antidrug campaign remain classified; thus we can only speculate about how much leeway they were given.

After the issuance of NSDD 221, supporters of the drug war redoubled their calls for the military to play an expanded role. After all, the principal function of the defense establishment is to neutralize serious threats to American security, and the president had certified that the drug trade posed such a threat. Conservative columnist James J. Kilpatrick exemplified the more militant attitude when he endorsed using the military in the drug fight: "Our soldiers, sailors and airmen are being paid to protect the national security. Let them earn their pay."[64]

Although using the military to help disrupt the supply of illegal drugs had the potential to entangle U.S. forces in difficult struggles in drug-source countries, such missions also offered opportunities to test equipment, personnel, and tactics. In the summer of 1986 Reagan's new strategy was put to the test when the United States dispatched six high-performance Black Hawk helicopters and 160 troops to Bolivia to assist the government of that country in its attempt to eradicate a network of cocaine-processing laboratories. American forces participated in the eradication effort—Operation Blast Furnace—for more than four months before they were withdrawn.[65]

Although administration spokesmen denied that Operation Blast Furnace was meant to be the prototype for similar measures elsewhere in Latin America, reports circulated that the administration had approached the governments of Colombia, Ecuador, and Peru about using U.S. troops.[66] Some drug war enthusiasts saw Operation Blast Furnace as the long-awaited first step toward greater use of the military in the campaign against narcotics. Former DEA administrator Peter Bensinger stated: "Five years ago, when Congress enabled the military to become involved in the fight against drugs, many of us hoped that military equipment, personnel, and technology would be put into the field—as they finally have been in Bolivia. But Bolivia is only one front in this war."[67] The dramatic escalation of the drug war in Latin America had begun.

The Reagan administration's policy accurately reflected public attitudes in the United States. A CBS-*New York Times* poll taken in April 1988 showed that half of the respondents considered drug trafficking to be the number-one international problem.[68] Given that belief, it was hardly surprising that Washington intensified its antidrug crusade in Latin America and regarded the drug trade as a national security issue.[69] That trend would become even more apparent during the next administration.

CHAPTER TWO

ESCALATING AND MILITARIZING THE DRUG WAR:
THE BUSH AND CLINTON YEARS

As the 1980s drew to a close, the Bush administration showed every indication of favoring an even more vigorous supply-side war on drugs than did its predecessor. Indeed, the declared objective of William Bennett, the first head of the newly created Office of National Drug Control Policy (the White House "drug czar"), was to reduce the amount of cocaine coming into the United States over a ten-year period by improving drug crop eradication measures, interdiction, and enforcement in the drug-source countries.[1] The administration seemed especially intent on pursuing campaigns in the Andean region, the source of most of the illicit drugs. Two events in December 1989 illustrated that the new administration also intended to have the U.S. military play a more active role in that effort. The first signal was the invasion of Panama, which was at least partly motivated by anger at the alleged drug-trafficking activities being pursued by the regime of Manuel Noriega. The second was a White House decision to station an aircraft carrier battle group in the waters off Colombia to help track and intercept drug shipments.

Enlisting the military in the crusade against drugs was the logical outcome of the militancy that had been generated in the

United States during the Reagan years, and it was an implicit admission that all previous methods of fighting drugs had failed. Those diverse supply-side and demand-side initiatives had no significant beneficial effect on the country's "drug problem." Despite an increase of nearly 400 percent in federal spending on antidrug efforts during the 1980s—from $1.2 billion in 1981 to more than $5.7 billion in 1989—usage was actually higher at the end of the decade than it had been at the beginning (although it had declined modestly after 1985).[2] Most troubling of all, the violence associated with the black market in drugs continued to escalate. As proponents of the war on drugs saw their strategies fail, they began to exhibit intense frustration that translated into a desperate search for "tougher" measures that would somehow achieve the victory that had proven so elusive. Predictably, many drug warriors began to look to the military as a panacea for both the domestic and international campaigns. The term "drug war" was fast becoming something more than an emotionally evocative metaphor.

As early as 1981, efforts were made to enlist the armed forces in the drug war. That year Congress passed legislation authorizing the president to employ the military in antidrug activities, albeit in a limited fashion, by amending the Posse Comitatus Act of 1878, which prohibited the use of military personnel to enforce civilian laws.[3] While most members of Congress were interested in using troops primarily to bolster the interdiction effort along the coasts and the U.S.-Mexican border, some drug-war enthusiasts soon began to advocate an even wider role for the military. In May 1984, for example, Senator Paula Hawkins (R-FL) proposed sending American troops to South America. She urged President Reagan to "offer whatever resources are necessary including U.S. military personnel to the government of Colombia in their war on illegal drugs."[4] A few years later, a *Washington Post* staff writer suggested deploying the National Guard on the streets of the nation's capital to stem the drug trade and the growing violence associated with it—an idea that was endorsed by some members of the city council.[5]

Most Americans still seemed wary about involving the military—especially in the domestic phase of the war on drugs. Critics pointed out that military forces are trained to seek out and destroy an enemy in wartime; they are not trained in the nuances of civilian law enforcement, much less the subtleties of constitutional law. Equally important, uniformed leaders and most civilian officials in the Department of Defense resisted attempts to conscript their institution for any aspect of the drug war, because they believed that it would divert attention and resources form the military's primary mission—protecting the United States from the Soviet Union and its allies. As cold war tensions eased as a result of Mikhail Gorbachev's more conciliatory foreign policy and internal reforms, however, some incentives for declining to enlist in the war on drugs disappeared.

A crucial step in militarizing the antidrug effort was Reagan's approval in April 1986 of the National Security Decision Directive declaring drug trafficking a threat to the security of the United States.[6] Public and congressional enthusiasm for greater military involvement in the drug war also accelerated in the late 1980s, with measures being passed by the House of Representatives in 1986 and by both chambers in May 1988 directing the Department of Defense to secure American borders against illegal drugs. The House version of that legislation—rejected by the Senate in 1986 and softened in conference after passage in 1988—even ordered the president to deploy within 30 days enough military equipment and personnel to halt the penetration of U.S. borders by aircraft or vessels carrying narcotics. The measure gave the secretary of defense 45 days after deployment to "substantially halt" the drug flow.

Those requirements were so wildly unrealistic that when that amendment cleared the House in 1986, it drew a derisive response from Senate Armed Services Committee chairman Sam Nunn (D-

GA), who stated that it would require returning the entire navy to American waters as well as a massive redeployment of air force and army units.[7] Pentagon spokesmen echoed those comments, noting that any serious attempt to seal the borders against drugs would require at least 90 infantry battalions, 50 helicopter companies, 50,000 army ground support personnel, 110 Airborne Warning and Control System (AWACS) planes, 150 cruisers, and hundreds of combat aircraft.[8] Those estimates were based in large part on a RAND Corporation study for the Department of Defense that concluded that the military would be an ineffective tool for stopping the flow of drugs into the United States.[9] The daunting military logistics impelled journalist Jonathan Marshall to comment that the House "might just as well have demanded that the National Weather Service bring rain to drought-stricken areas of the country within 45 days."[10]

DEEPENING THE DRUG WAR IN LATIN AMERICA

Nevertheless, pressure mounted throughout 1988 and 1989 to use the military, as exasperated members of Congress chastised Pentagon leaders who remained reluctant to entangle their institution in the murky struggle against drugs.[11] Yet U.S. policy appeared to change little until the assassination of Colombian presidential candidate Luis Carlos Galán on August 18, 1989, and the subsequent offensive against the Medellín cartel launched by the Colombian government. Within days of the Galán assassination, the Bush administration offered $65 million in emergency military aid to Bogotá, and that step was followed by the announcement of a broader "Andean Initiative" in early September. The Andean Initiative centered around Bush's pledge to militarize the drug war's supply-side campaign. "Our message to the drug cartels is this: The rules have changed. We will help any government that wants our help. When requested, we will for the first time make available the appropriate resources of America's military forces."[12]

Contrary to its official justifications, the administration was not merely responding to the bloody events in Colombia. It had already decided to escalate the war on drugs by providing more aid to indigenous military establishments in the Andean countries. U.S. policymakers also sought to create the foundation for a larger role by Washington's own armed forces. As early as the spring of 1989, President Bush alluded to probable U.S. military involvement when he met with Latin American police officials. At that meeting he expressed a willingness to dispatch U.S. military advisers to aid in tracking the drug cartels "to the ends of the earth."[13]

A more significant step was taken during the president's vacation at Kennebunkport, Maine, in August 1989 when he signed a new NSDD modifying the one approved by Reagan in April 1986. The new directive not only outlined a vast expansion of aid—especially military aid—to the Andean countries (it was, in fact, the program that became the Andean Initiative), it also included new rules of engagement for U.S. forces. Previously, members of the U.S. Special Forces from the U.S. Southern Command in Panama who had been training indigenous antidrug strike forces in Bolivia and Peru had been restricted to their base camps; they were prohibited from accompanying the South American units on patrol. The new NSDD allowed U.S. forces to go out on "routine" patrols in areas considered secure. One senior White House official predicted that the new NSDD would enable the United States to deploy "several hundred" U.S. military trainers, advisers, and support personnel in the Andean countries—a point confirmed when Bush announced the Andean Initiative in early September.[14]

It is extremely unlikely that such a comprehensive plan for a drug war offensive was formulated only after the Galán assassination. A more probable scenario is that the basic elements of the plan had been under consideration for weeks or even months and that the administration merely used the assassination as a pretext for implementing its strategy.

There were some apparent limitations on the extent of the U.S. military role in the hemispheric drug war. The administration did insist that there were no plans to use American forces in a combat capacity.[15] The president also stressed that requests from the host governments were a prerequisite for the introduction of U.S. military personnel.[16]

Nervous critics in Latin America and the United States had reason to wonder how effective the latter limitation would be in light of events during the final months of 1989. A November 3, 1989, legal opinion issued by the Justice Department at the request of the White House insisted that U.S. military forces had the authority to pursue and arrest drug traffickers overseas, even without the consent of the host government. That ruling came some two months after a U.S. Special Forces team was mobilized to apprehend reputed Colombian drug kingpin Pablo Escobar, who was reportedly in Panama. The mission was abandoned largely because the Bush administration feared that it might violate U.S. law (specifically the Posse Comitatus Act) as it was then interpreted.[17] The November 3 reinterpretation apparently removed that obstacle. In addition to the Justice Department's ruling, the administration's tendency to tout the invasion of Panama as a great victory in the drug war and the decision to deploy a carrier battle group off Colombia's coast without bothering to obtain Bogotá's consent suggested Washington's growing willingness to use its military power unilaterally.[18]

The Andean Initiative immediately allocated over $260 million in military and law enforcement assistance for Colombia, Peru, and Bolivia. That amount represented only the first annual installment of monetary and military aid that would exceed $2 billion over a five-year period and include various weapons systems designed to give the Latin American militaries an edge over the well-armed drug cartels. Additional U.S. Special Forces, along with other military advisers, also were sent to the region to train law enforcement and military personnel.

Not only did the administration and Congress support the use of U.S. troops, but there was a high degree of public support as well. One national poll indicated that 74 percent of Americans endorsed Bush's plan to send military advisers to Colombia. More ominously, 36 percent favored sending combat forces, even if some of those soldiers might be killed.[19] There was a similar outpouring of support for the intervention in Panama—especially after it was described as a decisive victory in the drug conflict.

It was apparent that Washington intended to exert maximum pressure on the governments of drug-producing countries to "request" U.S. military assistance. The United States had a great deal of leverage to produce such requests, even though most Latin American officials continued to argue that crop substitution programs and development programs, rather than militarizing the drug war, represented a better strategy. In particular, the threat of economic sanctions hung over the heads of "uncooperative" regimes.

Sometimes the pressure took more subtle forms. For example, more than two months before the Colombian government requested emergency military aid, the Bush administration had signaled its intent to provide increased levels of military and economic aid to the Andean countries to combat drug trafficking.[20] In the immediate aftermath of the Galán assassination, Attorney General Richard Thornburg and White House Chief of Staff John Sununu emphasized that the administration probably would approve direct U.S. military involvement if Bogotá reversed its long-standing position and requested such assistance.[21]

Even the most obtuse officials in Bogotá could scarcely have failed to pick up such repeated hints. The Bush administration's none-too-subtle pressure placed the government of President Virgilio Barco in a difficult position. Barco responded by asking the United States for military equipment and, as an apparent concession to Washington, a limited number of advisers; to placate nationalist feelings in his own country, he reiterated that there was no need for U.S. combat forces.

The Bush administration's effort to militarize the drug war was a risky strategy.[22] Perhaps most damaging, it tended to undermine the stability and legitimacy of the fragile democratic systems in the hemisphere. Left-wing insurgent groups lost no time in exploiting the opportunity to portray incumbent governments as stooges of the United States. Such allegations had resonance among nationalistic populations that resented Washington's overbearing attitude.

Washington's assistance to Latin American military establishments also increased the threat to incumbent democratic governments. Traffickers maintained significant ties to elements of the military in several drug-producing countries.[23] Moreover, increased military aid inevitably enhanced the power of the military sector vis-à-vis the civilian sector. One especially troubling feature of the emergency aid package to Colombia that Bush announced in August 1989 was that so much seemed to have little relevance to the drug war. Eight Huey helicopters were to be used for transportation of troops and equipment, small arms (such as machine guns, antitank weapons, and grenade launchers) were provided, and $8.5 million was slated for fixed-wing aircraft.[24] While Hueys plausibly could be used in the drug war, there was no similar rationale for fighter planes. When questioned by Congress about the tactical role of the latter in a conflict fought primarily on the ground, drug czar William Bennett could provide no concrete justification but nevertheless dismissed critics' concerns. He apparently believed that the mere fact that Colombia requested the planes was sufficient reason to provide them. Such a policy on the part of the United States gave Latin American militaries carte blanche to fulfill their "wish lists."

THE DRUG WAR TURNS HOT: THE INVASION OF PANAMA

A new and more militant phase of the drug war took place in late 1989 when U.S. troops invaded Panama and ousted that country's dictator, Manuel Noriega. One important reason for the invasion was the mounting evidence of Noriega's involvement in the drug trade. Ironically, the Panamanian strongman had been on the CIA's payroll throughout the 1980s, and a succession of U.S. officials had praised his efforts on behalf of the drug war as well as his role in supporting Washington's campaign against Marxist forces in Central America. By the late 1980s, though, even Noriega's friends in the U.S. government could no longer ignore evidence of his collusion with drug traffickers, his apparent murder of a prominent political opponent, and other egregious offenses (see chapter 5). Although it may have been tolerable for the United States to collude with a suspected drug trafficker in the early and mid-1980s to pursue other foreign policy objectives, at the end of the decade it was no longer acceptable. As the evidence against Noriega burgeoned, the Bush administration imposed economic sanctions on Panama. When that strategy failed, the administration backed an abortive coup by disaffected elements of the military in October 1989. That approach, too, failed to achieve its objective. The United States then decided to take direct action.

On December 19, 1989, U.S. troops invaded Panama and, in a matter of days, captured Noriega. The ostensible reason for the military assault was an incident a few days earlier in which Panamanian security forces had killed an off-duty U.S. Marine, Lieutenant Robert Paz, during an altercation in Panama City.[25] During and after the invasion, though, U.S. officials repeatedly cited evidence of Noriega's involvement in drug trafficking as a reason for taking action against him. White House Press Secretary Marlin Fitzwater stated that military action was justified by the necessity to safeguard American lives, to uphold U.S. rights under the Panama Canal Treaty, and to apprehend Noriega as a drug trafficker.[26] U.S. Ambassador to Panama Deane Hinton was more blunt, calling the invasion "the biggest drug bust in history."[27] More than two years after the incident, President Bush was still justifying it in similar terms. At a news conference in April 1992, he asserted that as a result of the invasion, Panama was "on the mend with encouraging economic growth rates, reduction in drug trafficking and a new commitment to democracy."[28]

Throughout Latin America, the invasion of Panama was also seen as a major escalation in Washington's antidrug campaign as well as the latest manifestation of Washington's long-standing habit of using military force against its smaller neighbors. Not surprisingly, it was extremely unpopular with governments and populations throughout Latin America. The willingness to defy Washington, though, was anemic and was soon overcome by new offers of U.S. financial aid to pursue antidrug initiatives.

SWAPPING THE COLD WAR FOR THE DRUG WAR

The invasion of Panama was the high-water mark to date of efforts to involve the U.S. military in a large-scale fashion in the war on drugs. In fact, the attempt by elected officials to enlist the military in that campaign was highly controversial. U.S. military leaders were initially extremely reluctant to become involved. Pentagon officials as well as field commanders voiced doubts about the wisdom or effectiveness of such a mission. The Joint Chiefs of Staff repeatedly argued that the diversion of military resources and manpower would have adverse effects on readiness and on the Department of Defense's principal mission—defending against the forces of hostile powers. Secretary of Defense Frank Carlucci stated that position bluntly in June 1988 when he resisted congressional pressure for a bigger antidrug role for the military: "The primary role of the Defense Department is to protect and defend this country from armed aggression. Nothing must stand in the way of our readiness or our preparedness to perform this task."[29]

Defense experts openly disagreed with contentions that Latin American drug trafficking should be viewed as a mortal threat to U.S. security. Former secretary of defense Caspar Weinberger, for example, cautioned that "calling for the use of the government's full military resources to put a stop to the drug trade makes for hot and exciting rhetoric. But responding to those calls, as Congress is on the verge of doing, would make for terrible national security policy, poor politics, and guaranteed failure in the campaign against drugs."[30]

Many uniformed officers seemed equally disturbed by the implications of U.S. military involvement—especially in the volatile Andean region. Particularly compelling was the analysis of officials actually stationed in Latin America, who voiced concern about becoming political pawns in a seemingly endless struggle. Underlying such resistance was the fear that the military might get bogged down in a Vietnam-like conflict.

Despite the manifest reluctance of military leaders, military involvement in the drug war—especially in interdiction efforts—had increased gradually but inexorably. Approximately $5 million was earmarked for such purposes in the 1982 defense budget; by 1990 that figure had grown to more than $567 million.

The incentives for the military to join the war on drugs increased dramatically at the end of the 1980s. As the Cold War came to an end, members of the national security bureaucracy, those who profited from a large military establishment, and cheerleaders for "inspiring" national crusades all began to see the drug war as a useful substitute. Using the military to combat drug trafficking both in the United States and in other countries created a justification (or more accurately a pretext) for maintaining bloated military spending and personnel levels.

A striking correlation existed between the demise of the Cold War and the military's willingness to participate in the drug war.

With the collapse of the Soviet adversary, the Pentagon faced the prospect of sizable losses in personnel and cherished weapons systems, as well as prestige and power, unless it had an alternative mission. The drug war was a plausible alternative mission. To at least a limited extent, a heightened role in attacking Latin American drug trafficking could fill a void—with the drug lords replacing the Soviet evil empire as the "necessary enemy." One early sign of a change of attitude among members of the national security bureaucracy was that outright opposition to military involvement in the drug war was gradually replaced by an emphasis on increased funding as a condition for involvement. Pentagon spokesman Dan Howard exemplified that position when he stated, "We're prepared to do more. But that requires resources." An analysis by the Joint Chiefs of Staff indicated that $14 billion was needed to purchase 66 additional AWACS aircraft and that $6.2 billion was needed for effective operation of border patrol planes and ships.[31]

Another sign of changing sentiment was the attitude of Bush's Secretary of Defense, Dick Cheney. In marked contrast to his predecessors, Cheney was receptive to the idea of greater military participation in the drug war. He quickly implemented Bush's NSDD in September 1989 by establishing new guidelines for an expanded role. The purpose of his directive, Cheney stressed, was "to make clear to everyone in the Department that this is a high national security mission for us, and therefore it deserves greater allocation of resources in terms of time and energy and perhaps equipment and troops and personnel than has been true in the past."[32] Shortly thereafter Admiral William Crowe, the departing chairman of the Joint Chiefs, delivered forceful farewell comments in which he emphasized the military's willingness to do battle against the new threat to national security and asserted that the American people would have to give up drugs. The willingness of Crowe, generally regarded as the most politically astute Joint Chiefs chairman in many years, to embrace the drug war explicitly signaled that the officer corps' resistance to a high-profile role for the military in that struggle was crumbling.[33]

Participation in the Andean Initiative also opened a way for the military and its defense industry allies to justify the procurement of questionable weapons systems. Defense consultant Dov Zakheim, a former deputy undersecretary of defense in the Reagan administration (and an even higher-level Pentagon official in the George W. Bush administration), touted the V-22 Osprey—a hybrid fixed-wing aircraft and helicopter used to transport troops—as an "innovative response" to demands for military operations "in scenarios where precise measurement of benefits is impossible." Zakheim left little doubt about the scenario he had in mind. He noted that the danger of a North Atlantic Treaty Organization (NATO)–Warsaw Pact war was increasingly remote and that the Osprey would make little sense in that setting in any case. Zakheim observed, however, that "the United States finds itself involved in an unanticipated conflict, a drug war that threatens to consume ever greater defense resources for programs whose effectiveness cannot be measured in the old, conventional ways."[34] Coincidentally, the Osprey had been earmarked for extinction by economy-minded officials in the Bush administration, in spite of feverish lobbying by the Marine Corps. As the military role in fighting drug trafficking threatened to expand, requests for superfluous personnel and weapons systems had a greater chance of prevailing, despite the end of the Cold War. Indeed, more than a decade later, opponents are still trying to drive a stake through the heart of the Osprey program.

The drug war offered another, more subtle, potential benefit to the national security bureaucracy. During the latter stages of the Cold War, U.S. military doctrine emphasized the need to engage and prevail in low-intensity conflicts. The collapse of the Soviet empire greatly undermined the principal justification for that strategy, but the war on drugs in Latin America provided an alternate reason. Operation Blast Furnace proved to be an ideal exercise for honing such skills. The troop deployments connected with the Andean Initiative gave the United States an ongoing military presence in a region where low-intensity conflicts were occurring and were likely to continue to occur. By providing technical expertise and equipment to Latin American militaries, U.S. officials were able to further yet another objective—strengthening allied forces that might be needed in low-intensity conflicts. That motive may have been the reason why so much of the Andean Initiative assistance was directed to the military establishments in the recipient countries even though the police forces had the primary responsibility for antidrug efforts.[35]

Civilian proponents of the drug war were generally more candid than government officials in acknowledging the usefulness of the drug war to the U.S. military establishment. Most participants in a special seminar conducted at the behest of the House Armed Services Committee in August 1988 stressed that a military role in the war on drugs would require a substantial increase in funding. William J. Taylor, vice president for political and military affairs at the Center for Strategic and International Studies, pointed out the potential advantages of the military's new mission in a post–Cold War setting:

> Defense spending has not only declined recently, it will decline a great deal more in the foreseeable future. This will occur because there is a declining perception of military threat in the Congress and among the American public, and because there will be increasing demands for spending on social programs. There will be new initiatives to reduce U.S. military troop commitments worldwide. If the DOD [Department of Defense] leadership were smart about the coming environment, they would approach the Congress with a military "social utility" argument which says that military manpower should not be further reduced because the Congress is mandating increased military involvement in the "war on drugs." They should, in fact, argue further that new funds should be

appropriated for these expanded missions which are socially use-ful.[36]

A few months earlier, neoconservative writer Irving Kristol had offered a similar rationale to members of the national security bureaucracy: "If the Pentagon cares about its military budget, as it surely does, it ought to be interested in demonstrating to the American people that this budget is being well spent. It has had—thank goodness—little opportunity for any such demonstration in recent years, which is why its budget is now at risk. The Pentagon should see [the troop] proposal as an opportunity to be seized, not a nuisance to be avoided."[37]

A steady escalation of rhetoric from individuals of varying political persuasions emphasized the drug trade as the new, exceedingly dangerous threat to national security. Typical of the genre was the warning by Representative Charles B. Rangel (D-NY), chairman of the House Select committee on Narcotics Abuse and Control, that if the United Sates did not thwart the drug traffickers, it could face horrendous consequences. Rangel offered his own version of the "domino theory" : "If Colombia falls, the other, smaller, less stable nations in this region would become targets. It is conceivable that we would one day find ourselves an island of democracy in a sea of narco-political rule, a prospect as bad as being surrounded by communist regimes."[38] Other propo-nents of the drug war were equally lurid in their portrayals of drug trafficking as a grave threat to national security. Peter Bensinger asserted that "the most important war in this century, certainly in the last 50 years, is the war on drugs."[39]

Several observers saw the drug war fast emerging as a substi-tute for the communist threat. *Washington Post* columnist Jim Hoagland was perhaps the most perceptive in noting that transi-tion: "Instead of beginning his presidency by dispatching military advisers to Vietnam to contain communism, as John F. Kennedy did more than two decades ago, Bush has dispatched military trainers to Colombia to fight drug traffickers. History may come to record Bush's decision as a symbolic turning point in America's world role."[40] In the course of criticizing Bush for lack of vigor in foreign policy, Hoagland's colleague Stephen S. Rosenfeld mused that "you would think that combating the drug scourge would be a pretty good surrogate for fighting communism." [41] Proponents of the drug war both inside and outside the administration seemed to have made that connection.

The obsession with the antidrug crusade as the moral equivalent of war during the Bush years was a variation on a theme that began to emerge several years earlier. Throughout the early and mid-1980s, various right-wing hawks built elaborate theories of a "narco-terrorist" or "narco-communist" threat to American security.[42] Some of the most outspoken proponents of that view, including analysts Michael Ledeen and Rachel Ehrenfeld, alleged that there was a vast conspiracy directed by the Soviet KGB. Most of their political allies in the Reagan administration never went that far, but they did repeatedly attempt to link the highest levels of the Cuban and Nicaraguan governments with the drug trade, implying that those connections were part of a concerted Leninist strategy to undermine freedom and democracy throughout the Western Hemisphere.[43]

As relations between the United States and the Soviet Union gradually improved during the Gorbachev era, allegations of Soviet complicity faded. Conversely, more evidence emerged that the Cuban government was deeply implicated in drug trafficking, although it was still not certain whether the principal motives were ideological or financial.[44] In any case, the image of a narco-terrorist or narco-communist link helped strengthen the impression that the war on drugs was a true war against a serious threat to national security.

The significant change in the Bush years was that drug trafficking per se was increasingly portrayed as an independent national security threat rather than as merely a subset of a larger communist threat. One important effect of the drugs-as-a-security-threat image was to garner support for U.S. military intervention in the Western Hemisphere among political factions that were normally opposed to such conduct. For example, evidence linking Manuel Noriega to drug trafficking impelled liberal Democrat senators John Kerry (D-MA) and Christopher Dodd (D-CT) to advocate vigorous U.S. measures to remove him from power.[45]

The war against drugs was not a perfect substitute for the fading Cold War, but it had several characteristics that could help sustain a large national security bureaucracy. As did the Cold War (and its predecessor World War II), the drug cartels provided the image of an utterly evil adversary, which provoked a visceral response of hostility in most Americans. In addition, just as the Cold War's ideological component frequently served as a pretext for U.S. intervention in the Third World in pursuit of more mundane political and economic objectives, so too the drug war could become a cover for renewed U.S. activism—especially in the Western Hemisphere.

But, in marked contrast to earlier conflicts, the most important characteristic of the drug war was the lack of a discernible termination point. Indeed, there was no clear concept of what would constitute "victory," and those who viewed the drug war as a new cash cow for the national security bureaucracy likely preferred such ambiguity. No matter how great the decline in drug trafficking, they could always claim that only a battle had been won, not the war, and that even more vigorous (and expensive) measures were justified since progress was being made and the elusive final victory was just around the corner. Conversely, a lack of progress always could be cited as evidence of the need for more resources and a redoubled effort to meet the mortal threat to U.S. security posed by drug trafficking. Proponents of a more vigorous U.S. military role often emphasized the inherently indeterminate duration of the drug war. As one expert noted, "This is going to be a decades-long war."[46]

FROM CARTAGENA TO SAN ANTONIO

The Andean Initiative was followed by a vigorous public relations offensive culminating in a drug policy summit attended by Bush and the presidents of Colombia, Peru, and Bolivia in Cartagena, Colombia on February 15, 1990. Even the U.S. invasion of Panama failed to derail that summit, despite some anxious moments. The Declaration of Cartagena that emerged proclaimed the formation of an "anti-drug cartel." It committed the four governments to a comprehensive multilateral strategy to fight all facets of the drug trade. The Andean regimes pledged to increase their efforts to disrupt trafficking patterns, prevent the diversion of essential chemicals to drug production operations, and discourage illicit coca cultivation. The United States pledged to reduce the domestic demand for drugs and to increase assistance to the Andean countries to reduce the supply of illegal drugs, develop alternative sources of income for coca growers, and enhance interdiction capabilities.[47]

Although the Cartagena summit was a public relations extravaganza, it produced relatively few substantive policy changes. Bush pressed his counterparts to use their militaries against the drug cartels and to adopt more vigorous crop eradication programs. They responded with impressive but nonbinding promises. The Andean leaders sought to exploit Washington's eagerness for an escalated drug war to obtain multibillion-dollar developmental aid programs. Bush merely responded by stressing the additional military and economic aid that would flow to recipient countries under the Andean Initiative.

There is no question that the administration's Andean Initiative produced increased aid dollars for drug source countries in Latin America. Counternarcotics assistance for Colombia during the first year included $21 million to support the National Police as the lead antinarcotics force; nearly $72 million in foreign military assistance (FMF) programs to provide equipment, services, and training for the counternarcotics efforts of the armed forces; and $3.7 million in economic and developmental aid. (Those figures were in addition to the $65 million in emergency aid that the Bush administration dispatched to Bogotá in the autumn of 1989.) Antinarcotics aid to Bolivia included $15.7 million in programs to strengthen law enforcement and interdiction capabilities; $39.1 million in FMF funds to support the antidrug role of the armed forces (plus $7.8 million in Department of Defense equipment, services, and training); and $40.5 million in economic assistance.

The initial levels of aid for Peru were considerably more modest: $20 million in law enforcement support and $4.3 million in economic support.[48] That difference did not reflect a belief among officials in either country that the drug-trafficking problem in Peru was less serious than elsewhere in the Andean region. Quite the contrary. Peru at the time was the principal source of coca leaf, and the government in Lima faced two radical left-wing insurgencies (the Túpac Amaru Revolutionary Movement and the Sendero Luminoso) that had at least some ties to narcotics growers. But relations between Lima and Washington had become quite strained over the drug issue. U.S. officials repeatedly expressed dissatisfaction with the administration of Peruvian president Alan García for its lack of enthusiasm in prosecuting drug eradication campaigns and made it clear that an increase in economic aid was contingent on a more cooperative attitude. At the same time, Lima contended that even the existing level of U.S. economic assistance, especially for crop substitution programs, was insufficient. In April 1990, shortly before leaving office, García stated bluntly that he would not sign any new antidrug agreement unless it included an increase in aid for crop substitution and debt relief.[49]

The dispute became even more acrimonious when García's successor, Alberto Fujimori, declined to have his country participate in the fiscal year 1990 FMF program to provide $35.5 million in military assistance for counternarcotics programs. Fujimori specifically objected that the U.S. plan did not make funding for crop substitution programs a major objective.

Peru's discontent underscored the point that, despite the increase in U.S. aid under the Andean Initiative, the sums still fell substantially short of what the recipient regimes had in mind. For all of its superficial solidarity, the Cartagena summit did not alter the fact that the United States and its hemispheric neighbors continued to pursue competing agendas on the drug issue.

THE CLINTON YEARS

The replacement of the Bush administration with the Clinton administration marked a subtle shift in U.S. drug policy throughout Latin America. That shift was more one of style than of substance, however. The new administration preferred to operate quietly rather than proposing high-profile ventures such as the Andean Initiative. Not until the United States signed on to Plan Colombia during Clinton's final year in office was there a comparable program accompanied by an abundance of publicity.

A quieter strategy, however, did not mean that President Clinton and his advisers were prepared to rethink the supply-side component of the drug war. Indeed, some of the most bruising "ugly American" pressures on hemispheric governments occurred during the Clinton years (see chapter 5). It was also during that period that the most spectacular source-country victories took place: the smashing of the Medellín and Cali drug cartels. Colombia, with Washington's strong encouragement, waged a war against those two drug-trafficking organizations, and by 1996 virtually all of their prominent leaders were in hiding, in jail, or dead.

In truth, Bogotá's offensive against the Medellín cartel began before Clinton. Angered by the assassinations of Luis Carlos Galán and other prominent Colombian political figures, as well as by a massive upsurge in violence orchestrated by the cartel in 1989 and 1990, the government began to strike back hard.[50] The highlight of that effort came in December 1993 when Colombian authorities shot and killed the infamous Pablo Escobar, the most violent member of the Medellín cartel hierarchy. At the time of Escobar's death, most of the other Medellín cartel leaders were also dead or imprisoned. The cartel had ceased to be the leading force in the Colombian drug trade.[51]

During the early 1990s the Bogotá government concentrated its efforts against the Medellín cartel because of its penchant for horrific acts of violence. At the same time, it tacitly tolerated the less-violent Cali cartel. Washington deemed that tolerance utterly unacceptable and pressured Bogotá to go after that organization as well. With the Medellín cartel smashed, the Cali cartel became the primary target in late 1994 and early 1995. Ironically, that effort was spearheaded by President Ernesto Samper—a man Washington accused of being in the pocket of the drug traffickers (see chapter 5). In little more than a year, the Cali cartel had been badly disrupted.[52]

Drug warriors in both Colombia and the United States loudly proclaimed a great victory with the defeat of the two leading drug cartels. The reality was much more sobering. The quantity of drugs coming out of Colombia did not decline markedly. Instead, the drug traffickers regrouped, forming smaller and less easily detected organizations. The Colombian drug trade became more decentralized and marginally less inclined to resort to violence against government officials and innocent civilians. In other respects, though, the smashing of the Medellín and Cali cartels produced few lasting results.

The lower-profile approach of the Clinton administration did not even mean that it was prepared to deemphasize the militarization of the war on drugs. In fact, the opposite was true; Washington slowly but inexorably escalated the emphasis on the military option. There was, however, a greater wariness about the direct involvement of large numbers of U.S. military personnel. The trend toward a blunt military strategy that was apparent during the Bush years gave way to a more indirect approach entailing U.S. training and logistical support for the security forces of the Latin American countries.

In 1993 and 1994 the United States was deeply involved in efforts to disrupt the "air bridge" of small planes linking the harvested coca crops of Peru and Bolivia with the cocaine-processing laboratories of Colombia. Washington operated military ground radars at various locations in the Andes and conducted airborne surveillance using air force AWACS aircraft. Data from those operations were passed along to Peruvian and Ecuadorean air forces, which then intercepted aircraft suspected of carrying drug shipments. Those planes were ordered to land, and if the pilots did not comply, they were fired on.[53]

At least 30, and by some estimates as many as 50, planes were shot down between 1994 and 2001, and drug shipments to the labs in Colombia unquestionably decreased. The principal effect, though, was not a serious, sustained disruption of the drug trade. It merely created another incentive for drug traffickers to relocate their sources of supply—the coca crops from Peru and Bolivia to newly planted fields in Colombia—closer to the labs and therefore more secure. Once again a "victory" in the war on drugs turned out to be little more than another manifestation of the push-down, pop-up effect.

Nevertheless, U.S. officials repeatedly hailed the program of assisting the Peruvian air force to shoot down planes suspected of carrying drugs as a great success. Disrupting the "air bridge" between Peru and Colombia supposedly was a grave setback to the drug traffickers. The hype suddenly subsided, though, in April 2001 when a Peruvian air force fighter shot down a Cessna over the rain forest in northeast Peru—a plane carrying American Baptist missionaries Roni and Jim Bowers and their two children.

The Bowers tragedy was entirely foreseeable. Indeed, at least one official in the Clinton administration anticipated such an event. The United States had begun to supply information on suspected drug flights to the Colombian and Peruvian governments as early as 1990, but Washington suspended that assistance briefly in 1994 when both countries announced policies to shoot down suspected craft. The Clinton Justice Department (as well as some elements of the State Department and Pentagon) worried that shooting at civilian planes was a violation of international law and that the United States could be held legally liable for any mistakes since it was involved in providing information. "Mistakes are likely to occur," several officials warned in internal memos, including the possibility of shooting down planes not involved in the drug trade.

But President Clinton, under strong pressure from drug warriors—including critics in Congress who derided him for being "soft" on drugs—disregarded the admonitions of his advisers. Instead, he looked for ways to restore the agreements without incurring the risk of U.S. liability. Near the end of 1994, the president proposed and Congress passed a law exempting U.S. government officials and employees from liability for any "mistakes" made while cooperating with another country's shoot-down policy in the war on drugs.[54]

In addition to its efforts to create havoc for the air bridge, the United States deepened its involvement in Colombia's effort to combat drug trafficking in the 1990s. Indeed, many of the elements that would characterize the much-touted Plan Colombia in 2000 and 2001 were in place on a smaller scale in the mid- and late 1990s. As part of a $112 million aid package announced in September 1996, Washington "donated" helicopters, observation planes, patrol boats, and other military hardware to Bogotá. In addition, the United States agreed to sell 12 Blackhawk helicopters.[55]

Beyond the transfer or sale of military systems, the State Department contracted U.S. firms to hire pilots to fly drug crop eradication missions in Colombia. Nevertheless, an underlying caution was still evident. Although U.S. aviators provided training and technical assistance to Colombian police and military on the herbicide spraying missions, there was an initial reluctance to have Americans fly the actual missions. For a brief period in 1996, a few U.S. civilian pilots did conduct such missions, but the administration abruptly pulled them after a month.[56] (The fact that the administration could order a halt to what was ostensibly a program operated by private companies demonstrated just how phony was the alleged distinction between governmental and nongovernmental portions of the U.S-directed drug war in Latin America.)

Washington provided even more direct military assistance and encouragement to neighboring Ecuador. Training missions blurred into joint military maneuvers. How such operations could entangle the United States in the murky politics of the Andean countries—and how Latin American governments exploit U.S. drug aid for their own purposes—became apparent in one such exercise.

> For two weeks in May, U.S. special operations forces used this isolated jungle region near the Colombian border to stage their biggest deployment in Latin America in years—an example of what the U.S. military is doing, and would like to do much more of, throughout Latin America. The idea was to train the Ecuadoran military to better fight two intertwined foes that frequently operate in the area: drug trafficking organizations and Marxist Colombian guerrillas. In the exercise, 143 elite U.S. troops and their 645 Ecuadoran counterparts used American-provided boats and Black Hawk helicopters in mock raids on targets such as a narco-guerrilla camp and a supposed cocaine laboratory. Overhead, A-37 combat jets raced after small airplanes to practice forcing down suspected drug flights. But at the operation's closing ceremony, the Ecuadoran military blared martial music and called the troops to arms—not against traffickers or guerrillas, but against their traditional rival, Peru, with which Ecuador has an unresolved border dispute. "We

will never cede even one millimeter of territory to the Peruvians," the loudspeakers boomed, as soldiers carried out their final drills alongside U.S. troops. "It is time for all of us to stand together against the enemy."[57]

In some respects, the vigorous prosecution of the supply-side phase of the drug war during the Clinton years was ironic. When that administration first took office, at least some of the new officials seemed to recognize that the strategy pursued by the Reagan and Bush administrations in Latin America had been a failure. One high-level official stated that "It's clear that we need some rethinking" about that approach.[58] There was even a healthy skepticism about enlisting the Latin American militaries in anti-drug campaigns. One senior official concluded, "The Bolivian military has never done anything whatsoever against narcotics traffickers, nor will it." In Peru, "not only has the army not done anything, it actually supports the traffickers." The Colombian military "has not been very effective either." The official charged that Latin American military organizations were "only interested in getting the goodies and the guns" from the United States while pretending to combat the drug trade."[59] Perhaps most revealing, spending on international drug control fell 57 percent, from $707 million in 1992 to $300 million in 1995.[60]

That wariness about the international component of the drug war seemed to be reflected in the administration's initial steps on the domestic front. One of the president's first actions was to slash the staff of the Office of National Drug Control Policy (ONDCP)—which had ballooned under President Bush to 146 people—by 80 percent. Administration policymakers also seemed to place greater emphasis on drug treatment rather than on either the supply-side campaign or draconian law enforcement measures to reduce demand. One ardent drug warrior, *New York Times* columnist A. M. Rosenthal, was so worried that he warned "the concept of a war against drugs is in danger of being dismantled," resulting in "creeping legalization."[61]

Even early on, though, there were mixed signs on both the domestic and international policy fronts. At the same time Clinton slashed the ONDCP staff, his overall drug-fighting budget continued the upward spending trend of his predecessors. And although some senior officials expressed skepticism about the efficacy of waging the hemispheric drug war, another senior official insisted that a strong eradication and interdiction program must continue and that the administration did not want to give the impression to Latin American political elites that Washington had written off the drug war.[62]

The administration's own ambivalence, combined with intense political pressure from domestic critics, soon aborted the flirtation with a more enlightened policy. As the years wore on, the Clinton administration prosecuted the drug war both at home and abroad with at least as much enthusiasm as its predecessors. A record number of drug offenders filled America's prisons, the U.S. military took a more active role in drug interdiction efforts along America's border with Mexico and in assisting the militaries of the Andean countries, and for the first time economic sanctions were imposed on a hemispheric neighbor (Colombia) for failing to cooperate adequately in Washington's drug war. And in the final year of his administration, President Clinton had the U.S. government sign on to pouring $1.3 billion into Plan Colombia, the most ambitious supply-side antidrug offensive to date.

Chapter Three

Plan Colombia:
A Dangerous New Phase in the Drug War

As originally envisioned by the government of Colombian president Andrés Pastrana, Plan Colombia was an ambitious blueprint to solve many of the country's economic problems as well as combat narcotics trafficking.[1] The centerpiece of the strategy was an economic development program to give hard-pressed peasants alternatives to involvement in the drug trade. The price tag for the plan was some $7.5 billion over two years, with the money coming from the United States, other major national donors (primarily the members of the European Union), the World Bank, the Inter-American Development Bank, and other international lending institutions.

The European and other international donors have been slow to provide funding. Indeed, as of the spring of 2001, it appeared that less than half of the projected $7.5 billion would be forthcoming. The United States, though, became an eager participant from the beginning, although its focus was somewhat narrower than Pastrana preferred.[2] Washington agreed to provide $1.3 billion to assist the government in Bogotá to combat drug trafficking. As designed, most of the U.S. money goes to the Colombian military to purchase hardware, provide training, and otherwise fund drug eradication efforts, not for general economic development. About 300 Green Beret troops are already in the country providing training for Colombian officers and enlisted personnel. The first installment in the transfer of 16 Blackhawk troop transport helicopters was delivered in July 2001, and a shipment of 25 Huey II helicopters was scheduled for delivery in 2002.[3] Washington has also provided 11 planes to conduct aerial fumigation of drug crops, and another 14 planes were scheduled to arrive in 2002.[4]

COLOMBIA'S MULTISIDED POLITICAL STRUGGLE

The political setting in Colombia is extraordinarily complex, as the government in Bogotá is involved in a struggle with no fewer than four factions. Explicitly arrayed against the government are two radical leftist insurgent movements, the Revolutionary Armed Forces of Colombia (FARC) and the National Liberation Army (ELN). Both have been designated as terrorist groups by the U.S. State Department. Violently opposed to FARC and ELN are the right-wing paramilitaries, most notably the United Self-Defense Forces of Colombia (AUC), also now designated by the State Department as a terrorist organization, largely bankrolled by prosperous ranchers who feel directly threatened by the guerrillas.[5] And finally there are various narcotrafficking organizations. Most of them have no strong political allegiances; they are primarily profit maximizers who are willing to form tactical alliances with whatever faction seems to be dominant in a particular region and, therefore, is in a position to advance or retard their business prospects. At times, they have worked closely with the rebel forces and paid "taxes" to FARC and ELN on drug crops and quantities of raw cocaine.[6] On other occasions and in other places, they have cooperated with the AUC against the rebels.

Not surprisingly, this political witch's brew has produced chaos and violence. More than 2 million Colombians have fled their homes to avoid the fighting. Some 35,000 civilians have died in the fighting over the past decade, and, according to Bogotá's official figures, more than 126,000 were made homeless by the war in 2000 alone. Some human rights groups place the latter figure at closer to 300,000.[7] In addition, thousands of murders each year may be connected to either the ideological struggle or the drug trade. The economy is a shambles with an unemployment rate estimated at 20 percent, capital flight is epidemic, and middle- and upper-class Colombians are beginning to leave the country in alarming numbers. Between 1996 and 2001 more than a million Colombians—out of a population of 40 million—emigrated. One reporter observes that lines "snake around the block near foreign consulates where people stand in line all night seeking visas."[8]

The strength of the guerrilla forces has surged in recent years. In 1985 FARC had some 3,000 fighters and was active in 25 isolated sectors. Today it has at least 20,000 better-armed fighters—the largest insurgent force in all of Latin America—and launches strikes all over Colombia. It controls a swath of territory in the south nearly the size of Switzerland.[9] The ELN is considerably smaller, but its forces dominate the territory in the northeast through which run Colombia's main oil pipelines. Between January and August 2001 alone there were 111 bombings of one of those pipelines, a level of disruption that caused a 30 percent drop in Colombia's oil exports.[10] The border area near Venezuela may be controlled by government forces in the daytime, but after dark it is usually under ELN control.

Into this snake pit now wanders the United States with its participation in Plan Colombia. The lack of realism underlying U.S. involvement is illustrated by the Clinton administration's original assurance that the funds would be used only to fight drug trafficking, not support the government's struggle against FARC and ELN. Critics point out the obvious: that the military hardware purchased can and will be used for both purposes. Indeed, most of the military operations ostensibly directed against narcotraffickers take place in areas that also have a large guerrilla presence. In many cases narcotrafficking organizations are allied with one or both of the guerrilla groups, and any action against the former will be considered by the latter as a blow against their cause. The functional distinction emphasized by liberal supporters of Plan Colombia is, therefore, ludicrously impractical.

Some officials in the Bush administration conceded that point early on. Robert Zoellick, a top foreign policy adviser to Bush during the 2000 presidential campaign and now U.S. Trade Representative, fairly scoffed at the distinction that the Clinton administration had imposed. "We cannot continue to make a false distinction between counterinsurgency and counternarcotics efforts," Zoellick stated. "The narcotraffickers and guerrillas compose one dangerous network."[11] Candidate Bush himself took a similar line, vowing that U.S. assistance "will help the Colombian government protect its people, fight the drug trade, [and] *halt the momentum of the guerrillas.*"[12]

Officially, though, the distinction between counternarcotics and counterinsurgency assistance remained U.S. policy until the spring of 2002. As late as September 2001, a "senior administration official" gave assurances that any expanded support, such as training additional units of the Colombian military, would be confined to the "existing mission" of combating the drug trade, not to bolster Bogotá's war against leftist rebels.[13] Other leaked comments, however, made it apparent that not all administration officials were in agreement about maintaining that distinction. A RAND Corporation study published in June 2001 also advocated abolishing the distinction between counternarcotics and counterinsurgency assistance:

> The United States recognizes the nexus between the guerrillas and the drug traffic, but sees the problem as essentially one of counternarcotics policy. As a result, U.S. efforts are focused on strengthening Colombian anti-narcotics capabilities while insisting that U.S. military assistance is not directed against the guerrillas themselves. U.S. policy therefore misses the point that the political and military

control that the guerrillas exercise over an ever-larger part of Colombia's territory and population is at the heart of their challenge to the Bogotá government's authority. The United States ought to rethink whether this distinction between counter-narcotics and counter-insurgency can be sustained, and whether Colombia and its allies can be successful in the war against drugs if the Colombian government fails to regain control of its territory.[14]

A new factor served to increase the incentive for the United States to aid the Colombian government in its counterinsurgency campaign as well as its antinarcotics efforts. As mentioned, both the FARC and the ELN are considered terrorist organizations by the U.S. State Department. Washington's hostility toward the Colombian rebels deepened in August 2001 when Irish Republican Army activists were found working with the FARC. The terrorist attacks on the World Trade Center and the Pentagon the following month—and the Bush administration's subsequent declaration of war against international terrorism—made it even more likely that the distinction between counterinsurgency and counternarcotics aid would be abolished. Perhaps indicative of the new attitude, Francis X. Taylor, the State Department's top counterterrorism official, insisted that FARC is "the most dangerous international terrorist group based in this hemisphere."[15] Both supporters and critics of aid to Colombia agreed that, if the distinction between counternarcotics and counterinsurgency aid was difficult to make, a distinction between counterterrorism and counterinsurgency measures would be virtually impossible. Representative Cass Ballenger (R-NC), chairman of the House International Relations Committee's Western Hemisphere subcommittee, stated that, in light of the September 11 attacks, "I don't think there'll be that much differentiation." Representative William Delahunt (D-MA) conceded that separating counterterrorism from counterinsurgency "would be a very difficult and delicate distinction to make."[16] Anne W. Patterson, U.S. ambassador to Colombia, admitted that "there's no question we are now focusing more on terrorism in Colombia."[17] Another official emphasized that Washington would become less supportive of the Colombian government's peace talks with groups that the State Department lists as terrorist.[18]

Pastrana's government did its utmost to exploit the heightened U.S. concern about terrorism. During a visit to the United States in November 2001, Pastrana repeatedly urged the United States to increase aid to his country to combat "narco-terrorists." He told U.S. officials and members of Congress: "There is a common enemy: the drug trade or narcoterrorism, which is the greatest financier of violence in Colombia and the world."[19] Lest anyone miss the linkage, he stated on another occasion that the narcotraffickers "finance the violence not only in Colombia but in Afghanistan."[20]

Pastrana found a receptive audience. Representative Mark Souder (R-IN), who chairs the House Drug Task Force, stated that the distinction between the drug war and counterinsurgency had "completely disappeared" in Colombia. "It's not just narcotics. It has developed into terrorism and we need to fight terrorism in our hemisphere," Souder told reporters after meeting with Pastrana. "As people practice terrorism and threaten the stability of a long-time democracy, it becomes more and more clear that this isn't just about drugs only, or about political power sharing. It is about terrorists who bully their way into the political system."[21] House Speaker Dennis Hastert made the linkage between the drug war and the war against terrorism equally explicit: "We will continue to work with President Pastrana and the good people of Colombia to rid their country of terrorism and take that plague of terrorism from our street corners as well."[22] Attorney General John Ashcroft praised Pastrana and emphasized that the United States regarded Colombia as "a staunch, steadfast ally in the war against drug trafficking and in the war against terrorism."[23]

Actions in the field were making the distinction among counternarcotics, counterinsurgency, and counterterrorism assistance moot in any case. Developments on the ground had increasingly confirmed a de facto linkage between antinarcotics offensives and military campaigns against rebel forces. In April 2001 Counter-Narcotics Battalion 1, an elite Colombian Army unit that had been trained by the United States specifically to conduct antidrug operations, had clashed with FARC guerrillas in southern Colombia. Nine rebels and one government soldier had been killed in the skirmish.[24] Other incidents occurred later in 2001 and in 2002.

In July 2001 press reports revealed that the United States intended to expand its military training role beyond the three counternarcotics battalions already operating in southern Colombia (largely outside those territories controlled by rebel troops).[25] That tacit avoidance of clashes with FARC and ELN units would end under a proposal being pushed by Ambassador Patterson. Under the new plan, the United States was to begin training additional battalions—probably one each year for several years—to go after drug labs protected by insurgent forces. Patterson implicitly conceded that Washington was using the drug war as a pretext to help the Colombian military strike at its Marxist adversaries. "We can do a lot under the counter-narcotics rubric," she told a group of reporters.[26]

Given all of these developments, it came as no great surprise that the Bush administration decided in March 2002 to ask Congress to remove all restrictions on U.S. military aid to Colombia, including those that restricted that assistance to counternarcotics measures.[27] Indeed, some members of the administration wanted to openly portray the new policy as part of Washington's global war against terrorism.

Whatever the initial intent, Plan Colombia inexorably draws the United States into Colombia's civil war. Indeed, the government in Bogotá apparently wants to draw Washington in. In an effort to reassure an uneasy American public and Congress, Pastrana gave repeated assurances that his country was not going to become a Vietnam-style quagmire for the United States.[28] U.S. policymakers have stressed the same theme. Clinton administration drug czar Barry McCaffrey stated flatly, "We are not offering to engage U.S. troops. It's not on the table. It's simply not going to happen."[29] He noted that the two governments had established guidelines that no more than 500 American soldiers and 300 civilian contract employees could be in Colombia at any one time. President Clinton emphasized that "a condition of this aid is that we are not going to get into a shooting war."[30]

Whether such intentions are enough to keep the United States out of a debilitating, Vietnam-style entanglement remains to be seen. It was not a reassuring development that the new Bush administration strongly resisted congressional efforts to place a mandatory cap on the number of U.S. military personnel and civilian contract employees who could be in Colombia at one time. The House of Representatives in July 2001 rejected the administration's bid to allow an unlimited number of civilian personnel to be in the country, which would have ended the FY 2001 cap of 300 American civilians. Instead, the House, on a voice vote, amended the administration's proposal, voting to cap the total number of military and contract personnel at 800. However, the amendment merely instructed the administration to inform Congress if and when it planned to exceed 300 civilian employees and to state the actual number it intended to send.[31] As a practical matter, the so-called cap provided no effective limit.

In addition, the Bush administration had already found a way to circumvent the cap of 300 American civilians, which was designed to keep the U.S. involvement in Colombia's turmoil at modest levels. Instead of hiring more Americans to fly the planes that conduct aerial missions to fumigate drug crops, DynCorp, the principal private firm hired by the State Department to conduct such missions, increasingly hired foreign pilots—at the direction of the State Department. By August 2001, DynCorp had 335 civilians working on various aspects of the antidrug campaign, but less than a third were U.S. citizens. (Another 60 to 80 American and other nationals worked for other firms under contract to the

State Department.) Critics admitted that while hiring foreign pilots and other personnel did not violate the congressional cap or the administration's pledge to limit the number of Americans deployed to Colombia, such hiring indicated a much more active U.S. involvement in the drug war (and, indirectly, the counterinsurgency effort) than administration officials had led Congress and the American public to believe.[32] That point became even more apparent when the Bush administration asked Congress to lift the numerical cap on both military and civilian personnel.

Despite his assurances, Pastrana clearly wanted Washington to play a role in ending the insurgency as well as in funding antidrug efforts. During a visit to Washington in late February 2001, Pastrana urged the Bush administration to begin participating in peace negotiations between his government and the two rebel organizations by attending a meeting scheduled to take place the following week.[33] Initially President Bush and other administration leaders firmly rebuffed that initiative.[34] Within days, however, U.S. policymakers seemed to have second thoughts. Trial balloons began appearing in the news media suggesting that, perhaps, the United States could play a constructive, albeit supporting, role in the negotiations—if the FARC was serious about wanting peace.[35] When peace negotiations broke down a year later, Washington's involvement in Colombia's civil war deepened in another way as the Bush administration expanded its support for the Colombian government's counterinsurgency efforts.

THE DRUG-TRADE FACTOR

Colombia probably would be a violent and turbulent place even without the drug factor.[36] The FARC and the ELN arose because of anger among the rural peasantry against the country's political system, and the insurgency would likely exist even if it did not derive funds from the drug trade. (Indeed the formation of the

FARC predates the onset of a vigorous war on drugs conducted by the Colombian government.) Moreover, similar left-wing insurgencies erupted in such countries as El Salvador, Guatemala, and Nicaragua in earlier decades even though drug revenues were not a major factor in any of those places. Likewise, the rise of the AUC occurred because of the resistance of more conservative Colombians to the violent inroads made by leftist forces and the inability of the government in Bogotá to repulse those incursions and control the affected territory. Again, the parallel with the rise of right-wing paramilitary groups in Guatemala and El Salvador is striking.

But the lucrative illegal drug trade in Colombia makes an already bad situation even worse. Both rebel organizations (and to a lesser extent the AUC) derive much of their revenues from the drug trade. (The other principal source of income comes from kidnapping wealthy Colombians and foreigners and holding them for ransom. Colombia has become the kidnapping capital of the world.) The bulk of the drug-related money appears to come from "tax levies" the groups impose on drug-crop farmers and the drug-trafficking organizations. According to Ralf Mutschke, assistant director of the criminal intelligence directorate of the International Criminal Police Organization (INTERPOL), the FARC collected $20 for each kilo of base cocaine produced in areas under its control, $30 for each kilo of crystal cocaine, and $2,500 for each use of a landing strip by planes bringing coca for processing or carrying the final product out of the country.[37]

But there is evidence that the FARC and the ELN sometimes are directly involved in trafficking. The strongest evidence emerged from raids conducted by Colombian military forces in early 2001 that uncovered documents, eyewitness accounts, and financial receipts showing that the rebels were directly engaged in the production and export of cocaine.[38]

One of the highest priorities of the Pastrana government was to separate the rebels from their trafficking allies. An important part of the government's strategy was a willingness to cede large portions of Colombia's territory to the FARC and the ELN. Pastrana ceded a large enclave in south-central Colombia to the FARC in 1999 and proposed a similar step in early 2001 with respect to a smaller 1,500-square-mile enclave for the ELN. The rationale was that the rebels might be more willing to negotiate if they had a sanctuary and were not under constant fire from army units. Such a territorial "carrot," Pastrana believed, could be the catalyst for productive negotiations on a power-sharing agreement to end the bloody civil war. A cynic might suggest that the concession was little more than an attempt to make public relations lemonade out of a quantity of unwanted lemons. After all, the government had not been able to effectively control the territory in question for years. Hence, there was less to such "concessions" than it might appear at first glance.

Nevertheless, Pastrana's initiative was hugely controversial in Colombia. Anticommunist peasants regarded the measure with great hostility, believing that the government had callously consigned them to the tender mercies of the FARC or the ELN.[39] More significant, the ceding of territory was fiercely opposed by the AUC, which regarded the initiative as appeasement and surrender on the installment plan. When the proposal for the ELN enclave surfaced, the AUC sent a stinging letter to Pastrana insisting that he had no such authority and pledging to fight to the death against such a concession. That letter, posted on AUC's website, warned that "The United Self-Defenses of Colombia are on total alert and our troops are willing to die or conquer, fighting subversion or whoever, in order to avoid a new demilitarized zone for our country."[40]

In April 2001 the AUC began to do much more than protest the Pastrana government's initiative. AUC fighters launched a major offensive against ELN strongholds and made considerable progress. The struggle centered on an effort to wrest control of Barrancabermeja, a river city of some 220,000 people 165 miles north of Bogotá.[41] Within days AUC forces had overrun much of the enclave that Pastrana had earmarked to be ceded to the ELN.[42] The AUC's successful offensive underscored both the weakness of the central government and the complexity of Colombia's civil war.

Critics in the United States also were scathing in their assessment of Pastrana's enclave strategy. Michael Radu, a senior fellow at the Foreign Policy Research Institute, concluded that "if there is a case study of how not to deal with a Marxist revolutionary challenge, Pastrana's policies could be the perfect model. After the 1998 surrendering of national sovereignty—no police, no army, no administrative government presence—over an area the size of Switzerland to the 17,000-strong FARC in exchange for vague promises of 'talks about peace talks,' the government has nothing to show for it." Radu was especially caustic about Bogotá's decision to try the same strategy with the ELN. "What makes the ELN deal so incredibly inane is that, unlike the still growing FARC, the ELN is on the ropes, militarily and politically. Long specialized in destroying Colombia's largest source of income, oil, by blowing up pipelines on a weekly basis, the ELN has largely been dislodged from most of its areas by the activities of the AUC."[43]

Ironically, the initial effect of the successful AUC offensive was to drive the FARC and the ELN closer together.[44] Previously the two rebel groups had feuded because of personality clashes and ideological differences. Although officially Marxist, the FARC has primarily served as a vehicle for a populist revolt by disgruntled peasants. The organization does not enjoy widespread support, and without the angry reaction of peasants to the war on drugs (especially the aerial fumigation of their crops), the insurgency might have been fatally weakened years ago.

The radical leftist orientation of the ELN is more strident, and its level of popular support is even more meager than that of the FARC. Founded by radical students and other admirers of Fidel Castro and the Cuban revolution, members of the ELN seem to take its revolutionary rhetoric and policies seriously. A convergence of the two organizations would be bad news for Colombia's beleaguered government. Not only would cooperation enhance the coordination and strength of insurgent activities, but an affiliation with the ELN might further radicalize the FARC and make a peace accord even less feasible.

Perhaps responding to criticisms of his attempt to negotiate with the rebels, Pastrana seemed to reverse course in August 2001. First, he broke off negotiations with the ELN. Then, in a move widely criticized by human rights groups both at home and abroad, he proposed and subsequently signed a new security law expanding the power of the military to deal with the insurgencies. Among other things, the new law gave the military supreme authority in areas declared to be conflict zones, superceding the authority of civilian governors and mayors.[45] The approval of the security act suggested that a new, and more violent, phase in Colombia's civil war might be on the horizon. That gloomy scenario became even more likely in January 2002 when negotiations between the Pastrana government and the FARC collapsed. Pastrana then announced an end to the sanctuary policy, and the army made preparations to retake the safe haven the FARC had been granted.[46] Only the eleventh-hour intervention by a United Nations mediator salvaged the negotiations even temporarily. That respite proved short-lived, however. A month later the negotiations broke down completely, and the army began operations in the former safe haven.[47] The election of Alvaro Uribe as Colombia's new president makes an intensification of the fighting a certainty. Throughout his campaign, Uribe had adopted an uncompromising position regarding both the insurgents and drug traffickers.

U.S. officials emphasize the importance of the drug trade to the leftist insurgent forces. Without the revenue derived directly from the rebels' own drug trafficking or the taxes imposed by them on drug-trafficking organizations, U.S. drug warriors contend, the insurgents would have a difficult time. "I don't think they could survive in their current form without it," concludes General

Charles Wilhelm, former head of the U.S. military's Southern Command.[48] Conservative estimates place the revenue flow to the FARC alone at between $515 million and $600 million a year.[49] Ambassador Patterson puts the amount at "several billion" dollars a year.[50] If even the lower figure is accurate, it would make the FARC the best-funded insurgency in the world today.

The massive flow of drug-related funds to the Colombian insurgent organizations should be somewhat embarrassing to drug warriors in the United States and Colombia. After all, when the Cali and Medellín drug cartels were broken in the early and mid-1990s, victories in that phase of the drug war were loudly proclaimed.[51] In reality, the traffickers merely adapted to the new environment and adopted a more decentralized form of business organization. Today some 300 loosely connected families control the drug trade, and Colombia still accounts for approximately 80 percent of all the cocaine produced in the world and two-thirds of the heroin consumed in the United States.[52]

HUMAN RIGHTS ABUSES

Human rights advocates in the United States and elsewhere have had grave reservations about Plan Colombia from the beginning. They worried that Washington was crawling into bed with some of the worst abusers of human rights in the Western Hemisphere. The U.S. Congress sought to deflect such criticism by attaching a number of conditions to the aid package, including a provision requiring the executive branch to closely monitor the behavior of Colombia's military and police forces.

As is often the case with congressionally imposed standards, those "requirements" have turned out to be little more than political window dressing. Indeed, Congress itself gave the executive branch a spacious legal escape hatch. Although the implementing legislation officially conditioned aid on certification by the secretary of state that Colombia was taking specific, tangible steps to improve the military's human rights performance, it also allowed a presidential waiver on national security grounds. That shell game has a dreary familiarity, since it has been applied to congressional restrictions with regard to many other situations throughout the Cold War and post–Cold War eras. The waiver provision effectively renders the so-called requirements meaningless. Sure enough, the first time the certification came due (in August 2000), President Clinton waived the requirement on the grounds of national security.

In his final days in office, Clinton was a bit more candid. He sent a letter to Congress along with a "progress report" on the human rights situation in Colombia. The report cited a number of positive developments, including the establishment of a Colombian equivalent of the U.S. military's Judge Advocate General Corps and the dismissal of some military officials. Nevertheless, the report conceded that the administration still was not satisfied that the Colombian military had purged its own ranks of violators or, as an institution, had shed its ties with right-wing paramilitary groups.[53] Despite such negative conclusions, however, the aid would continue to flow.

Such hypocrisy infuriates human rights groups such as Amnesty International and Human Rights Watch. A week before Clinton's report to Congress, representatives of those and other organizations had met with State Department officials and concluded that the rights situation in Colombia had actually deteriorated since the August waiver. Their calls to withhold the remaining aid went unheeded.

In fairness to the Colombian government, it has taken some steps to prosecute military and police personnel for the most flagrant abuses.[54] In December 2000 the state prosecutor's office charged 26 army and police officers as well as two local civilian officials with organizing massacres, disappearances, and other alleged human rights violations—most of them in collaboration with the paramilitaries. Although that seemed to be a step in the right direction, Robin Kirk, a researcher at Human Rights Watch, remained unimpressed. "We certainly welcome the state prosecutor's office's move, she said, "but these investigations have happened before. The prosecutor's office has done its job, but the military refuses to clean up its house. The pattern has been that jurisdiction is handed to the military and the cases end up being dismissed."[55] Moreover, the new security law signed by President Pastrana in August 2001 will make such prosecutions more difficult.[56]

Even Pastrana became alarmed at the growing strength of the right-wing paramilitary organizations and their willingness to commit horrific acts of violence. At one point he blasted the paramilitaries as a "veritable cancer spreading in our body politic." He conceded that AUC fighters were "responsible for 70 percent of the massacres." Equally troubling, the AUC's strength is expanding at an alarming rate. "While guerrilla numbers have risen 16 percent in the last two years," Pastrana stated, "the increase in AUC group members in that same period is estimated to have been five times greater."[57] He estimated that the AUC now had some 8,000 fighters.[58]

Human rights activists were again infuriated at an especially gruesome massacre over Easter weekend in 2001.[59] Some 200 AUC fighters used chainsaws and other weapons to mutilate and kill 40 villagers in western Cauca state. One angry Colombian human rights activist, Armando Borrero, described what he regarded as typical collusion between the army and the AUC as seen in dozens of previous cases: "It's a very similar situation. The massacre is announced. There is information. But at the moment it occurs, apparently no troops are in the area where the danger is the greatest."[60] Los Angeles Times correspondent T. Christian Miller, who wrote a detailed account of the massacre, reached a similar conclusion: "The massacre showed the exploding power of Colombia's paramilitaries, bent on wiping out by any means necessary the leftist guerrillas who have plagued the country for 40 years. It also showed the Colombian armed forces' history with right-wing violence. The military was seemingly powerless to stop the para-militaries entry into the region but was able to capture more than 70 of the [leftist] fighters as they fled."[61]

The AUC fighters are hardly the only ones guilty of commit-ting atrocities. In May 2001 FARC troops massacred more than two dozen farmers near Puerto Presquillo, in northern Colombia. As in the case of the earlier AUC rampage, the FARC assault was characterized by acts of shocking brutality. Many of the victims were hacked to death with machetes. The apparent motive for the FARC offensive was also quite revealing. Rebel forces invaded an area where a new coca crop had been used to generate income for the AUC. The massacre was also part of a larger FARC campaign to open a transportation corridor to the Caribbean and Panama to facilitate the flow of its own drugs and arms. Achieving that goal meant eliminating a stronghold that the AUC had seized more than five years earlier.[62] The horrific episode is merely one example of how the issues of ideology, drug trafficking, and human rights abuses all interact in the complex Colombian morass.

Human rights organizations are not the only critics of Plan Colombia. Governors in the coca-producing provinces, although strongly opposed to the Marxist guerrillas, condemn aspects of the plan. They reserve their harshest rhetorical fire for the aerial spraying campaign that Washington pushes with such enthusiasm. The governors warned in January 2001 that the operation would imperil the livelihood of thousands of poor peasants. Indeed, their worst fears were soon confirmed as the herbicide used in the spraying program killed acre upon acre of legal crops along with the coca plants (see chapter 6). Four governors escalated their criticism of the operation in March, reflecting the mounting anger of their constituents.[63] "The real problem is the terrible situation in which thousands of peasants live in Colombia," argued Guillermo Alfonso Jaramillo, governor of the southwestern province of Huila.

"We can't run over their livelihoods without giving them opportunities to grow other crops."[64] Unfortunately, the alternative pushed by the governors was the hoary and much-discredited crop substitution strategy.

PLAN COLOMBIA'S INHERENT FUTILITY

Predictably, both Colombian and U.S. officials touted "spectacular" early successes from the aerial spraying campaign. Just as predictably, details soon emerged to cast doubt on those claims. *Washington Post* correspondent Scott Wilson, traveling in Colombia just weeks after the most massive phase of the spraying offensive in December 2000 and January 2001, noted Bogotá's claims that some 40,000 acres of coca crops had been destroyed in one province, Putumayo, alone. Yet "in interviews around this village [El Tigre] . . . farmers said many drug plantations remained untouched, protected from spray planes in hard-to-reach valleys by jungle cover and guerrilla troops. Valleys full of coca were evident from the main east-west highway. And on almost every farm hit by the herbicide since December, small tents protected young coca plants for future cultivation."[65]

Evidence emerged in May 2001 that cast even more doubt on the effectiveness of the crop eradication strategy. A source within the Colombian government leaked information about revised estimates of the country's cocaine production. According to those revised estimates, Colombia is producing 800 to 900 tons of cocaine annually, not the 580 tons estimated by the U.S. State Department and the U.S. Drug Enforcement Administration.[66] If accurate, the new estimates mean that Colombia is producing more cocaine than the earlier U.S. estimates for total world production (780 tons).

Similarly, U.S. satellite data suggested that Colombia had approximately 340,000 acres under cultivation with coca when the latest phase of the crop spraying program got under way in December 2000. By May 2001 about 75,000 acres had been fumigated. But if the Colombian government study is correct, the actual acreage under cultivation is considerably higher. Aerial surveys conducted in the summer of 2001 detected extensive, previously unknown fields of coca (and poppy) in the vast, mostly unpopulated eastern plains of Colombia—often in rebel-controlled territory.[67] In short, even if one accepts the notion that the spraying completely eradicated the coca plants in the 75,000 acres affected, the reality is that the amount of acreage still under cultivation is greater than the total estimated when the campaign began. As the Colombian source put it, Plan Colombia had "not made a dent" in the country's output of cocaine.[68] "It's quite possible we've underestimated the coca in Colombia," conceded Ambassador Patterson. "Everywhere we look there is more coca than we expected. There's just more out there than we thought."[69]

Horacio Serpa, a leader of the opposition Liberal Party, contends that the long-term result has even been more dismal. "After spraying more than 500,000 acres (200,000 hectares) of coca, the area under cultivation is three times larger than it was five years ago," he charges.[70] He advocates an urgent reevaluation of the aerial spraying campaign.

As if the reports leaking out of Colombia were not enough to cast doubt on the effectiveness of Plan Colombia, Donnie Marshall, the head of the U.S. Drug Enforcement Administration, made a telling admission barely a week later. Marshall conceded that cocaine prices in the United States were not rising, despite the eradication efforts in Colombia. If those efforts were effective, they should have produced at least a modest supply shortage in the United States. That, in turn, should have created upward pressure on street prices for the drug. Yet Marshall admitted that prices had remained steady since December 2000, when eradication efforts under Plan Colombia went into operation.[71] Such is the fate of crop eradication "victories" in the war on drugs.

That should come as no surprise. Under U.S. pressure, Colombia has resorted to vigorous aerial spraying campaigns before. Each time the effort began with a flurry of professed optimism and determination; each time the campaign produced no lasting damage to the drug trade. In the early and mid-1980s, Bogotá conducted extensive fumigation strikes against both marijuana and coca crops. A decade later a new initiative was launched. Soon after assuming office in 1994, President Ernesto Samper (who, ironically, would soon be accused by Washington of being in league with the drug traffickers) pledged that all illegal drug crops would be eradicated in two years.[72] And now we hear similar confident predictions from the supporters of Plan Colombia.

Direct U.S. involvement in Colombia's antidrug effort began long before the approval of Plan Colombia. Trainers from U.S. Army Special Forces (the Green Berets) had been training units of the Colombian military for years in antinarcotics measures. American civilians (mostly retired military personnel) were also contracted by the State Department to fly some of the planes doing aerial spraying and other tasks. At least two ostensibly private firms in the United States were beneficiaries of such "outsourcing" contracts.[73] Plan Colombia merely increased the scope of those activities.

The risk exposure to those Americans in Colombia is also on the rise. Planes conducting the spraying have been fired on.[74] In February 2001 an armed search-and-rescue team, working under contract with the State Department, was also fired on as it plucked the crew of a Colombian police helicopter that had been disabled in a firefight with guerrillas trying to protect a coca crop. The search-and-rescue team included several Americans.[75]

SPILLOVER EFFECTS

The negative effects of Plan Colombia are not confined to Colombia. Indeed, one of the great dangers of the scheme is that it will cause Colombia's troubles to spill over the border into neighboring countries. The neighbors certainly are worried about that risk.[76] As soon as it became evident that the United States was financially backing Plan Colombia, and that Washington was primarily funding the military, antidrug component, officials in other countries began to express concern and objections. Not surprisingly, Venezuela's eccentric leftist president Hugo Chávez was one of the first and loudest critics. During a state visit to Brazil in August 2000, Chávez explicitly invoked the Vietnam analogy. "It would be very dangerous if the operation leads to a military escalation of the conflict," he warned. "It could lead us to a Vietnamization of the whole Amazon region." Chávez added, in a thinly veiled slap at both the Colombian and U.S. governments, "Some sectors in Colombia and other places may think that the conflict has a military solution. That is incorrect. Peace negotiations are the only way to achieve a solution."[77]

But Chávez was hardly alone in voicing apprehension about Plan Colombia. General Alberto Cardoso, chief security adviser to the president of Brazil, stated that it was of considerable concern to his country. The effects could include "the flight of guerrillas and the transfer of drug laboratories and plantations."[78] A short time later Brazil's foreign minister told U.S. Secretary of State Madeleine Albright that his country was not as committed as the United States was to Plan Colombia and would not be actively involved in any common international antidrug effort in Colombia.[79] Panamanian president Mireya Moscoso adopted a similar attitude of neutrality: "It is between Colombia and the United States . . . we are not going to get involved in this plan."[80]

On the eve of a meeting of South American presidents in September 2000, Bill Clinton urged them to endorse Plan Colombia. The chief executives refused to take that step. The joint declaration at the end of the summit expressed support for Pastrana's efforts to negotiate an end to the civil war, but the leaders pointedly refused to endorse Plan Colombia—especially its military component. At a press conference after the summit, Chile's president, Ricardo Lagos, made that distinction explicit. The presidents fully supported "the peace process, which implies negotiations," he said, but that was "distinct from the problem of narcotics trafficking."[81]

Seven weeks later, a meeting of hemispheric defense leaders showed that the wariness of Colombia's neighbors about the strategy Washington was pushing had not diminished. U.S. officials openly showed their impatience at such foot-dragging. In a closed-door session, Deputy Undersecretary of Defense James Bodner emphasized that Plan Colombia would go ahead with or without support from the other Latin American nations. "He complained about the lack of solidarity by South America, and he laid it on heavy," Representative João Herrmann Neto of Brazil's House Foreign Relations Committee, who had attended the meeting, later told reporters. Herrmann also related that some delegates bridled at both the U.S. position and the tone with which it was expressed. Herrmann himself described it as an example of "typical American superiority."[82]

Some of the warnings about Plan Colombia and the professed reluctance to endorse the scheme appear to be part of a cynical strategy on the part of various governments to extract more money from the United States. Ecuador's foreign minister, Heinz Moeller, was not exactly subtle about that point when he warned that it would be impossible to prevent Colombia's war from spreading to Ecuador (and other neighboring countries)—unless the United States came up with additional financial assistance. He thought that another $400 million to $500 million over a five-year period might be appropriate.[83]

Indeed, the lure of U.S. aid dollars eventually caused most Latin American leaders to embrace Plan Colombia, however reluctantly. By April 2001 even Hugo Chávez was on board. In contrast to his remarks a few months earlier warning of the "Vietnamization" of the Amazon basin and the advent of a "medium intensity conflict," Chávez stated that doubts about Plan Colombia "have now been clarified."[84] Coincidentally, his conversion took place barely two weeks after the Bush administration proposed to double the aid package to Colombia's neighbors. That package included some $10 million for Venezuela, even though the Chávez regime still had not agreed to allow U.S. planes on antidrug missions to transit Venezuelan air space.

Associated Press correspondent Jared Kotler noted the striking change that had occurred in the attitudes of various Latin American governments regarding Plan Colombia between summer 2000 and spring 2001:

> Only a few months ago, Colombia's neighbors were sounding loud alarms and hastily preparing for a drug war backed by Washington to send cocaine and guerrillas spilling over their borders. Ecuador girded for refugees and added troops along a lawless border. Brazil sent police and fretted about whether napalm would be dropped on the Amazon. With Green Berets training Colombian troops in the jungle, President Hugo Chávez of Venezuela warned darkly of a new Vietnam War in the making. Now, their complaints are giving way to pragmatism. By seeking U.S. aid and trade benefits for their collaboration in the war, the countries are trying to cash in on their fears.[85]

University of Miami professor Bruce Bagley states simply, "These countries are now negotiating for goodies."[86] In some cases, even the revised package offered by the Bush administration is not considered enough. Alejandro Toledo, elected president of Peru in June 2001, pledged full cooperation with the United States in antidrug efforts but added that he hoped the United States "not only supplies interest but also a bit more in the way of resources."[87]

But some influential Latin Americans have not muted their objections merely because their countries now hope to get U.S. aid funds. Even as Chávez and other politicians were announcing their conversion experiences, some 100 prominent Latin Americans, including Argentine Nobel Laureate Adolfo Perez Esquivel, sent President Bush a letter calling U.S. military aid and forced coca eradication in Colombia "misguided and harmful" and warning that the policy "will [adversely] affect the entire Andean region."[88] Ecuadorean congressman Henry Llanes, a prominent critic of his government's decision to allow the United States to run its antidrug surveillance flights out of a big air base at Manta, cites fear of a dangerous entanglement as one reason for his opposition. "We are compromising our neutrality in the Colombian conflict with the Manta base, dragging ourselves into a war between the Americans and their enemies in Colombia," Llanes warns.[89]

His fears are not unfounded. In January 2001, Ecuadorean troops had killed six men at an illegal drug lab near the border with Colombia. Evidence at the scene indicated that they were FARC members.[90] That marked the first armed clash between the Ecuadorean military and the Colombian rebels. Other incidents were not long in coming. In early February 2001 more than 500 Ecuadoreans fled their Amazon jungle homes after Colombian armed groups threatened their border hamlets. That incursion seemed to be in direct response to the earlier destruction of the labs.[91] In early June an Ecuadorean army unit clashed with ELN guerrillas some 13 miles inside the border. "I think it is a product of Plan Colombia, the guerrillas feel harassed and seek a place where they can act more calmly, which is worrisome," Vice President Pedro Pinto told reporters.[92] Pinto urged the United States to supply helicopters in addition to the planned $78 million in aid so that Ecuador could better patrol its border with Colombia.

Similar incidents have occurred along Colombia's border with Venezuela. In addition, Colombians fleeing the fighting between rebels and government forces—or between the rebels and right-wing paramilitary units—have crossed into neighboring countries. In one such incident in early February 2001, more than 400 people from four villages sought refuge in Venezuela after paramilitary

forces pillaged their homes.[93] Other victims have fled into neighboring countries to avoid outrages by the rebels. More than 100
refugees crossed the border into Panama after FARC guerrillas
killed the mayor of their Pacific coast village and terrorized them.[94]

In addition to the spillover of violence from Colombia's civil
war, there has been a spillover of the drug trade itself. Even as U.S.
support for Plan Colombia got under way in 2000, U.S. officials
were reporting a marked increase of drug trafficking in the upper
Amazon River region in Brazil as well as in Panama.[95] In the
autumn of 2000 the Brazilian government announced the start of a
three-year, $10 million effort, Operation Cobra, to combat the
increased drug trade that was being displaced from Colombia.[96]
Throughout 2000 there was a noticeable increase in U.S.-led
antidrug efforts throughout Central America, as that region
became the latest battlefield in the war on drugs.[97] Although the
financial commitment was modest—just $4.3 million in military
antidrug aid for the first year—the U.S. military presence was
growing. Not only were U.S. military trainers active in drilling
antinarcotics units in several Central American countries, but
Washington acquired the right to fly antidrug spy planes out of the
Comalapa air base in El Salvador. The U.S. military presence in
Central America is already beginning to resemble the level of
involvement during the 1980s. The principal difference is that the
target has changed. Then it was radical leftist guerrillas; now it is
drug traffickers.

The spillover effects have become serious enough that U.S. and
Colombian officials are explicitly addressing that phenomenon as
they assess the performance of Plan Colombia.[98] Colombia's neighbors are also demanding a larger piece of the funding pie. Originally, $180 million of the two-year, $1.3 billion aid package was
earmarked for neighboring countries, but Ecuador, Peru, Brazil,
and Panama all immediately complained that the sums were
inadequate. By late 2000 U.S. officials expressed agreement with
those complaints and promised that additional funding would be

forthcoming. Undersecretary of State Thomas Pickering was surprisingly candid in his reasons for the policy change: "As we increase our efforts in Colombia, there will be a tendency [for the drug organizations] to find new areas, either in Colombia or outside Colombia, in which to move the cultivation and production of cocaine and heroin."[99]

One would be hard-pressed to come up with a more concise description of the "push-down, pop-up" (or "balloon") effect and the inherent futility of the drug eradication component of the hemispheric war on drugs. (The effect occurs in other ways as well. For example, Plan Colombia's focus on coca eradication has produced one unexpected consequence: the diversion of resources away from stopping the country's flourishing heroin trade. Among other factors, the spraying of poppy plantations high in the Andes was put on hold so that more aircraft could be used to fumigate coca crops.)[100]

But Pickering did not draw the obvious conclusion from evidence of the push-down, pop-up effect. Instead, he cited the phenomenon as a reason for a broader and better-funded drug eradication program throughout the Andean region and beyond: "The need in the surrounding and nearby areas is going to increase. Enlargement of the programs through increased funding in a regional effort . . . is probably going to be necessary, and that's what informs our thinking in current budget planning. We are now thinking very clearly of a regional program . . . as a centerpiece of next year's effort to support the Andean region in its efforts to deal with cocaine, heroin and the associated multifarious problems in the region."[101]

In March 2001 the Bush administration proposed a significant increase in funding for Colombia's neighbors in the 2002 fiscal year budget. As part of a $731 million new "Andean Initiative" aid program, the administration earmarked $332 million for antidrug efforts in those countries. (It is perhaps symbolic of the intellectual sterility of the war on drugs that not only are the policies periodically recycled, but even the names of the various schemes are recycled. "Andean Initiative" is the same name given to the grandiose regional antidrug offensive waged during the administration of the elder Bush.) The new Andean Initiative request submitted to Congress included an additional $399 million for Colombia, $156 million for Peru, $101 million for Bolivia, and about $75 million for Colombia's four other neighbors—Brazil, Ecuador, Panama, and Venezuela.[102]

Although most members of Congress officially express support for waging the war on drugs in Latin America, the administration's proposal was not immune to the budgetary ax. Despite the enthusiastic backing of House Speaker Hastert, the version of the Andean Initiative passed by the House of Representatives cut the spending to $675 million. The Senate Appropriations Committee went even further, slashing the amount to $567 million and diverting the remainder to battle AIDS and other infectious diseases overseas.[103] If Colombia and its neighbors were hoping for a foreign aid bonanza by supporting Washington's drug-war initiatives, they may have to scale back their expectations.

ANOTHER NATION-BUILDING MISSION?

For all the claimed successes, Plan Colombia itself is already showing signs of trouble. It was certainly not an encouraging indicator that, barely months after the program went into effect, President Pastrana was already calling for a substantial additional infusion of financial support. In an interview shortly before his summit meeting with President Bush in February 2001, Pastrana asserted that perhaps as much as another $500 million a year was needed. Those funds, he argued, should go for economic development in the provinces where the aerial spraying programs were taking their greatest toll. It was a matter of justice and would merely compensate Colombia for the expenditure of its own money on what was largely a U.S. problem, he asserted. "We are a poor country. But we are spending $1 billion a year of our money to keep drugs off the streets of Washington and New York. We need more help." He added ominously, "This is a long-term plan, maybe 15 to 20 years."[104] That is not good news for Americans who worry that Plan Colombia is merely the first stage of what could become a long-term U.S. entanglement.

Nor is it encouraging that members of the Bush administration are openly discussing ways to expand the training of Colombian security forces beyond the three special counternarcotics battalions that have already received instruction under the first phase of Plan Colombia. Options being discussed include creating a fourth battalion of counternarcotics personnel or training an existing unit of the Colombian military. (U.S. officials are hesitant about the second option because of the human rights record of regular Colombian forces.) Resistance to expanding the U.S. involvement in Colombia comes primarily from civilian officials in the Pentagon. A revealing admission came from Peter Rodman, assistant secretary of defense for international security affairs. Rodman stated that Washington faced some "agonizing decisions" about its Colombia policy. "Are we getting deeper into a conflict or not?" he pondered. "I think that we as a country are not quite sure where we are headed."[105]

It is likely that such cautionary sentiments will be swept aside and that the United States will expand the mission in Colombia. An official who insisted on anonymity dismissed Pentagon reservations. Such concerns, he said, are "raised by civilian guys in the Pentagon who are new on the job, who are getting their feet on the ground." The official concluded, "Once they go to Colombia and see how it's done, they'll feel better about it."[106]

The antinarcotics effort embodied in Plan Colombia is beginning to look a lot like the nation-building missions for which President Bush and his foreign policy advisers have expressed a wariness bordering on outright aversion. Even Barry McCaffrey began to move beyond the drugs focus in early 2001 as he left office, arguing that Colombia was dying as a society. If America stood idle, he said, it would be like the neighbors of Kitty Genovese, the 1964 murder victim in New York City whose frantic pleas for help went unanswered.[107] Max Manwaring, a professor of military strategy at the United States Army War College, asserts that because of the fear of a Vietnam-style commitment, "we just concentrated on the drug thing and hoped the other problems would go away." Manwaring, for one, did not shy away from arguing that nation building is needed in Colombia. "We've got to go back to the term of nation building. Nobody wants to use it. Because that term is verboten. But that's what it is."[108]

But given America's miserable track record in nation-building missions throughout the initial post–Cold War decade, such a possibility ought to make Americans more rather than less nervous about their country's growing involvement in Colombia. If the debacles in Somalia and Haiti and the frustrating, increasingly futile ventures in Bosnia and Kosovo have demonstrated anything, it is that nation building may be an impossible task except under the most extraordinary circumstances (such as the political trans-formation of Germany and Japan under U.S. occupation after World War II).[109] Certainly the more recent attempts (as well as U.S. efforts in such places as Nicaragua and Haiti in the early 20th century) do not inspire confidence.

And Plan Colombia already shows signs of creating a nasty, anti-U.S. backlash among portions of the Colombian population. When Pastrana visited Putumayo in May 2001 to sell the "softer" (economic development) side of Plan Colombia, he was repeatedly confronted by groups of protesters, many waving signs showing a Colombian flag being subsumed by the Stars and Stripes, with the caption "Plan Colombia's achievements." Other demonstrators greeted the president with chants of "Pastrana subservient to the gringos."[110] "The United States thinks they're the boss here," one angry resident stated to a reporter. "We don't want fumigation, and we don't want money from Uncle Sam."[111]

Nor is anger at the United States confined to the peasantry. Columnist Roberto Pombo, writing in the pages of the highly respected Bogotá news magazine *Cambio,* bitterly denounced the fumigation campaign for destroying the livelihood of farmers, who have few options other than growing drug crops to make a living. Pombo denounced fumigation as a "failed campaign against drug traffickers, all by imperial order from the United States."[112]

Given the long-standing history of anti-U.S. sentiment in Latin America, the resurgence of such attitudes in Colombia is cause for concern. Latin American paranoia about U.S. imperialism, a fear that never slumbers too soundly to begin with, is beginning to resurface. And that development could have widespread, very negative ramifications. Even the June 2001 RAND Corporation report that advocated a hard-line policy against both the narcotics traffickers and the guerrillas questioned the wisdom of the aerial spraying campaign. The authors argued that U.S. officials should "review whether aerial fumigation of coca crops is the most effective means of reducing coca production at acceptable social and political cost. Alternative strategies, such as targeting bottle-necks in the drug refining and transportation network in Colombia, should be explored."[113]

Not only is antigovernment (and anti-U.S.) sentiment on the rise in Colombia, but the battle between government forces and their various adversaries is also spreading. The money flowing from the narcotics trade appears to be stoking the conflicts, but so too is U.S. aid under Plan Colombia. There is little doubt that the Colombian military has become more aggressive in its counterinsurgency campaigns and counternarcotics measures. As opponents of aid predicted, Plan Colombian monies could not fund one effort without indirectly supporting the other. As a result, a peaceful solution to Colombia's internecine struggles is even more remote than before. *Washington Post* correspondent Scott Wilson observes, "By almost any measure, more people are fighting more frequently in more parts of Colombia than at any point in the four-decade conflict."[114] Washington's policies are not solely responsible for that situation, but they certainly have contributed to it.

There is yet another troubling possibility in connection with Plan Colombia. If the effort fails to achieve its objective, pressure will mount on the United States to escalate its commitment. Even during these relatively early stages of the campaign, one can already hear arguments that America's credibility is on the line. In the cover letter accompanying the release of the RAND report, Edward R. Harshberger, director of the think tank's strategy and doctrine program, stated: "Should the Colombian government falter, the United States would be confronted with a strategic dilemma: whether to escalate its support of the Bogotá government or to scale it down, potentially at the cost of Colombia's tottering democracy. The latter approach would involve a significant loss of credibility and a degradation of the United States' ability to protect its interests in a critical region."[115] As we have seen in regions as diverse as Southeast Asia, the Persian Gulf, and the Balkans, once America's "credibility" is invoked, it is very difficult to stem the drive toward a major military commitment. In Colombia, another quagmire is beckoning.

CHAPTER FOUR

A MIX OF FLAWED STRATEGIES

The supply side of the U.S.-orchestrated drug war has emphasized three major components: (1) interdiction of drug-trafficking routes, (2) drug-crop eradication measures, and (3) crop substitution and alternative development programs. The mixture of the strategies changes from time to time, depending on which initiative is currently in fashion as the answer to the curse of narcotics trafficking, but all three elements are always present in some proportion. In reality, the specific mix does not really matter. All three strategies are hopelessly impractical.

Part of the problem is that the United States is asking the drug-producing countries to eliminate a significant portion of their economies. Just how important the illegal drug trade is to the economies of the Andean states and Mexico is a matter of some debate. Estimates vary widely. At the low end is the calculation by Colombian scholar Ricardo Rocha, who estimates that between 1982 and 1998, illegal drug trafficking typically accounted for approximately 3 percent of Colombia's annual gross domestic product (GDP).[1] Patrick L. Clawson and Rensselaer W. Lee III, analysts at the Foreign Policy Research Institute, estimate that the cocaine portion of the illicit drug trade alone accounts for about 7 percent of the combined GDP of Colombia, Peru, and Bolivia. While they acknowledge that such a figure is significant, they argue that the drug trade "is not the heartbeat that sustains the body economic."[2]

Other experts assert that the economic importance of the drug trade is substantially larger. For example, one estimate placed Bolivia's drug trade at 13 to 15 percent of GDP in the 1990s.[3] Another concluded that during the 1990s, cocaine exports accounted for 30 percent of Peru's total exports and that the drug industry in Bolivia provided up to 20 percent of the country's GDP and approximately 20 percent of the adult employment.[4] As just one indicator of the drug trade's prominence in Colombia's economy, Bogotá began to adjust its GDP figures in 1999 to include estimated income generated from growing illegal drug crops. Officials believed that drug exports could amount to between one-quarter and one-third of the country's legal exports—or as much as $4 billion a year.[5]

The magnitude of the drug trade and its portion of the economies of drug-source countries is inherently difficult to quantify, given the illegality of the trade.[6] But few experts would dispute that it constitutes a significant economic factor in the Andean countries, Mexico, and several other nations in the Western Hemisphere. And Washington's various strategies to wipe out or even meaningfully decrease the trade have met with scant success.

INTERDICTION: MUCH HYPE, LITTLE SUBSTANCE

Scarcely a month goes by without a major press story in the drug-producing countries or the United States about the interception of a large drug shipment. Typically, such busts are announced at well-promoted press conferences at which some or all of the seized contraband (often together with captured weapons and bundles of cash) are displayed. Time and time again, the news media disseminate reports about how the seizure will strike a serious blow against drug trafficking.

Proponents of interdiction are adept at spinning any result. If the amount of drugs interdicted goes up, that shows the effectiveness of law enforcement. Conversely, if the amount of drugs intercepted goes down, as it did on the U.S.-Mexico border following tightened security procedures in response to the September 11, 2001, terrorist attacks in New York and Washington, that too is hailed as a victory in the war on drugs.[7] U.S. Customs officials noted that between September 11 and September 23, some 8,700 pounds of drugs were seized—an 80 percent drop from the 44,160 pounds seized during the same period the previous year. In response to questions by *Washington Post* correspondent Mary Jordan, however, a spokesman for the U.S. Customs Service conceded that traffickers might be "sitting on loads in Mexico temporarily," and he could not discount the possibility that traffickers might be simply using alternate routes.[8] Unfortunately, most reporters do not ask the kind of probing questions that Jordan did, and government officials frequently score unearned propaganda victories.

Interdiction realities are far different from the picture painted by drug warriors. International interdiction has increased markedly over the past two decades, in part because of the improvement in radar and other detection methods. But there is little evidence that those efforts have materially reduced the amount of drugs reaching the United States.[9]

Interdiction can take place in three different areas, or "zones": the departure, the transit, and the arrival zones.[10] Farthest away from the United States is the departure zone, which includes the area in or immediately adjacent to the drug-source country. In the case of cocaine, for example, that country is usually Colombia. Responsibility for interdiction in the departure zone lies primarily with the authorities in the drug-source country, although U.S. law enforcement agencies (and increasingly the U.S. military) provide intelligence data and other assistance.

Drug shipments that make it out of the departure zone enter the transit zone, at which point the primary responsibility for interdiction shifts to the United States—although a considerable amount of cooperation with countries along the trafficking route is required. Most drugs leaving Colombia go by either ship or plane. Until recently traffickers preferred to fly a shipment out aboard a small aircraft. Indeed, before the mid-1990s, as much as 90 percent of the cocaine left Colombia in that fashion.[11] Drugs were also sometimes sent out on fishing trawlers or pleasure craft in the Caribbean. As interdiction efforts made those modes of transportation increasingly risky, other methods, such as sending drug shipments concealed in the cargo holds of commercial airliners or oceangoing commercial ships, have become more common.

The task of intercepting drugs in the transit zone is a daunting one, even with U.S. and Latin American authorities using over-the-horizon radar and other sophisticated detection hardware. More than 5,000 large ships are in the eastern Pacific Ocean on a given day, and an additional 1,000 or more are in the Caribbean. The odds of determining which dozen or so vessels might be carrying drugs are much worse than one would get in the typical casino. Planes also can exploit the enormous size of the transit zone. Smuggling planes typically can fly at altitudes of up to 10,000 feet as well as at very low altitudes. That fact alone means that the transit zone consists of more than 15 *billion* cubic miles.[12]

Drug shipments that make it through the transit zone (and the overwhelming majority do) enter the arrival zone. Occasionally that may mean an arrival at a U.S. port or airfield. During the 1970s and 1980s, it usually meant an arrival in the Bahamas or some other Caribbean locale close to the United States. More recently it means arrival at some location in Mexico. Unless it involves direct entry into the United States, primary responsibility for interdiction in this zone shifts from U.S. agencies to the law enforcement personnel of the country involved.

Even most law enforcement officials admit that only a small percentage of the drugs coming in from South America or Mexico is ever intercepted. The White House Office of National Drug Control

Policy has set a goal of interdicting 18.7 percent of the projected amount of drugs coming out of source countries in 2002 and 28.7 percent by 2007. Yet even officials tasked with fighting the drug war dismiss such goals as unattainable. Admiral James Loy, commandant of the Coast Guard and the designated "interdiction coordinator" in the U.S. counternarcotics campaign, is candid on that point, saying "I frankly don't believe that we are going to be able to reach those goals, given our current seizure rate of roughly 10 percent."[13]

The limitations of interdiction are a long-standing reality. In the mid-1990s, the U.S. Customs Service admitted that only 3 percent of the nearly 9 million shipping containers entering the United States were checked by customs inspectors. To take just one example, of the 5,000 trucks entering the United States daily from Mexico, only about 200 are inspected.[14] Most drug traffickers are perfectly willing to chance those odds.

Moreover, seizures of drug shipments generally have a very modest effect on the street price. The extent of the impact varies, depending on where in the production and distribution channel the disruption occurs. RAND Corporation analyst Kevin Jack Riley observes that "seizures made at the lower-risk stages of production will affect drug prices less than seizures made at the higher-risk stages of shipment and retailing."[15] In other words, interdiction in the source country or departure zone (early in the production channel) will have little effect on the retail price.

The bottom line is that interdiction at any point in the supply chain is extremely difficult and largely ineffectual. Riley aptly notes that "just as German forces outflanked the Maginot Line, drug traffickers have surmounted the interdiction barrier."[16]

"VICTORIES" THROUGH ERADICATION

Frustration with the limited effects of interdiction efforts is one factor that has led U.S. and Latin American officials to place more emphasis on crop eradication. Riley notes the working of that logic with respect to the cocaine trade: "Coca is the essential ingredient in cocaine, and without it the traffickers would be driven out of business. Coca plants themselves represent the most visible—and, thus, vulnerable—point in the production chain. Certainly coca fields are much easier to detect than small bundles of cocaine."[17]

The United States has supported both forced eradication of drug crops and compensated eradication programs. Both versions have encountered serious problems. Forced eradication risks alienating sizable portions of the population in drug-source countries. Vehement resistance to forced eradication by the peasantry in Bolivia was a major reason why successive governments resisted U.S. pressure during the 1980s. Peru under the government of Alberto Fujimori exhibited similar reluctance. The forced eradication component of Plan Colombia certainly is arousing a great deal of public opposition and confirms that the reluctance of the Bolivian and Peruvian governments was well founded.

But compensated eradication has its own difficulties. Among other problems, it can become a vehicle for milking the United States of aid money. In Bolivia, for example, the United States established a compensation level of $2,000 for every hectare (2.471 acres) of coca taken out of cultivation. That level was set in November 1986. By the early 1990s, coca growers were pressing for an increase to $6,000 per hectare, to reflect the higher potential value of coca on the illegal market. U.S. officials strongly opposed increasing the compensation level, arguing that $6,000 per hectare would act as an incentive to plant new coca and cash it in.[18]

Both U.S. and Latin American officials never seem to lose their touching faith in the efficacy of crop eradication programs. In January 1976 the official in charge of Operation Condor in Mexico predicted confidently that, with the use of herbicides, "before mid-year we are going to completely end the cultivation of drugs in this country."[19] A quarter century later, the claims made for the eradication efforts in Peru, Bolivia, and Colombia are only a shade less audacious.

The attitude of U.S. officials about the progress of the international phase of the drug war has a dreary consistency. Setbacks are ignored or explained away; every sign of success is touted, often to the point of absurdity; and victory is said to be just around the corner—if the current policies continue awhile longer. The proclamations of prospective breakthroughs occur so frequently that one is reminded of the person who asserts that it is easy to quit smoking: after all, he has done so numerous times.

Those who might be tempted to give credence to the optimism about progress in the hemispheric drug war oozing from recent editions of the State Department's annual *International Narcotics Control Strategy (INCS) Reports* should approach the issue with more than a little caution. For one thing, there is some doubt about the accuracy of the U.S. data. Part of that uncertainty reflects an inherent problem of trying to measure the size and scope of an illegal industry; all figures are little more than educated guesses. But in some instances the State Department's figures diverge sharply from the estimates produced by international agencies and other non-U.S. sources. Perhaps most troubling, the U.S. figures tend to show much greater progress in the drug war than do the other estimates. For example, from the mid-1980s to the mid-1990s, the figures on coca acreage in Peru cited in reports by the United Nations (UN), the Peruvian Ministry of Agriculture, and a respected private consulting firm all showed a steady rise. The State Department's figures, on the other hand, showed the amount of acreage to be flat or declining. The divergence was so great by 1994 that the UN estimate was nearly twice that of the estimate contained in the *INCS Report*.[20]

Those inclined to believe the current government's evidence of progress and predictions of ultimate victory would be wise to revisit similar language found in reports issued during the first Bush administration. As did their Clinton administration succes-

Table 4.1

NET PRODUCTION OF COCA LEAF

	Year		
Country	1984	1989	1990
Bolivia	49,200	68,300	64,400
Colombia	11,680	33,900	32,100
Ecuador	895	150	120
Peru	60,000	137,300	138,300
Total Coca	121,775	239,650	234,920

Source: INCS Report Summary, February 1, 1985; and INCS Report, March 1991.

sors, Bush administration officials conceded that there had been occasional setbacks and disappointments in achieving supply-side objectives. Nevertheless, they insisted that, on balance, the war was going well. The State Department's 1992 INCS Report, for example, exuded confidence, asserting that "for the second year in a row, the USG-led anti-drug effort registered important gains."[21]

The State Department's 1991 report also indicated that declines had occurred in several categories of global illicit drug production in 1990. Even the government's own statistics, however, showed that the declines were quite modest; indeed, in some categories they may simply have been statistical aberrations. Moreover, even if the declines from 1989 to 1990 were real, they followed years of dramatic increases. Table 4.1 illustrates the longer-term trend in the net production of coca leaf (production figures are in metric tons).

Moreover, the official figures did not fully convey the anemic results of the U.S.-directed campaign against the drug supply. In its 1991 report, the State Department made a most significant change in its methodology, noting that "mature" coca bushes—those 2-15 years old and capable of producing full-leaf harvests three or four times a year—had yields significantly higher than the "average" yield that the department had used for its previous production

Table 4.2

NET PRODUCTION OF COCA LEAF

(REVISED METHODOLOGY)

Country	Year		
	1989	1990	1991
Bolivia	77,600	76,800	78,400
Colombia	33,900	32,100	30,000
Ecuador	270	170	40
Peru	186,300	196,900	222,700
Total Coca	298,070	305,970	331,140

Source: INCS Report, March 1992, p. 28.

estimates. Because the percentage of mature bushes was especially high in Bolivia and Peru (the two leading source countries), the change in methodology had a dramatic effect on total production figures. Indeed, the State Department conceded that it may have substantially underestimated the potential yield in the Andean region.[22]

The 1992 report confirmed the magnitude of those earlier faulty estimates. As shown in metric tons in Table 4.2 the revised methodology revealed quite different—and far more sobering—net production figures.

Only according to the *Alice in Wonderland* logic of the U.S. government could an increase from 240,000 metric tons (original methodology) in 1989 to 331,000 metric tons (revised methodology) in 1991 be considered evidence of success. Given the depressing data on net production, U.S. officials understandably preferred to emphasize other measures of alleged progress. Thus, cocaine seizures "surged ahead," according to the 1992 report, and total land devoted to the cultivation of coca fell from an estimated 211,800 hectares in 1991 to 206,240 in 1992, which the State Department described as "a significant decline."[23]

Table 4.3

AMOUNT OF DRUG-CROP LAND ERADICATED

Country	Coca Cultivation		
	Cultivated	Eradicated	Net
Bolivia	53,386	5,486	47,900
Colombia	38,472	972	37,500
Ecuador	120	80	40
Peru	120,800	0	120,800
Total Coca	212,778	6,538	206,240

Source: INCS Report, March 1992, p. 27.

Again, though, the department's own data belied its optimistic conclusions. Despite intense pressure from Washington, the percentage of drug-crop land eradicated by source countries was quite limited. The figures on coca cultivation for 1991, given in Table 4.3, illustrate the point (Figures are in hectares).

Those figures probably overstate the results of the eradication programs. Previous eradication estimates were scarcely more reliable than the infamous "body counts" used by the Pentagon to measure the progress of the Vietnam War. Drug-source countries had every incentive to magnify the effectiveness of their eradication efforts. "Successful" programs maximized their chances of securing an increased flow of U.S. aid funds. Conversely, unsuccessful programs risked charges of lack of cooperation, which could lead to the termination of aid and the imposition of economic sanctions.

When confronted with the fact that their own data did not provide evidence of significant progress in the supply-side campaign against drugs, U.S. officials resorted to an almost existential definition of success. Citing the "pivotal role of national will," the State Department insisted that "one cannot measure success in absolute, quantitative terms." Rather, what is crucial is that the governments of source countries are making a serious effort: "For example, if despite intensive control efforts an illegal crop has been

Table 4.4

LAND IN COCA CULTIVATION

	Year		
Country	2000	1997	1993
Bolivia	14,000	15,800	47,200
Colombia	136,200	79,500	39,700
Peru	34,200	68,800	108,800
Total Coca	184,400	194,100	195,700

Source: INCS Report, March 2001, "Overview," p. 15.

expanding at an annual rate of 20 percent, reducing that expansion rate to 10 percent represents important progress."[24]

The notion that it is a sign of success if an already bad situation continues to deteriorate, albeit at a somewhat slower rate, is dubious. But the policy blindness exhibited by U.S. officials about both the international and the domestic aspects of the drug war led to just such claims.

If much of the language in the 1991 and 1992 reports seems familiar, that is because it is. With minor modifications, it could be inserted in the 2000 and 2001 reports. The optimistic spin continued to be evident, even in the face of stubborn facts. The 2001 report, for example, stated that "the year's most noteworthy accomplishment was to keep the Andean coca crop from expanding significantly."[25] Since the total coca acreage—185,000 hectares—was virtually the same as the total in 1989, more than a decade earlier, it was a dubious definition of success. A similar spin was evident in the discussion of achievements in Bolivia and Peru. Pointing to "dramatic reductions" of coca growing in Peru and Bolivia, the report emphasized that "both countries saw cultivation drop to unprecedented lows in 2000." Read on in the report, however, and one discovers that "the major drug syndicates' campaign to expand coca cultivation in Colombia again offset the reductions in Bolivia and Peru." Indeed, those syndicates "have not

Table 4.5

COCA LEAF HARVESTED

Country	Year		
	2000	1997	1993
Bolivia	13,400	70,100	84,400
Colombia	583,000	347,000	31,700
Peru	54,400	130,200	155,500
Total	650,800	547,300	271,600

Source: INCS Report, March 2001, "Overview," p. 17.

only expanded coca cultivation, they have achieved extraordinary levels of efficiency in extracting cocaine from coca leaf."[26]

In reality, the U.S.-funded antidrug efforts in the Andean region merely rearranged the cultivation shares among Bolivia, Peru, and Colombia. The aggregate total amount of land under cultivation has changed very little.[27] Table 4.4 illustrates the trend (all figures are in hectares).

The figures are even less encouraging if one calculates the amount of coca leaf actually harvested rather than the land devoted to coca-leaf cultivation. Table 4.5 clearly shows the steady upward trend in production since the early 1990s (all figures are in metric tons).

Things do not get much better when one examines the metric tons of cocaine that would be produced from the harvest. Table 4.6 shows the trend.

As noted in chapter 3, the figures for 2000 apparently underestimated the amount of cocaine production in Colombia. If that is true, the actual Andean production may have been substantially greater than 777 metric tons. Even if the State Department report is taken at face value, the trend since the early 1990s hardly supports the notion of serious progress in the war against coca.

Another example of the "up the hill and down again" phenomenon was the grudging admission by U.S. officials in December

Table 4.6

COCAINE PRODUCTION

	Year		
Country	2000	1997	1993
Bolivia	43	200	240
Colombia	580	360	65
Peru	154	325	410
Total	777	885	715

Source: INCS Report, March 2001, "South America," pp. 6, 17, 28.

2000 that coca production in Peru was again on the rise—perhaps by as much as 15 percent in the coming year.[28] Peru supposedly had been a drug war success story in the 1990s. U.S leaders had praised the drug eradication efforts of President Fujimori's government, even when serious human rights abuses accompanied such efforts. In addition, Washington had helped fund crop substitution and economic development programs to lure peasants away from growing drug crops.

There was actually less to the Peru success story than there appeared. Even if the figures documenting the decline in acreage devoted to coca cultivation were accurate (a questionable assumption), much of the decline was caused by a fungus that blighted the crop. Moreover, in those areas in which the blight did not strike, coca growers learned to increase crop yields. And finally, much of the coca production had not disappeared; as the data in the 2001 INCS Report indicates, it had merely moved across the border into Colombia.

The data with respect to opium and marijuana (cannabis) also fail to show meaningful progress in the supply-side campaign of the drug war. Indeed, the situation over the past decade and a half has become worse with regard to opium. Table 4.7 shows the trend of opium production in Latin America since the mid-1980s (all figures are in metric tons).

Table 4.7

OPIUM PRODUCTION IN LATIN AMERICA

Country	Year			
	1999	1997	1993	1987
Colombia	75	66	—	—
Guatemala	—	—	—	3
Mexico	43	46	49	50
Total	118	112	49	53

Source: INCS Report, March 2001, "Overview," pp. 17-18.

The data on marijuana production show a modestly better trend. Instead of getting noticeably worse over the past decade and a half, it has merely stayed the same. That is undoubtedly seen as a great victory according to the standards of America's drug warriors. Table 4.8 shows that, despite a massive eradication effort, marijuana production has remained stubbornly resilient (all figures are in metric tons).

The new figures in the latest report, issued in March 2002, provide little more encouragement. The potential cocaine output in Peru did decline modestly from 154 metric tons to 140 metric tons. But the figures for Bolivia pointed in the opposite direction, going from 43 metric tons to 60 metric tons.[29] The figures on opium output in Mexico are also troubling. The potential yield soared to 71 metric tons from 43 tons two years earlier.[30]

There is also one extremely curious aspect to the 2002 report. The State Department asserted that the figures for coca and opium acreage and production in Colombia were not available in time to be included in the report.[31] Critics were justifiably skeptical about that explanation and suspected that the remarkable omission occurred because the data would have indicated a surge in the supply of both drugs. That suspicion deepened when, only a week after the 2002 report appeared, the White House conceded that its estimates showed that the amount of acreage in Colombia devoted

Table 4.8

MARIJUANA PRODUCTION

	Year			
Country	2000	1997	1993	1987
Mexico	7,000	8,600	6,280	5,933
Colombia	4,000	4,133	4,125	5,600
Jamaica	—	214	502	460
Belize	—	—	—	200
Others	3,500	3,500	3,500	1,500
Total	14,500	16,447	14,407	13,693

Source: INSC Report, March 2001, "Overview," pp. 17-19.

to coca had grown to 419,000 acres (169,800 hectares)—a whopping 24.7 percent increase—despite Plan Colombia's aerial spraying effort.[32]

With considerable understatement, the White House spokesman admitted that the Colombia figures showed "that our efforts to date have not yet produced the results that we had hoped to achieve."[33] Not to be discouraged, though, the spokesman went on to say that the surge in coca acreage showed "the need for sustained U.S. engagement."[34] One wonders what amount of evidence would be required before U.S. officials might concede that the supply-side strategy was not working.

Drug policy analysts Patrick L. Clawson and Rensselaer W. Lee III describe the many unintended consequences associated with drug-eradication programs. They note that eradication in existing production areas may simply drive farmers into more remote areas, "thereby opening up new production areas—a pattern that has been repeated numerous times in both Bolivia and Peru."[35] Eradication also may encourage farmers to make every effort to increase yields on the remaining acreage. Between 1990 and 1995, for example, the area cultivated in coca in Bolivia fell 3 percent while the amount of leaf harvested rose 10 percent.[36] Clawson and Lee also note that eradication can be a de facto coca price support program. After all, the whole point of eradication is to reduce the supply of coca. Basic economic laws of supply and demand suggest that prices for the remaining crops would then tend to rise. Clawson and Lee point out that the voluntary acreage reduction programs so popular with both U.S. officials and leaders in the Andean countries "are similar to the crop acreage reduction programs that the U.S. government uses to raise the income of wheat farmers. It is not clear why Washington thinks that a crop reduction program raises the income of Midwest wheat farmers but lowers the income of Andean coca farmers."[37] Riley echoes their point: "Compensation establishes a floor price. When coca prices are above the compensation price, farmers have no economic incentive to eradicate. When prices are below the floor, the compensation provides the farmers an income and thus helps underwrite the downside risk associated with coca farming. In other words, the only way a farmer will not benefit is if he grows no coca at all."[38]

THE CROP SUBSTITUTION MIRAGE

As evidence mounts that eradication and interdiction efforts produce minimal results and that "victory" in the drug war is as elusive as ever, policymakers invariably start to place greater emphasis on crop substitution and economic development programs. We have gone through that cycle several times during the past three decades.

Even to many critics of the drug war, crop substitution appears to be a less draconian way to seek to reduce the supply of illegal drugs. Its rationale is to give Latin American *campesinos* viable economic alternatives to participation in the illicit cocaine, marijuana, or opium trade. But the record of crop substitution programs should dissuade U.S. officials from continuing to pursue that panacea. Neither the narrow version (providing financial subsidies to induce farmers to switch to legal crops) nor the broader concept (providing infrastructure assistance to make legal agricultural— and nonagricultural—enterprises economically viable) has achieved worthwhile results.

Over the years, U.S. officials have repeatedly worked with their Latin American counterparts to induce growers to abandon the cultivation of drug crops for legal alternatives. They have suggested a prolific array of substitutes, including bananas, maize, rice, coffee, citrus fruit, and various grains. Economic realities usually doom such efforts. For example, farmers can make 4, and sometimes more than 10, times the income growing coca than they can raising legal crops.[39] Drug policy scholar LaMond Tullis provides an even higher estimate of the advantage. He contends that, in many areas "illegal-drug growers can make from ten to fifty times more in provisioning the illegal drug market than they can in any other agricultural pursuit."[40] Although the income advantage varies greatly from country to country (and region to region within a country) as well as on the type of drug crop in question, the advantage is usually quite substantial. It is not comforting when two leading analysts conclude that in Colombia, UN "data on net income from various crops show that the only crop anywhere near coca is opium poppy."[41]

Drug crops have other important advantages. Coca and marijuana (and even opium poppies) can be grown in remote regions with poor soil—places in which alternate crops are not economically feasible. Clawson and Lee note that the advantage is especially evident with regard to coca: "Coca is a hardy and adaptable perennial shrub. . . . It flourishes on steep slopes and in infertile acidic soils, that is, in conditions that restrict the growth of other crops. Coca can grow almost anywhere in tropical South America and in tropical regions of the world generally."[42] That fact alone underscores the inherent difficulty confronting both eradication and crop substitution initiatives.

Drug crops also can yield faster returns. Coca bushes can be harvested a mere 18 months after planting and can provide maximum yields in three years or so. A well-tended bush can also produce for as many as 25 years.[43] Many alternative cash crops require four or more years from planting to first harvest. Coca provides up to six harvests a year whereas most other crops come into season just once a year.[44]

In addition, coca tends to be easier to market. Harvested leaves spoil relatively slowly, and they do not damage easily during transport.[45] Moreover, as one farmer in Peru's Upper Huallaga Valley bluntly told international officials: "Buyers go to the farms to get the coca. If I plant any other crop I must get it to market and spend money transporting it. That does not happen with coca."[46] The importance of the cash-and-carry policies of coca buyers in countries with inadequate transportation systems should not be underestimated. The trip from the Upper Huallaga Valley to Lima, for example, is a grinding 35-hour journey, primarily in second gear.[47]

Because they operate outside the law, drug-crop growers do not have to deal with many of the obstacles that farmers of legal crops must endure. Those obstacles include poor transportation infrastructure, lack of access to credit, lack of reasonable and consistent government standards for recognizing titles to property (as well as a lack of efficient enforcement of property rights), and volatile, unpredictable markets for agricultural products. Buyers for trafficking organizations merely purchase the crops, pay the growers well, and haul off the crops. Not surprisingly, a significant percentage of Latin American farmers prefer to do business that way even if it means dealing in an illegal product.

Although they express some optimism for the potential of crop substitution programs, Clawson and Lee concede: "Many barriers stand in the way of switching from coca to legal crops, such as fragile ecologies with dubious potential for legal cultivation, isolation from major markets, severe political and law and order problems, and the ease of growing and selling coca."[48] A United States Agency for International Development (USAID) study was even more pessimistic: "The crop substitution strategy . . . has been unsuccessful in introducing substitute crops and in controlling illicit cultivation, at least in the limited span of a typical development initiative. Viable substitute crops are difficult to identify given the generally unfavorable climatic conditions and poorly developed infrastructures that characterize most remote poppy- and coca-growing areas. In many instances, there are not alternative crops that can be grown profitably."[49] Even when there are crops that theoretically can compete with coca and other drug crops, there are usually problems that undermine their competitive advantage. Brookings Institution scholar Paul B. Stares notes one typical problem: "Some crop substitution programs have reported higher overall returns from certain licit crops. Studies have also identified other agricultural products that have the promise to be just as profitable, if not more so. The basic problem, however, is that these more lucrative crops are typically consumed locally, and local markets are not large enough to sustain a large-scale shift in production."[50]

Sometimes well-meaning initiatives by U.S. aid workers lead to disastrous results for Latin American farmers. A few years ago officials for USAID convinced peasants in the Upper Huallaga Valley that growing achiote (a local food crop) would be more profitable than growing coca. The farmers proceeded to plant achiote in large quantities. When it came time to sell, however, the price had plummeted and, thanks to USAID prodding, there was so much overproduction that some of the achiote could not be sold at all.[51] Needless to say, the farmers were not thrilled at the results of that crop substitution program.

Similar developments occurred in Bolivia. U.S. experts talked one group of farmers into planting ginger. After accumulating 40 tons of the plant, they were urged to halt production because there was no market for that much ginger. The coca farmers who had switched to bananas, grapefruit, and pineapples fared no better.[52] James Painter, BBC correspondent for Latin America, describes the crop substitution fiasco in the Chapare engineered by Washington and La Paz in the early 1990s: "The Chapare is full of rotting oranges, lemons, and grapefruit. Oversupply, high transportation costs, and long distances to markets mean that often it is simply not worth a farmer's even picking them off the ground where they fall."[53]

Even when some coca, marijuana, and poppy growers are willing to take their fields out of production in exchange for U.S. financial largess, there is little to stop other entrepreneurs from entering the market. Indeed, even current producers often simply pocket the money and resume operations in another location.[54] There are indications that Bolivian, Peruvian, and Colombian participants in crop substitution programs have done exactly that. Ironically, aid from the United States or the indigenous government may provide growers with additional capital to expand their production.

The mounting evidence of the failure of crop substitution programs has impelled U.S. officials to emphasize broader alternative economic development programs to induce farmers and laborers involved in the drug trade to pursue other options.[55] Such programs have fared little better than crop substitution efforts. In fact, economic development projects can simply provide additional capital and other benefits to those who have no intention of abandoning the drug trade. For example, aid monies to improve the transportation infrastructure in recipient countries by building modern roads into remote areas make it easier for drug farmers to get their crops to market and may open new areas to drug cultivation. That situation became so evident in Bolivia's Chapare region during the late 1980s and early 1990s that USAID stopped funding road construction projects. The Drug Enforcement Administration (DEA) took even more drastic action, actually blowing up existing roadways in the Chapare.[56]

Building manufacturing facilities in such regions (even in those rare cases in which the projects are economically justified) also tends to have a supplemental rather than a substitutional effect. In other words, drug-crop farmers do not give up their traditional livelihood and replace it with their new jobs; they merely add the income from that new job to the existing illegal source of income.

The bottom line is that the black market premium in the illegal drug trade creates an irresistible temptation for a substantial portion of the agricultural sector in drug-producing countries. Drug-trafficking organizations can outbid the competition from buyers of legal crops, and usually can do so quite easily.[57] The notion that the potential income from bananas, maize, or citrus fruit can compete with the potential income from coca, marijuana, or opium poppies is about as realistic as assuming that a burger flipper at McDonald's can earn as much as a software designer for Microsoft.

True, some farmers will refuse to be drawn into the drug trade because of its illegality. Some may object to drug trafficking on moral grounds; others may simply want to avoid it out of fear of criminal penalties or other government retaliation. But many will swallow any moral qualms they might have, and even incur the risk of criminal sanctions, given the sizable profit potential. And the drug-trafficking organizations can bid up the price to whatever level is necessary to ensure an adequate supply of the product. Crop substitution programs, like eradication and interdiction efforts, ignore some of the most basic principles of economics. That is why they are inevitably doomed to fail.

Both U.S. and Latin American leaders have been impervious to that reality. Crop substitution schemes have been tried and found wanting for more than a quarter of a century—an extraordinarily long record of failure. To be blunt, crop substitution strategies have worked no better than other exercises in central economic planning around the world. One would think even the most determined officials would finally learn that lesson.

Unfortunately, that does not seem to be the case. Shortly after his election as president of Peru in June 2001, Alejandro Toledo emphasized crop substitution as a solution to the plague of commerce in illegal drugs. He stated that alternative crops—coffee, cocoa, cotton, rice, bananas, and papaya—were the way forward in the battle against coca leaf production. Indeed, he added a wrinkle to the usual crop substitution strategy. Toledo stressed, "I believe in crop substitution that generates work. That means pulling up coca leaf. People will be paid to pull it up. And then, in a second phase, come other crops."[58] In other words, he wanted to create a make-work, public works program out of crop substitution. He apparently was unfamiliar with the concept of opportunity cost as well if he believed that pulling up coca plants was the most efficient use of time for Peruvian workers.

Yet even Toledo implicitly acknowledges that alternative crops cannot compete economically with coca absent artificial advantages. And it was apparent whom he thought ought to fund those advantages. "Let's hope there could be a 'haven' price for substitute crops" and that the United States provides more resources for the program, he said.[59]

The experience of Plan Colombia in one portion of Putumayo province illustrates some of the problems with the crop substitution strategy. The "carrot" portion of Bogotá's carrot-and-stick approach there was a combination of economic development projects and direct financial incentives to farmers who were willing to sign pledges renouncing the growing of coca. (The "stick" was the aggressive spraying of coca crops.) At one village, Villa Garzon, people lined up to greet President Andrés Pastrana and to sign such pledges in exchange for initial payments of up to $100 per family. Many of them wore "Coca-free Putumayo" T-shirts provided by the government to highlight the president's visit.[60]

Some peasants stated that they would honor the pledge—although whether they actually would do so over the long term was doubtful. Others were cynical from the outset. One farmer, Wilmar

Ospina, told reporters bluntly that he would like to consider other crops, but he could make $10,000 a year from coca—far more than from any alternative crop and an enormous sum by Colombian standards. Indeed, the government's promised compensation (up to $870 per family in the form of tools and agricultural supplies) was less than the value of a single harvest from one hectare of coca.[61] (To make matters even worse, the bulk of the government's meager compensation packages had yet to be disbursed by the beginning of 2002.)

Nor did the spraying campaign put small growers such as Ospina out of business. Ospina was annoyed that planes had sprayed his coca in January 2001, even though he had only five acres under cultivation and the government had promised to confine its spraying to fields at least five times that size, which authorities assumed belonged to the big drug cartels. He also echoed the complaint of many other peasants that the spraying had killed his banana plants. But Ospina also learned from the experience. By lightly washing the coca leaves shortly after fumigation and then treating them with chemicals, he was able to save a significant portion of the crop. Perhaps more to the point, within weeks he was busily planting the illicit leaf again.[62]

Matters have not fared much better for one of Plan Colombia's showcases: a palm-heart cannery near the town of Puerto Asis. Plan money is being used to buy palm grown by local peasants switching from coca. But even local officials admit that Putumayo's soil and climate offer no alternative crop that earns as much money as does growing coca.[63] Indeed, even outside the main coca-growing areas such as Putumayo, coca is becoming more and more prominent, sometimes displacing Colombia's most pervasive legal crop, coffee.[64]

In a March 2002 confidential report, the U.S. State Department provided an extremely pessimistic assessment of the crop substitution component of Plan Colombia. The report concluded that farmers in southern Colombia who had signed agreements to eliminate coca in exchange for aid payments had in fact eliminated little or none of the crop, nor did they show any intention of doing so. But what policy conclusions did U.S. officials derive from this sobering assessment? They decided to largely abandon the crop substitution scheme in favor of two other options: to intensify the aerial spraying campaign to convince Colombian peasants that their coca would be wiped out (and they would therefore suffer financial devastation) if they tried to continue growing the crop and to build large infrastructure projects to provide jobs outside of agriculture and to improve overall living conditions of people in the coca-growing areas.[65] One would be hard-pressed to come up with two more utterly sterile proposals. Both tactics have been tried repeatedly in numerous drug-source countries in Latin America, and both have failed repeatedly to produce lasting beneficial results.

The blunt assessment of crop substitution programs made by Mexican scholar María Celia Toro a decade ago still applies: "No agricultural product can be made as profitable as any commodity that is to be sold on the black market. The gap between the prices of legal and illegal crops is enormous. Short of decriminalization or legalization, little can be done to eliminate the economic incentives that spur drug production and smuggling."[66]

THE PUSH-DOWN, POP-UP EFFECT

Interdiction, eradication, and crop substitution/alternative development all have one thing in common: They have failed to produce a significant, lasting decline in the supply of illicit drugs. To take just one example, during the 1980s and early 1990s, as Washington's spending on counterdrug efforts soared, the street price of a kilogram of cocaine declined from $300,000 to $150,000. In other words, despite the massive combined efforts of the United States and drug-source countries in Latin America, supplies of the drug became even more plentiful.[67] Riley explains the economic reasons for that phenomenon: "The source country cost components of the price chain, such as leaf, paste, and base are but a small fraction of retail prices. Even huge price increases in these components, such as a tenfold rise in leaf prices, will barely affect retail prices."[68] Even brief "success" in eradicating or interdicting the raw materials for cocaine, thereby increasing retail prices, will have a perverse economic impact within a relatively short period of time. "Unfortunately, the same large price precipitated by a massive eradication or interdiction program also serves to ultimately undue the policy's effects. High retail prices (which also imply high intermediate product prices) signal that there are profits to be made in drug production and drug trafficking. Those traffickers that can successfully get a shipment to the United States might now make three, four, five or even ten times as much as they might have made previously. Thus, the higher prices that result from interdiction and eradication also serve to encourage traffickers to expand production."[69]

Other drug policy experts have observed the same phenomenon. Illegality provides what analyst James Inciardi describes as the "crime tax," the difference between what a product would cost in a legal market and an illegal market.[70] Cocaine selling for, say, $100 a gram on the streets of an American city might well be marketed for $5 to $10 dollars in a legal, competitive environment. La Mond Tullis stresses the perverse effects of the crime tax. "The 'tax' is reaped principally by traffickers, who pass a sufficient amount of it on to induce peasant growers and minor underlings to flock to the drug enterprise with abandon. Thus, illegality makes it almost impossible to devise a policy mix (risks and incentives) that would generally induce growers to abandon their crop."[71]

What successes have occurred have been both short term and localized. In a pattern that has occurred again and again, the principal impact of supply-side offensives has been to rearrange production locales or trafficking routes. When the United States pressured Turkey in the 1970s to eradicate the cultivation of opium poppies, which were being used to make heroin, Mexico soon replaced Turkey as the leading supplier of heroin to the United States. In 1972 the amount of heroin coming into the United States from Mexico was 10 to 15 percent of the total supply; by 1975 Mexican sources accounted for 80 percent.[72] Following the crackdown in Mexico, poppy cultivation spread across the border into Guatemala and became a major component of the drug industry in Colombia as well.[73]

During the 1970s, Washington also pressured Mexico to wage a vigorous offensive against marijuana production. That offensive, Operation Condor, appeared to be a solid success over the short term.[74] The supply of Mexican marijuana for the U.S. market declined from 75 percent in 1976 to barely 4 percent in 1981.[75] But that achievement hardly created a marijuana shortage. Colombia promptly replaced Mexico as America's leading supplier of that drug, and that development, together with an increase in marijuana cultivation in the United States itself, meant that there was no overall decline in the supply. In the 1980s, when Colombia responded to U.S. pressure by going after marijuana farmers, Mexico regained its status as the leading exporter of marijuana.

While U.S. officials have touted the decline in coca cultivation in Peru and Bolivia during the mid- and late 1990s, that decline has been largely offset by a surge of cultivation in Colombia. The recent anti-cocaine offensive in Colombia, symbolized by Plan Colombia, is accompanied by reports of new coca fields in Ecuador, Panama, Venezuela, and Brazil. The recent price surge for coca in Peru is yet another manifestation of the push-down, pop-up effect in response to Plan Colombia. In late 2001 and early 2002 the price for coca leaf had shot up to over $4 per kilogram (from less than $2 two years earlier). That price rise also reflected the inherent bankruptcy of crop substitution programs. "That's really high," stated James Willard, director of antinarcotics affairs at the U.S. embassy in Lima. "For it to be competitive with coffee or cacao, it needs to be around $1."[76] In other words, even when the supply-side campaign in Peru had been a "success" and had driven the price for a kilo of coca leaf below $2, farmers could still make more money from growing coca than they could from growing competing crops.

Interdiction efforts produce a similar phenomenon. The disruption of the traditional drug-trafficking routes through the Caribbean in the 1980s led to a diversion of the trade through Mexico. Shooting down suspected drug planes over Peru and other measures taken to disrupt the "air bridge" of coca shipments to processing labs in Colombia merely impelled the drug-trafficking organizations to subsidize the growing of coca in Colombia, thus minimizing the transportation problem. The focus on preventing small planes from carrying drugs from Colombia and Mexico into the United States has merely caused the traffickers to adopt new techniques. Some traffickers have even built their own minisubmarines in an effort to bring their product to market.

The prohibitionist strategy distorts the drug trade in other ways, most of which make the problem even more severe or intractable. Riley notes two examples of such distortions resulting from Washington's eradication and interdiction initiatives: "[A]ttempts to control production of drugs in foreign countries can lead to adverse consequences in the consuming country. In one striking example, the high potency of marijuana now available across the United States is largely the result of traffickers' efforts to reduce the bulk of their contraband and evade intense interdiction programs that operated in Mexico and Colombia in the 1970s and 1980s. . . . Similarly, a crackdown on cocaine markets in Colombia in the early 1980s may have augmented the spread of crack by temporarily restricting the supply of chemicals needed to convert base, a cracklike substance, into cocaine."[77] Riley concludes, "Both the marijuana and crack cases may be examples of the 'Iron Law of Prohibition,' which notes that as law enforcement efforts increase, so does drug potency."[78]

Indeed, as another observer of the phenomenon points out, a similar process occurred with alcohol during the Prohibition era.

Bootleggers increasingly moved away from marketing beer (which was fairly bulky) in favor of hard liquor—including the 190-proof White Lightning, "the crack of the 1920s."[79]

The track record of supply-side initiatives should lead to an inexorable conclusion. No matter how the components of the supply-side strategy are configured, the strategy itself is hopelessly flawed. It may be a cliché to speak of rearranging the deck chairs on the *Titanic,* but no other image so perfectly captures the supply-side strategy that Washington has pursued with such dogged yet futile determination for more than three decades.

OTHER ILLUSORY OPTIONS

Yet a shift away from a supply-side strategy toward emphasis on a "demand reduction" approach offers little more hope of success. The United States has flirted with that shift on occasion, most notably during the initial year or so of the Clinton administration. Some elements of the George W. Bush administration also appear to favor that approach, although it is still a minority viewpoint. The reality is that the specific mix does not matter very much. Demand reduction in the United States would have only a modest impact on the global drug trade. In fact, it would have less of an impact today than it would have had a decade or two ago, because other regions are greatly increasing their consumption of drugs. While the U.S. market may be relatively "mature" (with the prospect of little or no growth in the coming years), other markets are just beginning to boom.

For example, U.S. government experts estimate that 220 tons of cocaine flowed to Europe in 2000—double the amount estimated in 1996. Thirty-five percent of Colombia's cocaine now goes to Europe.[80] A growth in demand is also taking place in portions of the developing world. Even Islamic fundamentalist

Iran now concedes that it has a serious drug consumption problem.[81]

Paul Stares points out that with economic globalization, it will become even easier for drug-trafficking organizations to penetrate these new markets: "The expansion in trade, transportation networks, and tourism has not only made it easier for them to distribute drugs to the long-established markets of North America and Western Europe, but it has also opened up new parts of the world to exploit."[82] The growth of U.S. trade with Mexico is one example of the phenomenon. As trade between the two countries has expanded, thanks to the North American Free Trade Agreement (NAFTA), more drug shipments are entering the United States "riding piggyback" on legitimate cargo shipments. During the fiscal year ending September 30, 2001, border agents found 68,532 pounds of illegal drugs (primarily marijuana and cocaine) in 19 seizures of shipments from *maquiladoras,* assembly plants in the Mexican border states that import material duty free and then produce products for export. That quantity was triple the amount of drugs seized during the previous 12-month period.[83]

Stares also points out that, in most portions of the developing world (and the United States), the first two decades of the twenty-first century will see a sharp increase in the number of teenagers and young adults in the population. Those are the age groups most likely to experiment with illegal drugs. The social dislocations caused by the transition to market economies in both the former communist world and the developing world are also likely to produce an abundance of personal stresses that increase the incentives for drug use.[84]

All of those factors have important implications. The illegal drug trade is almost certain to be a growth industry globally for the foreseeable future. With consumer demand outside the United States spiking upward, even the best-case scenario for demand reduction in this country offers little hope for a meaningful impact on Latin America's drug exports.

The growth of the drug trade in Europe and other areas outside the United States also has led to new affiliations among drug traffickers and other criminal elements, such as the growing cooperation between Mexican trafficking organizations and the Russian mafia that came to light in the spring of 2001. (The Colombian drug cartels had discovered the potential benefits of such an affiliation nearly eight years earlier.) In addition to helping Latin American traffickers market their products throughout Eastern Europe and the former Soviet Union, Russian mobsters are adept at laundering drug monies through banks they control in Russia and elsewhere.[85]

The core problem with the drug war's supply-side strategy, according to Stares, is that "drugs can be produced too easily in too many places for source-country suppression efforts to have any significant or sustained effect on worldwide supply of drugs, certainly while the demand exists."[86] The failure of interdiction, eradication, and crop substitution/alternative development strategies to make a serious dent in the drug trade has led some frustrated advocates of prohibition to grasp at another option: targeting the financial resources and profits of the drug-trafficking organizations. Stares argues that such an attack "has far more potential to do harm to their operations and deprive them of what ultimately motivates their activities."[87]

One method of such an attack would be more vigorous prosecution for money-laundering and other financial offenses. The goal of such a campaign is relatively straightforward: to deprive the narcotrafficking organizations of profits from illicit activities. There is little doubt that without an effective money laundering system, the drug trade would be badly damaged if not crippled entirely.[88] But the optimism surrounding this latest front in the drug war seems as misplaced as the earlier enthusiasm for interdiction, eradication, and crop substitution. Even Stares admits that the "growing integration of the global financial system, with its rapidly expanding array of services and instruments, has also provided traffickers with more opportunities to launder money and to invest in other activities—licit or illicit."[89] That trend is almost certainly likely to accelerate in the future.

The bottom line is that, no matter what the specific configuration of tactics, the supply-side campaign against illicit drugs is doomed to fail. As long as there is a substantial global demand for those drugs, the supply will continue to flow.

CHAPTER FIVE

WASHINGTON'S "UGLY AMERICAN" TACTICS

Not only has the supply-side component of the U.S.-orchestrated war on drugs been futile, it has created needless tensions and animosity in Washington's relations with Latin American countries. One of the most urgent tasks facing the Bush administration is to repair the damage caused by the bullying tactics of its predecessors.

Although U.S. officials like to stress the economic aid component of the war on drugs in both Plan Colombia and such predecessors as the Andean Initiative in the early 1990s, there have always been more "sticks" than "carrots" in Washington's policy. Whenever the carrot of U.S. aid dollars fails to secure cooperation from Latin American governments, Washington also can resort to the stick—threatening to terminate aid and impose economic sanctions.

The United States has used a repertoire of other bullying tactics. Washington frequently pressures Latin American governments to dismiss officials who are deemed corrupt—or merely insufficiently enthusiastic about prosecuting the war on drugs. U.S. leaders have exerted enormous pressure on nations throughout the hemisphere to extradite accused drug traffickers to the United States for trial, a position that implies a vote of no confidence in the criminal justice systems of Latin American countries. The U.S.

government also has asserted the right to apprehend accused drug traffickers and conduct money-laundering "sting" operations on the territory of its hemispheric neighbors without the consent—and sometimes even without the knowledge—of the host government. The most prominent example of the former tactic was the 1989 invasion of Panama to capture Manuel Noriega and bring him to the United States. The most prominent example of the latter tactic was Operation Casablanca in Mexico during the late 1990s. Those were by no means the only episodes, however.

Such attempts to apply the principle of extraterritoriality to U.S. drug laws has been an especially sensitive issue with Latin American nations. To both the governments and the populations of those countries, U.S. actions are reminiscent of the bad old days of flagrant imperialism by the "Colossus of the North" during the early decades of the twentieth century.

THE DECERTIFICATION THREAT

The Drug Abuse Acts of 1986 and 1988 require "source" countries (drug-producing or drug-transiting nations) to participate in eradication and interdiction programs to be eligible for U.S. foreign aid funds and various trade preferences. The number of nations that must fulfill that requirement has been growing in recent years and now includes countries not generally perceived as major players in the drug trade.

The certification process mandated by Congress requires the president to determine annually whether the government of a drug-source country has cooperated sufficiently in eradication and interdiction efforts. In certifying cooperation, the president is obliged to consider a variety of factors, but the principal question is whether the actions of a foreign government have resulted in the maximum achievable reductions in illicit drug production. Although the standards give the president considerable latitude, and he can even waive the requirements if he states explicitly that doing so is in the national interest, there is considerable pressure to decertify recalcitrant regimes. Congress also has the power to reject the president's determination of compliance for a specific country.

If the president does not certify that a drug-source country is in compliance—or if Congress overrules his certification—some sanctions are imposed automatically. The mandatory sanctions include:

- Suspension of 50 percent of all U.S. assistance (except humanitarian aid and international narcotics control aid) for the current fiscal year
- Suspension of all types of aid (except those in the exempt categories) during subsequent fiscal years
- A requirement that U.S. representatives in multilateral development banks vote against loans to the offending country
- Denial of a sugar quota (which provides eloquent testimony to the political clout of the U.S. sugar lobby)

In addition to the mandatory sanctions, several penalties may be imposed at the discretion of the president. Some of the more potent discretionary sanctions include:

- Denial of "most favored nation" (i.e., normal) tariff treatment to goods exported by the decertified country to the United States
- Imposition of duties of up to 50 percent on exports to the United States
- Curtailment of air transportation between the United States and the decertified country.[1]

The mere threat of decertification gives the United States a potent diplomatic and political weapon against reluctant Latin

American governments. Although the dismal record of U.S. bilateral and multilateral assistance programs suggests that recipient countries would be better off without the crutch of foreign aid, the abrupt withdrawal of U.S. subsidies would create major economic disruptions. The imposition of trade sanctions would have an even more devastating impact on nations whose economies are heavily dependent on access to the U.S. market. For example, 24 percent of Peru's exports go to the United States; the figures for Bolivia and Colombia are 21 and 38 percent, respectively, and for Mexico an astonishing 85 percent—boosted in recent years by that country's membership in the NAFTA.[2]

Washington often has employed the threat of decertification to pressure the governments of drug-source countries. Actual decertification is relatively rare and typically is confined to countries in which the United States has little influence in any case. For example, in both 1990 and 1991 President George H. W. Bush recommended the decertification of only four nations: Afghanistan, Iran, Syria, and Burma. With the possible exception of Syria in 1991, U.S. relations with those states were exceedingly strained or nonexistent, and there was utterly no prospect of aid programs, with or without certification. Similarly, of the 24 countries under review in 2001, the new Bush administration officially decertified just four: Afghanistan, Burma, Haiti, and Cambodia. The latter two were then given a waiver for national security reasons.[3] In other words, the only countries to which the penalties of decertification actually applied were Afghanistan and Burma. Washington had long treated both states as pariahs for other reasons.

The one notable exception to the record of decertifying only pariah states was the formal decertification of Colombia in 1996 and 1997. In that case, though, the underlying reason seemed to be a personal vendetta by U.S. officials against Colombia's president, Ernesto Samper.[4] For a brief period following his election in 1994, Washington at least officially regarded Samper as an ally in the war on drugs and even occasionally praised him for his antidrug efforts.

Then evidence emerged that officials in Samper's election campaign organization had taken money from suspected or known drug kingpins. Further investigation led U.S. officials to conclude that Samper himself had known about the financial connection with drug-trafficking organizations and that he may have personally accepted such funds not only in the presidential campaign but throughout much of his political career.

The U.S. reaction was furious and uncompromising. Washington in essence cast a vote of no confidence in Samper's administration and indicated that the president should resign. When Samper refused to step down, the United States sought to isolate him in every manner possible.[5] That included denying him a visa to travel to the United States—an action that previously had been taken against only one democratically elected head of state, Austrian president Kurt Waldheim (because of his apparent Nazi affiliations during World War II).

The truth of the allegations against Samper may never be known. There did indeed appear to be evidence of financial support from drug traffickers, but given the pervasiveness of the drug trade in Colombia's economy, it is doubtful whether that was unusual in the country's political system. Indeed, probably few politicians of any prominence in Colombia are entirely free of the taint of drug money from political supporters. But some U.S. officials were wary of Samper from the outset. Earlier in his career, Samper had openly asserted that legalization should be considered as a policy option, especially if more repressive actions proved ineffective.[6] As the level of violence in Colombia rose at the end of the 1980s, he had called for dialogue with the traffickers, pleading "Let's not turn Colombia into the Vietnam of the war on drugs."[7] Although he had recanted his flirtation with legalization before his successful run for the presidency, some U.S. drug warriors considered him unreliable at best.

In that sense, the pattern of U.S. hostility was similar to that shown a few years earlier toward Colombia's prosecutor general,

Gustavo de Greiff. Almost as soon as de Greiff began flirting with a discussion of legalization, evidence suddenly emerged allegedly tying him to drug traffickers. A U.S. diplomat bluntly described him as "a thorn in our side."[8] And indeed he was. De Greiff stated that the drug war "does not have victories, only failure. Despite spraying and manual eradication, the areas of cultivation have not diminished, only increased. Drug interdiction doesn't even reach 10 percent of the drugs that reach international markets. We kill the big capos, we put them in jail, we extradite them to the U.S.—and yet prices don't even move overseas. . . . We have to study legalization." He added: "Change frightens people. There are a lot of vested interests in the drug war. There are a lot of people who would lose their jobs with legalization."[9] It was not surprising that U.S. drug warriors considered Gustavo de Greiff a very dangerous man.

Perhaps Washington's campaign to make de Greiff and Samper pariahs was honestly motivated, and it is even possible that both men may have been in league with drug traffickers all along. But it is also possible that their real "crime" was daring to contradict the United States on drug policy.

Whatever the motive, Washington decided to punish Samper by decertifying Colombia. "This is a decertification not of Colombia, but of President Samper," said Marc Thiessen, spokesman for Senator Jesse Helms (R-NC), chairman of the Senate Foreign Relations Committee and a political figure who had lobbied hard for the decertification decision. "This is a vote of no confidence for him, not the country."[10]

An anonymous high-level Clinton administration official also stated that the action was directed against Samper rather than Colombia as a whole. Other U.S. officials went out of their way to show that the decertification was directed against Samper personally. Even as the decertification went into effect, U.S. Drug Enforcement Administrator Thomas Constantine telephoned Colombia's defense minister to praise the military's antidrug efforts and to compliment the work of national police commander General José Serrano and the country's chief prosecutor, Alfonso Valdivieso.[11]

U.S. objections apparently went beyond Samper's alleged financial links to traffickers. Indeed, the U.S. definition of a "lack of cooperation" in antidrug efforts (the legal basis for decertification) seemed to be very broad. "Samper, on the one hand, was saying he was cooperating with us, but under the table he was cooperating with [Colombia's] Congress to pass laws, so impunity [for drug traffickers] is even more total. That was untenable."[12] The U.S. arrogance was breathtaking; an elected president's decision to support bills in the country's national legislature was now deemed an unpardonable offense if Washington did not like the legislation.

The Clinton administration's lack of respect for Colombia's democratic institutions was evident in other ways. In the spring of 1996, Samper became the first president to go through an impeachment trial, as the Colombian congress considered the drug corruption allegations against him. In what the country's media described as the "trial of the century," lawmakers absolved Samper of those charges. The vote in the House of Representatives clearing him of wrongdoing was overwhelming: 111 to 43.[13] Instead of accepting that result, however, the Clinton administration regarded the vote as evidence that the Colombian congress, as well as Samper, was corrupt. "The decision to clear Mr. Samper leaves unanswered many questions regarding pervasive narcotrafficker influence on Colombia's institutions and it will not resolve the resultant crisis of confidence," the State Department responded tersely.[14] Samper's critics in the U.S. Senate called for stepped-up sanctions against Colombia, warning that if the Clinton administration did not take such action, Congress might well take matters into its own hands.[15]

Ironically, instead of defying the United States, Samper sought to get back into Washington's good graces by intensifying an aerial spraying campaign against coca crops. The reaction of peasants in the coca-growing regions was strikingly similar to their response to the more extensive campaigns a few years later under Plan Colombia. *Christian Science Monitor* correspondent Mary Matheson described the fiasco:

> Eager to please a disenchanted U.S. government, President Samper is refusing to cave in to the demand by the peasants to stop fumigating their illegal crops, used to make drugs. But now he must find a way to defuse the anger among peasants that his measures have provoked. In mid-July more than 50,000 peasants from several remote states in southern Colombia began to converge on large towns to protest the fumigation of their fields of coca . . . and poppies. . . . By early August the demonstrations had turned violent. . . . Demonstrators burned vehicles and tried to block local airstrips to disrupt the local economy. And the Army blew up the few roads leading to the main towns in the area to obstruct the way of marching demonstrators.[16]

Matheson observed that "with a review of Colombia's decertification due next month, and the threat of U.S. economic sanctions ever more likely, Samper is being careful not to misstep" by appearing to be weak in the war on drugs.[17] U.S. officials apparently did not consider the long-range consequences of pressuring a political leader to make war on his own population to satisfy Washington's demands.

Samper also worked hard to placate Washington on the most politically sensitive issue of all in the drug war: the extradition of Colombian suspects to the United States for trial. In December 1997, after weeks of political arm twisting and back-room deals, Samper persuaded the Colombian congress to approve legislation overturning a 1991 decision to eliminate the extradition treaty with the United States. The measure was not retroactive, but it was nevertheless a huge concession to Washington. With the passage of the new extradition statute (and with mounting evidence of alarming gains by antigovernment guerrilla forces), the administration took Colombia off the decertification list in 1998.

Samper's attempt to regain Washington's favor proved futile; he remained a pariah as far as U.S. officials were concerned. On the other hand, U.S. attempts to use the decertification stick to force Samper to resign also failed. He served out his term of office despite the Clinton administration's hostility. The feud was a thoroughly disagreeable episode in U.S.-Colombia relations. Longtime observer of Colombian affairs Bert Ruiz notes: "Historically, Theodore Roosevelt and William Jefferson Clinton were the only two Presidents in the chronicles of the United States to publicly belittle Colombia for the entire world to see. Both American Presidents pursued policies that scandalized Bogotá. In addition, Roosevelt and Clinton had no respect for the leaders in Bogotá and took assertive actions to advance self-serving American objectives. The major difference between the two Presidents was that Roosevelt had the Panama Canal to show for his deeds and Clinton ended up empty handed."[18]

The results were actually worse than that. Washington's bullying tactics engendered tremendous bitterness in Colombia. Myles Frechette, the U.S. ambassador and one of the most enthusiastic proponents of the anti-Samper strategy, became a lightning rod for that anger. Interior Minister Horacio Serpa, a political associate of Samper's, dubbed Frechette a "sick gringo." Liberal Party senator Jaime Dussan was even more direct, calling Frechette a "son of a bitch."[19] The hostility became so intense and pervasive that Frechette expressed fears for his safety.

It also became increasingly evident that the U.S. policy of decertifying and isolating Colombia had backfired in another way, as the two leftist guerrilla groups and the principal right-wing paramilitary organization exploited the weakness of Samper's government to increase their activities and expand the territory under their control. The change in policy in 1998 showed that U.S. officials and Colombia's critics in Congress were having second thoughts about continuing the decertification strategy. In fact, a growing number of voices in Congress were warning that Colombia was spiraling downward and the country's democratic system might collapse entirely without a new infusion of antidrug aid.

Except for the Colombia episode, though, the threat of decertification and its attendant penalties—rather than actual decertification—has been Washington's preferred method of coercion. It is certainly used against a wider range of regimes and with greater effect. David Beers, chief of the State Department's International Narcotics and Law Enforcement Bureau, openly boasts of the intimidating effects of the certification process: "Prior to the March 1, deadline for certification each year, we have seen countries introducing legislation, passing laws, eradicating drug crops and capturing elusive drug kingpins. The timing is no coincidence."[20]

Sometimes messages of U.S. displeasure are sent to hemispheric regimes even when their cooperation is officially certified. In its 1988 drug strategy report to Congress, for example, the State Department stated that although the law required justifications only for countries given a "national interest certification," it had "taken an unusual step and provided justifications for two countries that are certified as fully cooperating. We are sending a signal to Colombia and Mexico."[21] The subsequent tone of the report made it clear that the "signal" was that Washington was increasingly unimpressed with the seriousness with which the two regimes were waging the drug war. Only the most obtuse Colombian or Mexican officials would have failed to discern the underlying threat: Unless greater cooperation was forthcoming, subsequent reports might recommend decertification and its resulting penalties.

Similarly, Washington announced that it was "postponing" $94 million in military and economic aid to Peru for FY 1991 because it could not obtain an agreement from the new government of President Alberto Fujimori on a coordinated antidrug strategy.[22] As is noted in chapter 6, Peru sought a program that placed greater emphasis on economic assistance and less on military aid. The U.S. action was notable because Peru had been officially certified as cooperating with U.S. efforts. The timing of the announcement was also revealing; it occurred in the midst of intensive negotiations with Lima concerning the composition of antidrug programs. Postponing the delivery of aid monies, therefore, was most likely a tactical maneuver by Washington to gain a decisive advantage in those negotiations.[23]

In recent years, the certification process has come under increasing fire from diverse political sources. Drug-war hard-liners in Congress assert that the process is often a sham, and that Mexico, in particular, has been certified despite tepid (at best) cooperation with U.S. efforts. Conversely, Latin American governments and officials at the Organization of American States (OAS) argue that the certification process is too rigid and that alternative incentives to promote cooperation ought to be explored. In February 2001 the OAS issued a country-by-country "report card" on the progress of the war against drugs. The report also argued that the approach embodied in its new Multilateral Evaluation Mechanism (MEM) was superior to the U.S. certification system. "We are certain this method of evaluation will have more legitimacy," asserted the OAS secretary general, Cesar Gaviria. He added, "Almost every country in the hemisphere thinks the unilateral process is inconvenient. This is a method of cooperation."[24]

A few years earlier, Washington would simply have rejected the criticism and spurned the suggested alternative. This time, though, dissatisfaction with the certification system had reached the point that the reception was far milder. Indeed, the new Bush administration welcomed the report. "It will become increasingly apparent to policy people in the hemisphere that our national interests are better served by this evaluation mechanism than by a system based on confrontation," said Edward H. Jurith, acting director of the Office of National Drug Control Policy.[25] That attitude had been foreshadowed by the skepticism about the certification process that Secretary of State Colin Powell had expressed during his confirmation hearing before the Senate Foreign Relations Committee.

Even some members of Congress seem receptive to scrapping the certification system. Just two days before the OAS issued its report, Senators Christopher Dodd (D-CT.), John McCain (R-AZ), and Chuck Hagel (R-NB) introduced legislation to suspend the certification process for two years while governments in the Western Hemisphere worked to develop a less divisive way to counteract the drug trade. A number of senators, including nearly all from the southwestern states, introduced a more limited bill that would give a one-year waiver to Mexico, thus reducing the pressure on the new government of President Vicente Fox.[26]

Moving from a unilateral to a multilateral evaluation system does little to overcome the core problem of the hemispheric war on drugs: the inherent, destructive futility of a prohibitionist strategy. But it might help eliminate some of the worst Ugly American tactics. That is because the unilateral certification process has been the foundation for Washington's bullying tactics and other unsavory practices.

SOME STRANGE BEDFELLOWS

In the course of waging the war on drugs, the United States has made common cause with an assortment of dubious regimes. One of those relationships was the evolving cooperation during the 1990s between Washington and the government of Peru's autocratic president, Alberto Fujimori. The trend toward democracy in Latin America experienced a major blow in April 1992 when Fujimori declared to the nation that he had assumed exclusive control of the government in a "self-coup" (*autogolpe*) with the support of the military. His revamped regime moved quickly to shut down all independent branches of the government: dissolving the Peruvian Congress and eviscerating the justice system by summarily dismissing 13 Supreme Court justices as well as all the judges on the Tribunal of Constitutional Guarantees. During the early years of his authoritarian rule, the U.S. State Department and Justice Department frequently condemned the regime's human rights abuses. As the Fujimori government pressed its campaign against the Maoist Sendero Luminoso guerrillas, there was an abundance of such abuses.[27]

Fujimori's offensive against the Shining Path also impacted many of the peasants in the Upper Huallaga Valley and other remote locales who grew much of the coca crop and at least countenanced if not actively supported the guerrillas. As the effort to stamp out the Shining Path gained momentum in the mid- and late 1990s, Washington began to look on Lima's autocratic regime with greater tolerance. Indeed, from the standpoint of U.S. officials, Fujimori's decision to unleash the military offered the promise of a dual benefit. Not only did it promise to weaken a dangerous radical-left political force, but it also seemed to be disrupting the source of the bulk of the cocaine flowing from the Andean region. Between 1996 and 1998, the acreage under coca cultivation in Peru dropped by 40 percent. By 1999 the decline reached 56 percent. U.S. officials used terms such as "amazing" and "astonishing" and were quick to credit the Peruvian government.[28] In truth, the principal reason for the decline was a fungus that swept through the Peruvian coca crop during those years.

During the 1990s the U.S. military assisted the Peruvian government interdict planes carrying drugs out of Peru to processing facilities in Colombia.[29] U.S. radar monitoring of suspect flights was crucial to that operation. By 1998 Washington was significantly expanding its drug-war financial aid to the Peruvian government in other ways. Under one program, a five-year, $60 million effort, the United States sought to greatly expand Peru's force of river patrol boats to combat the drug trade in the Amazon basin. At that time, the Peruvian military had just 16 such boats. The U.S. aid would provide an additional 54 boats as well as funds to train the military personnel needed to man them.[30]

The Fujimori government's prosecution of the drug war was more apparent than real, however. Indeed, as far as the Peruvian military was concerned, the principal offense of those peasants involved in growing coca was not that they were involved in the drug trade but that they helped fund the Shining Path. A cynic might even argue that the military's real complaint was that too many peasants paid off the Shining Path instead of the military. Throughout the 1990s allegations surfaced repeatedly that Vladimiro Montesinos, the head of the National Intelligence Service, used his office to shield friendly drug traffickers even as the military used force against drug-crop peasants who were deemed enemies of the regime. After Fujimori fell from power and fled the country in late 2000, those allegations soared in number.[31] Evidence emerged that Montesinos may have received as much as $1 million from a leading Mexican drug cartel.[32] At the same time, he and his intelligence apparatus were apparently receiving up to $1 million a year from the CIA.[33]

Despite the unsavory nature of the Fujimori-Montesinos regime, U.S. praise for Peru's antidrug efforts increased steadily throughout the 1990s. Between 1995 and 1998, the price of coca leaves had fallen by half. That drew praise from U.S. ambassador Dennis Jett, who said that Peru had "demonstrated that the battle can be won against an enemy that doesn't respect frontiers or laws."[34] It did not seem to bother Washington unduly that it was cooperating with a regime that had used the military to undermine democracy in Peru.

The U.S. government's relationship with another authoritarian ruler, Panamanian dictator Manuel Noriega, followed a somewhat different course. Throughout the 1980s, Washington's relationship with Noriega was a curious one. For years there appeared to have been close cooperation as the Panamanian strongman assisted Washington in its drive to undermine the leftist Sandinista regime in Nicaragua and prop up the right-wing government of El Salvador against Marxist rebels. General Noriega also had received praise from the Drug Enforcement Administration for his cooperation in helping to stanch the flow of narcotics through his country. The latter was no small consideration, since Panama was a major transit point in the illegal drug trade. Yet throughout this period there was evidence that the Medellín cartel paid the Panamanian Defense Forces $1,000 for every kilogram of cocaine transshipped through Panama.[35] Since Noriega tightly controlled the Defense Forces, it is highly improbable that he was not in on the take.

Cooperation between Washington and Noriega began to break down in 1987 when Roberto Díaz, a retired high-ranking Panamanian military officer and a former Noriega confidant, publicly accused the general of trafficking in narcotics. U.S. intelligence agents and some DEA agents had made similar accusations for years, but they were disregarded by policymakers in the Reagan administration. Díaz's charges, though, had such a high profile that U.S. officials could not have dismissed them even if they had been so inclined. In addition to allegations about trafficking in drugs, Díaz also accused Noriega of setting up the 1984 murder of a leading opposition politician who had spoken out against Noriega's involvement in the drug trade. After Díaz's revelations, thousands of Panamanians took to the streets demanding Noriega's ouster, and the Civil Crusade, a coalition of civic, labor, and business organizations, called a series of strikes.[36] A short time later the U.S. Senate passed a resolution denouncing Noriega, who retaliated by orchestrating a violent demonstration against the U.S. embassy. The Reagan administration promptly began to terminate its association with the Noriega government, and relations became increasingly strained.

The chill deepened in February 1988 when two federal grand juries in Florida indicted Noriega on drug charges. Indeed, one declared purpose of the December 1989 U.S. military operation in Panama was to apprehend Noriega and take him to Florida for trial.

Even before that episode, the Bush administration applied economic sanctions against Panama (which mainly devastated the anti-Noriega urban middle classes) in an effort to force Noriega from power. Only when that tactic failed did the United States invade Panama and seize its onetime client.

The willingness of U.S. administrations to collaborate with the most odious dictatorships in the war on drugs is a long-standing and continuing pattern. It is also one that extends well beyond the Western Hemisphere. Despite its overall policy of attempting to isolate Burma's military dictatorship, the United States maintained cooperation with that regime on antidrug initiatives throughout the 1990s and the initial years of the twenty-first century. Washington even sought to cooperate with the infamous Taliban regime in Afghanistan and praised its effort to eradicate the cultivation of opium poppies.[37] In reality, the Taliban gave its order to halt cultivation to drive up the price of opium the regime had already stockpiled.[38]

Even if the Taliban had tried to stem cultivation for honest reasons, U.S. cooperation with that regime should have been morally repugnant. Among other outrages, the Taliban government prohibited the education of girls, tortured and executed political critics, and required non-Muslims to wear distinctive clothing—a practice eerily reminiscent of Nazi Germany's requirement that Jews display the Star of David on their clothing. Yet U.S. officials deemed none of that to be a bar to cooperation with the Taliban on drug policy. Washington's approach came to an especially calamitous end in September 2001 when the Taliban regime was linked to Osama bin Laden's terrorist attacks on the World Trade Center and the Pentagon that killed more than 3,000 people. Moreover, evidence quickly emerged that the Taliban all along had been collecting millions of dollars in profits from the illicit drug trade, with much of that money going into the terrorists' coffers.[39] Rarely is there such graphic evidence of the bankruptcy of U.S. drug policy.

When it comes to waging the war on drugs, though, no moral or ideological impediment has seemed sufficient with regard to any regime. In recent years the United States has even cooperated with Fidel Castro on drug matters—a policy that inexplicably drew praise from two Council on Foreign Relations Task Force reports on policy toward Cuba.[40] Former drug czar Barry McCaffrey also thinks that such cooperation with the Castro regime is a splendid idea.[41]

UNCLE SAM: BULLY OF THE HEMISPHERIC PLAYGROUND

Although the United States might prefer cooperative relationships (even with unsavory regimes) on the drug issue, it has frequently resorted to bullying tactics. The threat of decertification and the attendant economic sanctions was, for example, the principal leverage the elder Bush's administration used to persuade the Andean governments to militarize the drug war. On that issue, as on so many others, U.S. officials ignored the long-standing antipathy of Latin American populations to U.S. military pressure.

The actions of U.S. drug enforcement personnel and the indigenous antinarcotics units funded and trained by Washington have also come in for criticism. As noted in chapter 3, the human rights record of the Colombian military has been so dubious that the Pentagon has been reluctant to train regular Colombian battalions in counternarcotics work, insisting instead on preparing only carefully selected "elite" battalions. But the Colombian military is hardly the only governmental organization in Latin America with a troubling human rights record. The conduct of antinarcotics forces in Bolivia and Peru—and sometimes even the conduct of U.S. personnel themselves—has been cause for concern.

For example, serious questions have been raised about the conduct of the DEA and (even more so) the Leopards and other elite Bolivian antinarcotics units trained by the United States. A woman from the small town of Chimore describes a drug raid on her home: "One day in March 1990, the DEA and UMOPAR [Bolivian antidrug forces] did a joint raid on all the houses in Chimore. They knocked on our door at 5:00 A.M. When we didn't open, they just kicked it down and forced their way in. My daughter was on her own downstairs doing her homework. I was still in bed upstairs. 'Why did you come to the Chapare,' they asked her. They opened all the drawers and helped themselves to what they wanted, even my daughter's bras and knickers."[42]

Unfortunately, that was not the only instance in which the DEA played the role of Ugly American in Bolivia. The agency's highhanded actions during a 1991 raid (involving 20 DEA agents and 650 Bolivian police) that wrested the town of Santa Ana from control of the traffickers provoked angry outbursts from Bolivian opinion leaders. "The special force for the fight against drug trafficking serves only U.S. interests," fumed the prominent Catholic radio station Fides the day after the raid. "UMOPAR is not at the service of Bolivia, it is at the service of the U.S. Our government should put the DEA in its place."[43]

Indeed, one of the most frequent complaints in Bolivia and other Latin American countries is that U.S. law enforcement agencies show no respect for the national sovereignty of the host countries and act as if they are operating in the United States. James Painter, a BBC correspondent for Latin America, describes the neo-imperial quality of U.S. antidrug operations. "In practice, it is U.S. officials, and particularly the DEA and military personnel in the U.S. embassy in La Paz, who control Bolivia's interdiction efforts. It is most often the DEA that plans operations, executes and usually leads drug raids, and coordinates and often monopolizes antinarcotics intelligence." The gap between official policy and the reality on the ground is striking, according to Painter. "DEA officials stress that they are merely helping the Bolivian government in its efforts, but it is quite clear that they call the shots."[44]

The intensification of the drug war has played into the hands of left-wing insurgent movements as well as right-wing authoritarian elements in Latin American military establishments that sought to undermine the tenuous democratic systems in those countries. Radical leftist groups especially have sought to use U.S. drug war policy demands as a focal issue to discredit existing regimes.[45] Playing on nationalistic sentiments, those groups appointed themselves the "true" voice of the people and portrayed the democratic governments as U.S. lackeys that are willing to implement Washington's policies regardless of their dire effects on Latin Americans.

In Colombia, U.S. actions—especially Washington's demands that Colombia extradite accused drug traffickers to the United States for trial—early on created "a mood of anti-imperialism that our guerrillas have failed to achieve in decades," remarked noted Colombian newspaper columnist Enrique Santos.[46] The extradition issue has been a source of intense controversy (as well as a catalyst for violence) since the early 1980s. Under immense U.S. pressure, the Colombian government passed an extradition statute in 1985 only to have Colombia's Supreme Court invalidate the measure. In 1990 Colombia succumbed to U.S. pressure once more and implemented an extradition measure. But that cooperation was again suspended a few years later because of continuing intense public opposition.

In Peru, the Shining Path guerrillas used the U.S.-sponsored coca-crop eradication program in the Upper Huallaga Valley to solidify their power among the local peasantry. Peruvian officials in the late 1980s conceded that "efforts to destroy the coca fields have hurt the popular support among peasant growers and created a crucial source of funding [for the guerrillas] from fees collected for protecting the drug trade."[47]

The Fujimori government understood that connection and focused its efforts on counterinsurgency efforts against the Shining Path while looking the other way with regard to coca farmers who were not in league with the guerrillas. During the early and mid-1990s, Fujimori's regime did just enough in the drug war to fend off decertification, although in some years (e.g., 1995) the country did not receive full certification but was instead given a "national interest" waiver.[48] Only after the Shining Path was badly weakened did Lima devote more effort to the drug war (in part because of its desire to get U.S. antidrug funds).

The relationship between leftist insurgent movements and trafficking organizations has always been complex.[49] While conflicting interests generally inhibit the formation of overt alliances—for one thing, the traffickers tend to be politically conservative—there is strong evidence of informal cooperation. Most notably, both factions share the desire to rid their countries of an American presence and prevent extradition of accused criminals to the United States. The primary danger of the U.S.-directed drug war, though, is not that it helps cement an explicit narco-guerrilla alliance but that it enables the leftists to gain popular support from beleaguered peasants. That pattern is emerging once again in Colombia as left-wing insurgents are exploiting discontent with the aerial eradication component of Plan Colombia.

The United States has engaged in a variety of abrasive acts that have damaged relations with Latin American countries. One of the worst is that U.S. ambassadors in source countries have repeatedly demanded the dismissal of officials they suspected were involved in drug trafficking or merely opposed the war on drugs.

An interview by ABC News correspondent Peter Jennings with Bolivian president Jaime Paz Zamora in 1992 suggested the extent of U.S. "influence" on political appointments in that country.

> JENNINGS: Does the American ambassador in Bolivia have the power to make or break police officers, military officers, even politicians?
> ZAMORA: [through interpreter] Without a doubt.

JENNINGS: Does this mean that if the U.S. ambassador doesn't like a man you've appointed to government, he can ask you to get rid of him?

ZAMORA: [through interpreter] Yes, in practice it works that way.[50]

Paz Zamora could have added that he would have virtually no choice but to accede to U.S. "requests." It was revealing that when Jennings asked the U.S. ambassador about the extent of his power, he did not deny that he could get rid of officials he deemed offensive. Indeed, less than two years earlier, three high-level officials in Paz Zamora's government had been dismissed or forced to resign because of U.S. pressure.

The dispute began when the government appointed army colonel Faustino Rico Toro commander of the country's antinarcotics forces. Washington voiced immediate and strong objections, noting that Rico Toro had served as chief of a crucial army intelligence unit during the notorious administration of President Luis García Meza in 1980-81 when drug traffickers had apparently penetrated the highest levels of the Bolivian government. The Bush administration's actions were not confined to diplomatic protests; it promptly suspended delivery of more than $100 million in aid.[51]

Washington's coercion resulted in Rico Toro's resignation within days, but U.S. officials did not stop there. Instead, the State Department "pressed its concerns" about other high-level Bolivian officials, making it clear that the aid spigot would not be turned back on unless some of those individuals left the government. The Bush administration's hard-ball tactics received an assist from Congress when Representative David Obey (D-WI), chairman of the House appropriations subcommittee that oversees foreign aid, announced that his panel was putting a "hold" on aid to Bolivia until the allegations of corruption by Bolivian officials were resolved. That pressure achieved the desired results; Interior Minister Guillermo Capobianco and national police commander Felipe Carvajal submitted their resignations.[52]

The most high-profile attempt to use coercive measures to force a change in governmental personnel was, of course, the campaign against Colombian president Ernesto Samper in the mid-1990s. That episode was notable for two reasons: It was directed against not only an elected official but the top elected official in the country; and it failed. But Samper was merely the most prominent target. Washington has shown time and again that if one wants to survive politically in Latin America, it is necessary to not deviate in the slightest from the U.S. orthodoxy regarding the war on drugs. That is not only an imperial mentality, it is not even a very subtle version.

Americans might be tempted to hail the results of such coercive diplomacy. It is quite possible that the various charges of corruption were accurate and the Latin American governments might be better off without the accused officials. Moreover, U.S. leaders take the understandable position that American tax dollars should not be used to support regimes that undermine Washington's policy objectives. Recipient regimes that assume otherwise ignore evidence that U.S. antidrug aid has more than a few strings attached.

But those who favor using such coercive tactics should consider the possible adverse consequences. It seems profoundly unwise for the United States to attempt to dictate the policies, much less the composition, of foreign governments. Such imperialistic pretensions are certain to be widely resented, especially in Latin America. Our hemispheric neighbors have not forgotten Washington's tendency to interfere in their internal affairs, a habit that was most pronounced during the early decades of the twentieth century but has never entirely disappeared, as the 1989 invasion of Panama and the 1994 occupation of Haiti confirmed. Given the renowned sensitivities of Latin American populations to any signs of domination by the "Colossus of the North," such trampling on national sovereignty is playing with political nitroglycerin. The perception that U.S. ambassadors are modern-day

Roman proconsuls implementing Washington's imperial edicts could undermine the legitimacy of the hemisphere's democratic governments and reawaken virulently anti-U.S. emotions throughout the region.

That is becoming evident with respect to Plan Colombia. Although the plan already has led to large and sometimes violently anti-U.S. demonstrations in Bogotá and other Colombian cities as well as in the rural areas most directly affected by the eradication campaign, Washington is not about to alter course. Lest the government of President Andrés Pastrana waver in its commitment to the aerial fumigation component of Plan Colombia because of rising public opposition, U.S. ambassador Anne Patterson warned that any backtracking would have immediate financial consequences. If the fumigation did not continue, she emphasized, "we won't give the level of assistance that Colombia needs."[53]

But the animosity at U.S. tactics is not confined to Colombia. Elements of Plan Colombia are exacerbating anti-U.S. sentiments in several other neighboring countries. The establishment of a major U.S. antidrug operation at an air base near Manta, Ecuador, has proven extremely controversial. In the early months of 2001, construction crews were busy at work lengthening a runway and building a variety of support facilities to accommodate new arrivals—U.S. E-3 AWACS planes. Smaller U.S. spy planes had operated out of the base for several years, and approximately 150 Americans were already stationed there, but the expanded operation would bring the total to more than 400. By the summer of 2001 Manta had become the main hub for U.S. surveillance flights over the entire cocaine-producing region in South America. Most revealing, the expanded facility allowed the full resumption of surveillance flights, which had been cut by two-thirds when U.S. forces were compelled to vacate Howard Air Force Base in Panama in the summer of 1999.

Ecuadorean critics of the program raise several objections. The fact that the United States pays no rent for using the facility is seen as evidence of a neocolonial privilege. Another source of anger is that the original deal had been signed with a president who was later overthrown and went into exile in the United States. It did not help matters that the expansion of the Manta base occurred at the same time that the Ecuadorean government adopted the U.S. dollar as the national currency—something that already rankled nationalistic elements. All of this led critics to warn that Ecuador was turning into America's "new Panama"— which is decidedly not meant as a compliment. Indeed, some opponents asserted that Ecuador was being treated as America's fifty-first state. Congressman Henry Llanes, a leader of the effort to block Washington's use of the base, asserted that Ecuador was fast becoming a "sold-out country." He expressed his fear that "we will pay with more than our pride."[54] Washington ignores such manifestations of nationalist resentment at its high-visibility profile in the drug war at its peril.

Perhaps the most odious example of Washington's "Ugly American" tactics was the U.S.-sponsored kidnapping of Mexican physician Humberto Álvarez Machaín, whom the DEA accused of participating in the 1985 torture and murder of DEA agent Enrique Camarena. The kidnapping of Álvarez was part of Operation Leyenda, a campaign launched after Camarena's death to bring to the United States by any means possible the 19 people allegedly involved in his killing.[55] (In addition, the United States launched Operation Intercept II, which threw the U.S.-Mexico border into the same type of gridlock as the original Operation Intercept during the Nixon years.)

Operation Leyenda reflected a growing attitude in the United States beginning in the mid-1980s that drug offenses, even when committed overseas, were properly a subject of U.S. criminal jurisdiction.[56] Indeed, the Drug Abuse Act of 1986 made it a crime to manufacture or distribute drugs outside the United States "with the intention of exporting them to U.S. territory."[57] Along with Operation Leyenda and its pressure on Mexico, Washington was putting enormous pressure on Colombia to extradite accused drug traffickers to the United States for trial. Latin American governments viewed this trend toward a bold assertion of U.S. extraterritorial criminal jurisdiction with understandable apprehension. But it was the logical outcome of the increasing militancy of U.S. attitudes about the drug problem. María Celia Toro observes: "Having defined drug trafficking as a matter of national security and having put international terrorists and drug traffickers on equal footing, the United States created an environment propitious for those (such as the emboldened DEA) in favor of taking the 'war on drugs' literally."[58]

Frustrated by problems in getting the Mexican government to extradite Álvarez to the United States for trial under provisions of the treaty between the two countries, the DEA offered a bounty for his kidnapping, a lure that produced the desired result in 1990. The U.S. Supreme Court finally considered the sordid affair in June 1992 and ruled that the extradition treaty did not bar U.S. authorities from using other means to bring an accused party to trial.

From the standpoint of constitutional law, the Court's decision was relatively narrow. The majority did not pass judgment on whether it was wise policy in terms of U.S. relations with hemispheric neighbors.[59] Throughout Latin America, however, the Court's ruling was widely interpreted as giving a green light to the U.S. executive branch to apprehend accused drug traffickers without the consent of the host countries. Ill-considered comments by Bush administration officials exacerbated that fear, and the *Álvarez* case became a new symbol of Yankee arrogance in the minds of many Latin Americans.

The aftermath of Álvarez's criminal trial made matters even worse. To the chagrin of the DEA, a federal judge acquitted the accused with caustic comments about the weakness of the government's case. Instead of quietly accepting defeat, Washington then demanded that Mexico put Álvarez on trial to honor the spirit of the extradition treaty—the same treaty U.S. officials had circumvented up to that point. Not only did the demand deserve a prize for chutzpah, it again inflamed anti-U.S. sentiment in Mexico and the rest of the hemisphere.

Latin Americans also recall the Justice Department's November 1989 ruling authorizing the U.S. military and law enforcement officials to apprehend accused drug traffickers in foreign countries without the consent of the host governments. From the perspective of those governments, it seems that the United States has arrogated to itself the right to use any methods to bring Latin American drug suspects to the United States for trial. Among other consequences, that perception has led to demands by Mexico and other Latin American governments that future extradition treaties include specific language prohibiting U.S. kidnapping enterprises and that existing treaties be modified to include such restrictions. Although the Clinton administration took the constructive step of assuring Mexico that there would be no repetition of the tactics used in the *Álvarez* case, relations between the two countries remained cool throughout the rest of Clinton's presidency. The *Álvarez* case was certainly not the only reason, but it was a factor.

Another factor was Operation Casablanca. Beginning in 1995 and continuing into 1998, the U.S. government ran a sting operation, setting up a front financial services operation offering to launder drug money for Colombian and Mexican traffickers. In one sense Operation Casablanca was a great success. As one expert on money laundering observed, "The sting captured a truly amazing collection of money launderers, drug traffickers, corrupt bankers, and assorted participants."[60] But the operation also was conducted without consulting the government of Mexico, and some aspects of the sting involved U.S. law enforcement activities on Mexican soil without the consent of that government. The reason for failing to bring Mexican authorities into the loop was obvious: Given how thoroughly the drug traffickers had penetrated Mexico's governmental institutions (see chapter 7), the sharing of information would have compromised the sting from the outset. Nevertheless, the government of President Ernesto Zedillo was outraged, and vehement diplomatic protests were sent to Washington as soon as the operation became public. Anger among the Mexican population was even more pronounced. Once again the United States paid a considerable price in damaged relations with a neighbor for vigorously prosecuting the war on drugs.

Operation Casablanca further fueled Mexican suspicions that the United States wanted to treat Mexico as nothing more than another arena for the jurisdiction of U.S. law enforcement. Other U.S. actions suggested that such suspicions were not unfounded. In March 1997 the U.S. House of Representatives voted to decertify Mexico unless that country showed a significantly greater commitment to the fight against illegal drugs within 90 days. The specific demands in the House resolution were most revealing. Mexico would lose its certification unless it: (1) allowed more U.S. narcotics agents into the country; (2) allowed U.S. law enforcement officers to carry weapons while in Mexico; (3) agreed to extradite Mexicans sought by U.S. officials on drug charges; and (4) allowed the U.S. Coast Guard to chase suspected drug traffickers into Mexican territorial waters.[61] The U.S. Justice Department and the DEA immediately sought to use the House vote as leverage to get Mexican officials to agree to those changes.

Mexican leaders did not react well to either the House vote or the subsequent pressure. President Zedillo blasted the House demands. "This is where we draw the line," he told Mexican reporters. "Our sovereignty and dignity as a nation are not negotiable."[62] A senior foreign ministry official was even more caustic about the attitude of U.S. law enforcement agencies. "North American drug officials say to us, 'Just let us alone to do whatever we want in Mexico.'" He fumed: "That's ridiculous. We're not going to allow a bunch of Rambos to overrun our country."[63]

One of the most telling examples of U.S. arrogance was the threatening posture Washington adopted when Jamaica considered decriminalizing marijuana in 2001. A special commission appointed by the government held extensive hearings on the issue and then issued a report recommending decriminalizing possession of small quantities of the drug. The U.S. response was swift and uncompromising. "The U.S. opposes the decriminalization of marijuana use," stated Michael Koplovsky, spokesman for the U.S. embassy in Kingston. "The U.S. government will consider Jamaica's adherence to its commitments under the 1988 UN Drug Convention when making its determination under the annual narcotics certification review."[64] U.S. officials maintained that decriminalization was not in keeping with Jamaica's obligations to combat drug trafficking.

Jamaican leaders were understandably miffed at the U.S. position. They pointed out that Jamaica's laws against trafficking in any drug, including marijuana, would remain on the books, and they affirmed that cooperation would continue against the international drug trade. Yet that was not enough for Washington; the U.S. government was attempting to dictate to the Jamaican parliament and public what domestic laws the country could have regarding simple drug possession. One angry senior Jamaican official said, "This is a matter that will be decided by the Jamaican parliament, and the island's sovereign parliament will not be swayed by external threats."[65]

Can the United States change course and overcome the longstanding temptation to use its great power coercively against its hemispheric nations in the name of pursuing the drug war? To its credit, the administration of George W. Bush seems at least dimly aware of the problem. Indeed, in terms of overall international policy, the president and his advisers recognize that some of Washington's actions have not been well received around the world but were seen instead as manifestations of arrogance and bullying. During the 2000 presidential campaign, Bush himself stressed the need for "humility" in U.S. foreign policy. The Western Hemisphere would be a great place to begin applying that principle. And repudiating the use of coercive measures to get Latin American governments to cooperate in the drug war should be the first step.

CHAPTER SIX

REAPING THE WHIRLWIND:
CONSEQUENCES TO LATIN AMERICAN SOCIETIES

In country after country in Latin America, governments that have responded to U.S. pressure and waged a war on drugs against their own populations have encountered evasion, opposition, and sometimes outright defiance. Several Latin American societies have been strained badly as public anger with the drug war has spilled over into broader opposition to incumbent governments and occasionally even the political system itself. The dangerous potential consequences have been most evident in Peru, with the surge in support for the Maoist Shining Path during the 1980s and early 1990s, and more recently with the mounting political chaos in Colombia. But other societies, including those of Bolivia, Ecuador, Panama, and Mexico, have also suffered, albeit to a lesser degree.

The bottom line is that the huge profit margins in the illicit drug trade have created powerful economic and political constituencies in drug-producing and drug-transiting countries. Those constituencies do not take kindly to government efforts to deprive them of their livelihoods. Washington has repeatedly been oblivious to that reality.

Instead, U.S. officials argue that trafficking in drugs per se threatens democracy in the hemisphere and the stability of Latin American societies. President Bill Clinton epitomized the conventional wisdom, arguing that "because of the rise of narcotraffickers and terrorist activities in Colombia and other countries, democracy is under great strain in Latin America."[1] On another occasion he urged other Latin American governments to support Plan Colombia because if the oldest democracy in South America could be torn down by the traffickers and their allies, "so can others." He asserted that all of Colombia's neighbors had a "deep and abiding interest" in seeing that the traffickers' efforts were defeated.[2]

That is the international version of the hoary argument of domestic drug warriors that the violence and other social pathologies afflicting many urban neighborhoods are caused by the sale and use of illegal drugs. Critics of the drug war have presented massive evidence to show that most of the worst dislocations actually are caused by the incentive structures created by a prohibitionist strategy combined with the harsh measures employed to enforce the drug laws. Drug use itself causes a relatively small percentage of the problems. Critics note further that many of the undesirable consequences associated with illegal drugs also were present when the United States experimented with alcohol prohibition in the 1920s and early 1930s and greatly diminished once the country abandoned Prohibition.

BLOODBATH IN COLOMBIA

One of the earliest victims of U.S. pressure to wage war on a powerful domestic political and economic constituency was Colombia. A succession of Colombian governments during the 1970s and 1980s resisted Washington's demands to extradite accused drug traffickers to the United States for trial. This was not a small issue for the traffickers. Given the degree of corruption in Colombia's judicial system, the drug lords were confident that convictions for trafficking offenses would be rare, and most of those would be overturned on appeal. In the unusual instance that a conviction would take place and be upheld on appeal, a drug lord would serve his sentence in something less than onerous conditions. The latter situation was confirmed in an especially flagrant manner when Pablo Escobar, a leader of the notorious Medellín cartel, agreed to surrender to the authorities at the beginning of the 1990s. Escobar was sentenced to serve time in a special mountaintop prison that had been designed to his specifications. The "prison" was little more than a glorified country club, and Escobar continued to run his business operations from its confines until he orchestrated an escape in 1991.

Such "punishment" did little to deter the Colombian drug lords. But the prospect of a trial in the United States—and a lengthy stay in a maximum security federal prison—was a different matter entirely. The drug lords made it their highest priority to defeat extradition treaties or extradition statutes. When a constitutional case on the extradition issue was pending before Colombia's Supreme Court in 1985, rebels from the leftist M-19 faction invaded the Supreme Court building and killed a number of people, including 12 Supreme Court justices. It was likely no coincidence that the justices assassinated were those who were most favorably inclined to approve the extradition statute. (This is just one of many instances in which drug traffickers and leftist guerrillas, the M-19 and, after that group made peace with the Colombian government, the FARC, have collaborated to serve mutual interests.)

When the Colombian government again showed signs of succumbing to U.S. pressure on the extradition issue in the late 1980s, the drug organizations (primarily the Medellín cartel) unleashed a massive wave of violence.[3] Thousands of innocent Colombians perished in the fighting between the drug lords and government police and military forces between the late 1980s and the mid-1990s. The worst period was the second half of 1989 and the first half of 1990. Following the assassination of Liberal Party presidential candidate Luis Carlos Galán in August, the government of President Virgilio Barco invoked a state of siege, bypassed the Supreme Court, and imposed extradition by decree. He then moved to confiscate many of the assets of the drug lords. Pablo Escobar and his fellow traffickers responded with a press communiqué proclaiming that henceforth the fight with the government was a blood feud. The communiqué was signed "The Extraditables." The level of violence soon far exceeded previous levels, with major bombing incidents every few days. In September an especially bloody massacre took place when gunmen machine-gunned the wives of police and army personnel as they shopped for groceries. The most horrific incident, though, took place on the morning of December 6. As people were headed to work, a truck loaded with a half ton of dynamite detonated in front of the police headquarters in Bogotá. The massive explosion heavily damaged two square miles of the city, killed 60 people outright and wounded nearly 1,000.[4]

The violence continued almost unabated into 1990, subsiding only when the country's new president, Cesar Gavíria, elected in May, cut a deal with the drug traffickers. If they agreed to turn themselves in, Gavíria assured them that they would be tried in Colombia, not the United States. That deal effectively ended extradition—much to the fury of U.S. officials. It did have a beneficial effect in one sense, however; violence returned to "normal" pre–August 1989 levels, despite the continuing efforts of the Gavíria government to undermine the Medellín cartel. Author Mike Gray offers a depressingly accurate summary of the upsurge of violence in Colombia in response to U.S. pressure to escalate the drug war: It "had damaged the country in ways that would endure for a generation. The best judges, the most incorruptible politicians, the most aggressive journalists, the bravest army officers had all been sacrificed to the war on drugs. Most of the survivors were thoroughly compromised. Given the choice of *plata o plomo* [silver or lead], they had understandably chosen *plata*. But once they took the cash, they found themselves on the payroll, and the resulting moral cancer infected everything in Colombia from the top down."[5]

After a brief decline following the defeat of the Medellín and Cali cartels in the mid-1990s, the violence began to escalate again toward the end of the decade and has continued into the new century. This time, though, there is an increasingly prominent political dimension as leftist insurgent groups take advantage of the situation.

BACKLASH IN BOLIVIA

Just as U.S. policymakers ignore the most obvious reason for the adverse domestic consequences of the drug war, they miss the most obvious connections between a prohibitionist strategy and negative public reactions in Latin American countries. Bolivia has been the most responsive to U.S. demands in recent years. Under President Hugo Bánzer, the La Paz government vigorously pressed drug-crop eradication measures. Government officials proclaimed that by the end of 2002 they hoped to destroy all illegal drug plantations. At the beginning of 2000, cocaine production was 70 tons a year—down from 250 tons before the latest eradication programs began in 1997.[6] By the beginning of 2001, it had dropped to 43 tons.[7] (Data in the U.S. State Department's latest *International Narcotics Control Strategy Report,* however, suggest that the Bolivian government's goal of complete eradication of coca is going down the same path as previous grandiose goals in other countries. In the 2002 report, cocaine production is back up to 60 tons.)[8]

Eradication efforts have not gone unopposed by Bolivian peasants who attempt to carry on a centuries-old tradition of cultivating coca. In April 2000 some 10,000 peasants gathered in El Chapare, in the heart of the country's coca-growing region, and demanded that the government stop the destruction of their crops.

Those demonstrations remained largely peaceful. The same was not true a year earlier, when the government sent thousands of soldiers and police into the area. The resulting clashes left more than a dozen people dead and scores wounded. In March 2000 another set of violent demonstrations erupted in Cochabamba, Bolivia's third-largest city.[9]

Bolivian government officials sought to downplay the significance of the opposition. Interior Minister Guillermo Fortún charged that drug traffickers were behind the demonstrations and that in the case of the Cochabamba disorders, demonstrators had all their expenses paid by drug-trafficking organizations—a charge that peasant leaders vehemently denied.[10] It is virtually impossible to assess the accuracy of Fortún's allegation, but U.S. officials adopt a similarly dismissive attitude. Yet even Fortún admits that the eradication plan hurts the nearly 200,000 peasants who make a living out of growing coca. He argues, though, that matters are improving as more and more peasants supposedly accept a government-sponsored program to develop alternative crops, such as coffee and bananas. Peasant leaders ridicule such notions and charge further that the government has done little to help create markets for those other crops.[11]

One peasant leader, Evo Morales, a left-wing Bolivian congressman and prominent candidate in the 2002 presidential election, charged that "the abuse of the military crop eradicators is intolerable." Morales noted that the government's program emphasized the development of other crops that would provide farmers with a decent living—but that most of the crops were unable to do so. He issued an ominous warning: "The decision of thousands of farm families has been very clear: the government must paralyze the eradication of the coca fields and come up with a true alternative, or else violent confrontations may occur because we are ready to die rather than surrender."[12] That sounds like something a bit broader than a conspiracy against the government conducted by a few well-heeled drug traffickers.

The demonstrations in 1999 and early 2000 were hardly the last instances in which Bolivian farmers exhibited intense opposition to drug-eradication efforts. More demonstrations occurred in the autumn of 2000, leading to the deaths of 10 people and the wounding of 120. The government estimated the economic losses caused by the unrest at $130 million—some 1.5 percent of Bolivia's GDP.[13] In a country as poor as Bolivia, such losses are no trivial matter.

U.S. leaders largely ignored the social unrest and praised the Bánzer government for staying the course in the drug war. Commenting on Bánzer's goal of eradicating all illegal coca crops by 2002, Secretary of State Madeleine Albright was effusive in her praise during a visit to La Paz. "I congratulated him. Coca eradication is a huge success and needs to be continued in a way that President Banzer has planned it. When that landmark is reached, Bolivians will have great cause to celebrate."[14]

Washington has backed up its words of praise with a variety of financial inducements. By 2000 the United States had tripled the amount of aid it was giving to Bolivia, reaching $115 million a year. In addition, Washington promised the country another $110 million in aid as an offshoot of Plan Colombia. Beyond the aid flows, the United States had waived Bolivian debts of $450 million since 1991 and was negotiating with La Paz and the International Monetary Fund to gain a waiver of an additional $1 billion in debt. Those are not trivial sums, but they must be measured against the economic losses entailed by the eradication effort. Bolivian experts estimate that the decline of coca production now costs the Bolivian economy some $500 million a year.[15] And the impact is felt disproportionately by poor farmers, exacerbating poverty and producing social unrest. U.S. aid does not offset losses of that magnitude. (Moreover, Washington declines to take other measures—such as substantially increasing Bolivia's textile quota—that would have a significantly greater economic impact.) The adverse economic impact of eradication programs likely explains the increasingly violent reaction of peasant growers.

The recent incidents are hardly the first time that Bolivian farmers reacted angrily to U.S.-sponsored antidrug efforts by the government in La Paz. There were ugly incidents as far back as 1986. During Operation Blast Furnace, U.S. and Bolivian antidrug units entered the small town of Santa Ana, in the heart of the coca-growing region, to search for traffickers and destroy reported drug labs. The drug fighters were forced to flee for their lives from an angry mob of some 3,000 people. That was an especially impressive turnout, since Santa Ana had fewer than 5,000 inhabitants. As the drug warriors left the area, shouts of "Kill the Yankees" could be heard clearly.[16] It was that reaction that convinced U.S. officials to have American military personnel play a more discreet role, which was the case in the subsequent, more prolonged Operation Snowcap.[17]

In addition to the economic motives for opposing the drug war, there are social factors. In Bolivia and other Andean societies, coca-leaf cultivation and use has had a long history and is regarded as legitimate by major portions of the population.[18] People frequently chew the leaf for a mild narcotic effect—which apparently, among other things, helps them deal with the effects of a high-altitude environment. Coca is sometimes brewed as tea. Whether correct or not, users assert that such uses give them a boost of energy. It is a very small jump indeed to assume that growing coca for the production of cocaine is also legitimate.

PROBLEMS IN PERU

Drug eradication measures especially provoke the wrath of hard-pressed farmers. And that is true in other countries besides Bolivia. Drug policy analysts Patrick L. Clawson and Rensselaer W. Lee III note that eradication programs undertaken by the Peruvian government in the 1980s at the urging of the United States helped the Shining Path movement "establish a powerful foothold among coca growers and other disaffected populations."[19] Alberto Fujimori, who became president of Peru in 1990, seemed to recognize the danger. One of his first acts as president was to dismiss the police general in charge of the eradication program. Virtually no mature coca was eradicated between 1990 and 1995 as Peru's antidrug effort shifted from eradication to interdiction. Fujimori candidly expressed the reason for abandoning forced eradication as a strategy. (Some voluntary, compensated acreage reduction programs remained in place.) "An effective program of repression that leaves the peasants without other alternatives would sharply increase the numbers of those in extreme poverty and could unchain a civil war of unsuspected proportions. . . . We will not repeat the errors of President Ngo Dinh Diem of Vietnam who, during the 1950s, pitted himself against the informal, common law order of the peasants. . . . We will not push peasants and their families into the arms of the terrorists and drug traffickers."[20]

Fujimori's approach worked reasonably well. Once the threat to their livelihood eased, Peruvian peasants began to turn on the Shining Path, and the organization was badly weakened during Fujimori's tenure in office. But since the downfall of his regime, the new government has responded to Washington's pressure and has redoubled its antidrug efforts. Perhaps not coincidentally, the Shining Path is now making at least a modest resurgence, and the old alliance between the guerrilla group and drug traffickers is also resurfacing.[21] One indication of the reemergence of the Shining Path was a major car bombing incident directly in front of the U.S. embassy in Lima just days before a scheduled visit by President George W. Bush in March 2002.

RESISTANCE TO PLAN COLOMBIA

The consequences of Washington's ham-handed pressure on Latin American governments has again become evident with Plan Colombia. RAND Corporation analyst Kevin Jack Riley observed in

1996: "No nation has paid a higher price for its cooperation with the United States in the war against cocaine than Colombia."[22] Given the level of violence that has afflicted Colombia as its government has battled the drug traffickers, Riley's statement was no exaggeration. Unfortunately, the societal costs now threaten to go even higher with Plan Colombia.

Beginning in December 2000, the government of President Andrés Pastrana used plan funds to launch a massive new campaign of aerial spraying of coca crops in Putumayo, the province along the border with Ecuador and Peru that accounts for at least half of Colombia's coca production. Drug-war boosters quickly cited the Putumayo offensive as a great success. General Charles Wilhelm, who until September 2000 had headed the U.S. military's Southern Command, noted that the campaign had resulted in the eradication of some 60,000 acres (24,000 hectares) of coca crops in the first two months. He also boasted that some 1,450 families had accepted an offer to halt coca production in return for a stipend from the Colombian government.[23]

But information soon began to surface that all was not well with the stepped-up eradication program. Previous aerial spraying campaigns had targeted large-scale coca plantations, but the new round focused on smaller plots farmed by peasants who had thus far declined the government's buy-out option. Throughout much of the province, small farmers regarded coca as a legitimate crop and grew it side by side with legal crops. There were indications that the spraying killed those legal crops, such as corn, yucca, and bananas, just as readily as it did coca plants. Local officials predicted widespread hunger in the area as a result of the destruction of food crops.[24]

U.S. bureaucrats were astoundingly insensitive about this point. Washington belatedly acknowledged that farm crops may have been damaged along with coca plants, but argued that the farmers had no one to blame but themselves. William Brownfield, deputy assistant secretary of state for Western Hemisphere Affairs, told journalists that drug crops often were camouflaged among legal crops. "In those situations, there is little remedy for the grower, because the presumption is that he or she did it intentionally for the purpose of protecting the illegal crop."[25] Needless to say, such legalistic quibbling was unlikely to sway peasants who had just seen not only their economic livelihood but even the food supply needed to keep their families alive wither and die.

In addition to the destruction of legal crops, farmers reported cases of cattle dying from the spray, fish kills in a nearby river, and even incidents of people experiencing health problems. White House drug czar Barry McCaffrey and other U.S. officials scoffed at such complaints, contending that the herbicide used, Roundup, produced by Monsanto, was harmless to both humans and animals. Yet the product was sold in the United States with warning labels advising users to apply it so that it did not come in contact with people, either directly or through drift. The Environmental Protection Agency also said that Roundup and similar products should be handled with caution and could cause vomiting, swelling of the lungs, mental confusion, and tissue damage.[26] Moreover, the product was never designed to be applied through indiscriminate, massive spraying campaigns in populated areas.

If the reports from Putumayo (and other regions in Colombia) turn out to be true, the aerial spraying offensive could turn out to be the twenty-first century equivalent of the Agent Orange disaster in Vietnam. But whatever the validity of the reports of ill effects on humans and farm animals, the spraying campaign is not likely to win supporters for the Bogotá government or the United States.[27] Already poor peasants who are reduced to the brink of destitution and starvation by Plan Colombia are prime candidates to be recruited by the FARC and the ELN. True, some may have been guerrilla sympathizers before; but now they have considerable incentive to be more than just sympathizers. To make matters worse, the pilots of the planes doing the crop dusting are operating under subcontract arrangements with the U.S. State Department—

thus making the United States an even more direct target of wrathful peasants whose lives were turned upside down by the eradication campaign.[28]

Putumayo is not the only part of Colombia where anger at the Bogotá government is soaring. Peasants in the northern province of Bolivar are reacting in the same way. "They sprayed all our crops and they sprayed our food too," one farmer near the small village of Pozo Azul told reporters. "Today, there are a lot of people who don't have a scrap of yucca to put on the stove," said another farmer. He affirmed that he had enough food for about two months, but after that he did not know what he would do to feed his eight children.[29] The local police inspector of Pozo Azul fumed, "If Pastrana wants peace he shouldn't cut off the peasants' arms like this." The farmer with eight children stated that "ninety percent of the people in the south of Bolivar are thinking of taking up arms [against the government].[30] That may have been only a slight exaggeration. A few days earlier more than 1,000 local farmers marched into the municipal center of San Pablo to demand that the Bogotá government alleviate their plight and help them avoid the specter of starvation.

Those were the largest demonstrations since the summer of 1996, when an earlier aerial spraying campaign triggered weeks of antigovernment protests. At one point in early August of that year, some 8,000 demonstrators battled military police for control of the airport in Puerto Asis in Putumayo.[31] On another occasion, Florencia, a city of more than 120,000 residents and the capital of Caqueta state, was virtually under siege. Cesar Mundaca, one of the farmers laying siege to the city, highlighted the futility of the aerial spraying campaign. "If they fumigate 20 hectares here, we'll cultivate 200 hectares over there," he said. "They'll have to get rid of the whole forest."[32]

The Colombian government's response to the burgeoning public protests against Plan Colombia is similar to that of the Bolivian government regarding its outraged farmers. In remarks strikingly similar to those of Bolivian interior minister Fortún, General Gustavo Socha, the head of Colombia's antinarcotics police, charged that "the drug traffickers are generating false information and forcing people to disseminate it."[33] When asked to provide specific examples of such a concerted disinformation campaign, however, Socha was unable to do so.

The aerial spraying campaign has become controversial even within Colombia's political establishment. In July 2001, six governors from some of the country's main drug-producing states forced a meeting with top officials in the Pastrana government after warning that current policies could provoke mass protests in their regions that would dwarf previous outbursts.[34] Conservative Party Senator Juan Manuel Ospina announced his intent to introduce legislation sharply scaling back the fumigation effort. Aerial spraying "has been absolutely ineffective in reducing or eliminating the areas under cultivation," he said in a media interview.[35] His bill also would provide expanded aid to induce farmers to switch to legal crops and would decriminalize small drug plots. At a congressional hearing, Comptroller Carlos Ossa called for fumigation to be stopped altogether, as did Eduardo Cifuentes, the federal government's human rights ombudsman, who noted that the government's offers of compensation for poor farmers was lagging far behind the pace of the spraying.[36] Another member of President Pastrana's own Conservative Party, S. Rafael Orduz, offered a succinct view of the aerial spraying campaign: "Our fumigation policy is madness."[37]

Perhaps responding to the growing antifumigation sentiment, Judge Gilberto Reyes of the Bogotá district court issued an order in late July 2001 temporarily suspending the spraying campaign.[38] That profile in courage was short lived, however. Although Reyes's initial order seemed to apply to the entire country, the following day his office issued a "clarification" that it applied only to Indian lands in the Amazon rain forest—a tiny percentage of Colombia's territory.[39] One can only speculate how much that clarification may have been due to pressure from the Pastrana government and the United States. In any case, the spraying missions resumed almost immediately, despite burgeoning public resistance in the affected areas. A week later Judge Reyes lifted his order entirely.

The potential for public disaffection with democratic political systems is not a danger only in Bolivia, Peru, and Colombia. As is discussed in chapter 7, Mexico, which has long been politically stable, is incurring serious risks by trying to combat the drug trade. In addition to the violence and corruption that have afflicted other drug-producing societies under a prohibitionist strategy, there are special risks of alienating the peasantry. According to Mexican scholar Miguel Ruiz-Cabaña I, "Prosecution under the [antidrug campaign] in rural areas for an extended period tends to wear out the state's image among the peasantry, which assumes the risk of cultivating illegal drugs. Depending on the specific circumstances, the government's agents in charge of eradicating crops—the army and the Federal Judicial Police—tend to be viewed with mistrust and suspicion by campesinos."[40]

CREATING A CLIMATE FOR CORRUPTION AND VIOLENCE

In addition to creating pressures for Latin American governments to alienate major portions of their populations by vigorously prosecuting the drug war, Washington's policies also have created the incentives and opportunities for massive corruption. Nowhere have the consequences become more evident than in Peru following the departure of authoritarian president Alberto Fujimori in 2000. Within months, 18 generals and more than 50 other high-ranking military and civilian officials were arrested on criminal charges—most having to do with drug-related corruption. The massive number of arrests led *Washington Post* correspondent Anthony Faiola to observe that "many of the people the United States worked with most closely to accomplish its goals—especially in the drug war—appear to have been working both sides of the street, forming a network of corruption right under the noses of their U.S. partners."[41]

The root problem of the political and social dislocations afflicting drug-source countries as the United States presses them to wage an ever more vigorous war on drugs is the prohibitionist strategy itself. Drug policy scholar LaMond Tullis provides a pithy summary of the consequences: "Successful business enterprises framed in illegality rouse the worst imaginable social and political outcomes. They infiltrate otherwise legitimate bureaucracies, buy public decisions, make alliances with terrorists, threaten or launch intimidating violent attacks on any who choose not to stand aside, create antistates wholly outside the rule of law, and contribute to sundry economic and social effects inimical to civilized life."[42]

Such effects undermine the ostensible goals of the United States for the hemisphere. Washington proclaims that it wants to see the spread of market economies, political democracy, the rule of law, and the invigoration of civil society. But the prohibitionist strategy works at cross purposes to all of those objectives. Latin America is reaping a social whirlwind from the wind of drug prohibition sown by U.S. policy.

CHAPTER SEVEN

MEXICO: THE NEXT COLOMBIA?

U.S. leaders are deeply alarmed at the situation in Colombia, fearing that the democratic political structure in that country could collapse. Their nightmare scenario is the emergence of a Marxist/narcotrafficking state characterized by extensive government involvement in all levels of drug trafficking and a corresponding political impetus to maintain an environment of corruption that provides financial profits for various groups in the state hierarchy.

Those fears are not unfounded, but U.S. policymakers have a serious problem brewing much closer to home. The prominence of the drug trade in Mexico has mushroomed in recent years. Some press reports contended that, by 1997, Mexican drug organizations were rivaling or even surpassing the strength of the Colombian cartels.[1] Two years later Thomas Constantine, head of the U.S. Drug Enforcement Administration, stated that the power of Mexican drug traffickers had grown "virtually geometrically" over the previous five years and that corruption was "unparalleled."[2] As just one indicator of Mexico's growing importance in drug trafficking, 7 of the 12 names listed on the U.S. government's May 2001 list of "international drug kingpins" were those of Mexicans.[3] (Under U.S. law, individuals and enterprises are prohibited from doing business with any individual listed as an international drug kingpin.)

And—as is always the case with lucrative black markets—the trade has been accompanied by escalating corruption and violence.

In a number of troubling ways, Mexico is beginning to resemble Colombia a decade or so ago.[4] Indeed, Mexicans are beginning to refer to the trend as the "Colombianization" of their country.[5]

The rise of Mexico's importance in the drug trade is the result of several factors that have facilitated increased ties among criminal networks and increased incentives for violence and corruption. Mexico had long played a significant role in marijuana production and trafficking. Indeed, during the 1970s the country was the leading source of marijuana consumed in the United States. Under U.S. pressure, the Mexican government waged a major offensive against marijuana production during that decade, including a spraying campaign using the herbicide Paraquat, a toxic chemical that acts as a leaf defoliant.[6] Not only did the eradication effort produce a drop in the supply of Mexican marijuana, it produced a sharp decline in demand, as American marijuana users feared the health effects of Paraquat contamination. Many marijuana traffickers switched their lines of supply from Mexico to Colombia, where they could acquire an unspoiled product. The outcome, though, was not an overall decline in either the drug supply or drug consumption. Instead, there was a classic example of the push-down, pop-up effect. Colombia promptly replaced Mexico as the leading exporter to the United States. Mexico regained its position in the 1980s following a crackdown on marijuana production in Colombia.[7]

The 1970s was also a crucial decade for Mexico's involvement in the heroin trade. Before that time, the overwhelming majority of heroin used in the United States came either from Turkey or the "Golden Triangle" of Southeast Asia. As one of its first actions in the war on drugs, however, the Nixon administration both bribed and pressured the government of Turkey to eliminate opium poppy cultivation. That campaign achieved a surprising degree of success. However, Mexico promptly replaced Turkey as America's leading heroin supplier. The eradication campaign against opium poppies in Mexico proved less successful. Poppy farmers began to shift their production to more remote locations and to use smaller, less easily detected plots of land.[8] Moreover, as RAND Corporation analyst Kevin Jack Riley points out: "Where once the Mexican drug industry was geographically contained, production now extends throughout the country."[9]

Mexico's extensive involvement in the cocaine trade is more recent than its role in either the marijuana or the heroin trade. It dates from the mid-1980s, when U.S. efforts made it more difficult for Colombian traffickers to transport their product via routes in the Caribbean. The initial involvement of Mexican drug kingpins was ominous in that it expanded cocaine markets and the economic and political interests of individuals participating in those markets over a much broader spectrum. That development became important later, especially between 1989 and 1992, when U.S.-led efforts to go after the financial resources of the Colombian cartels created a new opportunity for Mexican traffickers, who began to take payment in cocaine rather than cash. One result of that arrangement was that it gave Mexican traffickers a substantial stake in lucrative U.S. wholesale and retail markets. They soon moved to solidify that stake by creating or expanding syndicates of their own.[10]

Even President Bill Clinton acknowledged the existence of a push-down, pop-up effect with regard to Mexico. "We had a lot of success a few years ago in taking down a number of the Colombian drug cartels," he stated in late 1999, "but one of the adverse consequences of that was a lot of the operations were moved north to Mexico."[11] In February 2000 U.S. ambassador to Mexico Jeffrey Davidow created a furor when he contended that the country had become the world's "main headquarters for drug traffickers."[12]

Mexico's increasing prominence in the drug trade infuriates hard-line drug warriors in the United States. An April 1998 editorial in the *Washington Times* noted acidly, "There's a lot of 'cooperation' on drugs going on in Mexico these days, but it's not with the United States."[13] Roger Noriega, an aide to Senator Jesse Helms (R-NC) later charged that the executive branch's annual certification of Mexico as cooperating in the war on drugs had "become a farce." Helms followed up that assessment with a stinging letter to Secretary of State Madeleine Albright in February 2000 in which he charged that "the Clinton administration, for many years, has failed to apply the law faithfully when it comes to its annual March 1 certification of Mexico's anti-drug cooperation."[14] Helms and other congressional conservatives have long demanded that Mexico be decertified as Colombia was in the mid-1990s.[15] Indeed, the Republican-controlled House of Representatives voted 251 to 175 in March 1997 to overturn President Clinton's certification of Mexico unless the Mexican government was able to show within 90 days that it was making significant progress in the war on drugs.[16] Although the Senate declined to go along with the House action, the vote was a clear expression of anger among congressional conservatives.

Conservative Republicans have been the most critical of Mexico's role, but annoyance with drug-related corruption in Mexico is not confined to that portion of the U.S. political spectrum. Even some congressional Democrats, including Senators Dianne Feinstein (D-CA), Christopher Dodd (D-CT), and Robert Toricelli (D-NJ), have adopted highly critical positions on occasion—even going so far as to advocate decertification.[17]

Given Mexico's economic and political importance to the United States, it is highly unlikely that any administration would take that step, however. (Moreover, the economic sanctions that would have to be imposed following a decertification decision would seem to violate the provisions of NAFTA.)

THE ORGANIZATION OF MEXICO'S DRUG TRADE

As in Colombia during the 1980s and early 1990s, the drug trade in Mexico is dominated by a small number of tightly organized cartels. (The more decentralized structure that characterizes drug trafficking in Colombia today has yet to make an appearance.) Six regionally based cartels currently dominate the Mexican drug trade and have divided up the country into commercial territories. Although there is some overlap in those territories, such an arrangement minimizes competition and the resulting struggles among the various organizations.

- The Gulf cartel is so named because it operates all along the gulf coast of Mexico, from Tampico in the north, through the Yucatán Peninsula and southward to the border with Belize. It is run by Humberto García Abrego, the brother of the notorious drug kingpin Juan García Abrego, who is now in prison for drug offenses.
- The Juárez cartel operates mainly along the Caribbean coast, central Mexico, and along the Texas–Mexico border. Juárez, a city across the Rio Grande from El Paso, Texas, has Mexico's largest concentration of *maquiladoras*. That situation is perfect for drug trafficking, especially given the constant flow of truck traffic taking *maquiladora* products across the border to the United States. Led by Vincente Fuentes, the Juárez cartel deals in heroin and marijuana but gets most of its revenue from the transshipment of Colombian cocaine.[18]
- The Colima cartel operates in the western state of Colima and (in an isolated enclave) along the far eastern Texas–Mexico border.
- The El Mayo/El Chapo cartel is a relatively new gang formed by the merger of two smaller drug-trafficking organizations—one run by Ismael "El Mayo" Zambada and the other by Joaquin "El Chapo" Guzmán. It operates along the Pacific Coast and along the Arizona–Mexico border. That organization is also well placed to fill the void created by the recent weakening of the Arellano Félix cartel (see below).

- The Valdez cartel is an organization of drug smugglers in Mexico's restive southern state of Chiapas. Although there is no hard evidence of collusion between the drug gang and leftist rebels in Chiapas, reports of such collusion continue to surface.

- The Arellano Félix (or Tijuana) cartel was run until early 2002 by brothers Benjamin and Ramon Arellano Félix and operated primarily in the state of Baja California, especially the Tijuana area. It was the most violent of the Mexican drug organizations. It recruited gang members from Tijuana and nearby San Diego.[19] With the death of Ramon (killed in a shootout with Mexican police forces in February 2002) and the capture of Benjamin in March 2002, the future of the Arellano Félix organization is uncertain. Already other drug traffickers, including Ismael Zambada, are vying to fill the void created by the brothers' removal.[20]

Most Mexican gangs concentrate on the distribution of drugs produced elsewhere (primarily in Colombia) rather than on domestic production—although that is beginning to change. Given their focus, those organizations are seen as important allies by the Colombian drug traffickers. Many times the Mexicans act as middlemen in the drug trade; in charge of ensuring that the product makes it to the United States. In November 2000 Mexico's attorney general mentioned the existence of an alliance, thought to account for more than 20 percent of the cocaine smuggled annually into the United States from Mexico, between the Colombian FARC and the Arellano Félix cartel. Mexican officials speculated that the FARC sent cocaine to Mexico in return for the cartel sending weapons south. According to some intelligence analysts, the unusually large volumes of cocaine (8 tons in March and 13 tons in May) confiscated by the U.S. Coast Guard in two major seizures suggest that the alliance between the FARC and the Arellano Félix cartel may have been "significantly larger and more complex than originally described by Mexican and U.S. officials."[21]

Recently the level of cooperation between Colombian and Mexican traffickers ratcheted a notch higher. In early April 2001 Colombian president Andrés Pastrana and Mexico's new president Vicente Fox met and signed bilateral accords to fight drug trafficking. The measures focused on increased intelligence sharing and heightened provisions for financial monitoring and controls to combat money laundering. But at the same time Pastrana and Fox were meeting, the leaders of all the Mexican drug organizations, except for the Arellano Félix gang, held a summit to coordinate and adjust their efforts. In other words, as the Mexican and Colombian governments were forming an enforcement cartel, the traffickers were forming an overall trafficking cartel. Even more alarming, a group of Colombians were reportedly in attendance at the traffickers' summit serving as "consultants" to the Mexicans.[22]

The formation of such an overarching cartel is reminiscent of how the major drug organizations in Colombia colluded to battle that government's antidrug measures in the 1980s and early 1990s. Then in Colombia, now in Mexico, the traffickers always seem to be one step ahead of the authorities in terms of organization.

THE ESCALATION OF CORRUPTION AND VIOLENCE

One of the most troubling similarities between Mexico in the early twenty-first century and Colombia a decade or so ago is the explosion of corruption. Admittedly, corruption is hardly new to Mexico. What is new is the scale of the corruption. Author Mike Gray notes, "In the old days, *mordida*—the bite—was accepted as an efficient lubricator, a means of getting things done while sharing the wealth in an otherwise unequal society. But with the arrival of the narco-billions everything shifted gears."[23] Drug-related corruption in Mexico began to explode.[24] Already in the mid-1980s

Mexico was becoming the major transshipment route for the Colombian drug cartels in response to a U.S.-orchestrated crackdown against the previous favorite routes—through the Bahamas and other islands in the Caribbean. Guillermo González Calderoni, former commander of the Mexican Federal Police, notes that "in 1984, we seized 300 kilos of cocaine, and that set a record in Mexico. Never before had such a large shipment been seized." González Calderoni also acknowledges the link between the growth of the drug trade and the growth of corruption in Mexico. "I discovered that the Colombian traffickers were using Mexican dealers—marijuana traffickers—to move cocaine. From that moment on, the power of corruption definitely increased."[25]

The Drug Enforcement Administration and other U.S. agencies has long been concerned about evidence of corruption in Mexico's law enforcement agencies, but one event served to reveal its magnitude. In February 1985 DEA agent Enrique Camarena was kidnapped off the streets of Guadalajara. Most troubling, he had been snatched by uniformed men. Jack Lawn, DEA administrator from 1985 to 1990, described the significance of that episode: "We determined that the individuals who took Camarena off the streets were law enforcement personnel. That was particularly galling to me and to law enforcement throughout the nation, because when the system becomes so corrupted that the law enforcement community in the host country upon which you depend are part of the problem, then nothing is safe."[26] Lawn added that the corruption was not confined to low-level police functionaries: "Governors, ministers, corruption in the office of the attorney general of Mexico—very, very high up."[27]

The nexus between corruption and the drug trade, though, is revealed most clearly in the role played by ordinary police personnel. González Calderoni ably describes the process:

> You have to do what everyone else does in order to survive, so it's a
> common practice for police commanders to utilize their position to

get money. But they don't take money only for themselves. Quite often they must pay their superiors to get appointed. They also pay to get a job in a certain geographic territory.

For a border region, people will pay a lot of money. The border is the funnel. Tons and tons of drugs will have to go through, and the traffickers will want to pay to make sure that they go through. So for a border appointment you get charged $1 million. And then you would have to pay $200,000 or $300,000 per month to your bosses in Mexico City in order to remain in that position.

So what did the police officer need to do in these border areas after he bought the position? He would definitely have to work in drug trafficking in order to make back the money he paid to get there and also to cover the monthly expenses.[28]

As bad as the corruption in Mexico was in the 1980s, the trend has clearly worsened in the past decade or so. Both major and relatively minor officials have been implicated in the drug trade. In August 2001 the former security chief from the northern city of Mexicali was arrested for allegedly providing protection to the Arellano Félix drug cartel.[29] It was neither an isolated nor a relatively new phenomenon. Twelve years earlier the National Police commander, Luis Esteban Villalón, was caught with $2.4 million in cash in the trunk of his car. Later he was convicted of giving more than $20 million to another government official to buy protection for one of Mexico's most notorious drug lords, Juan García Abrego.[30] General José de Jesús Gutiérrez Rebollo, once Mexico's counterpart to America's White House drug czar, was jailed in 1997 for accepting bribes from Amado Carrillo Fuentes, the late head of the Juárez drug cartel.[31]

The Gutiérrez Rebollo episode was especially disheartening to U.S. drug warriors. When newly elected president Ernesto Zedillo took office at the end of 1994, it was apparent that the Federal Judicial Police were riddled with corruption. Indeed, that institution was so compromised that most police personnel never even bothered to pick up their paychecks, since their salary was such a minor portion of their real income.[32] The new reform police chief did not last long. Before he could implement plans to clean house, he was poisoned in his sleep. Although he lived through the assault, the incident left him paralyzed from the neck down.

Zedillo, in desperation, turned to the military, appointing Gutiérrez Rebello as Mexico's drug czar. It was a dubious move from the outset, for there was ample evidence that the Mexican military was as involved as the federal and local police forces in the drug trade. The general, though, seemed to have excellent drug-fighting credentials, having personally led a much-publicized raid against the leader of the Sinaloa cartel. U.S. officials greeted the appointment enthusiastically. U.S. drug czar General Barry McCaffrey fairly gushed with praise: "He has a reputation for impeccable integrity. . . . He's a deadly serious guy."[33] McCaffrey predicted a new era in U.S.-Mexican cooperation to battle the scourge of illegal drugs.

Three months later the Zedillo government announced that its new drug czar was in a maximum-security prison, charged with taking bribes and protecting the nation's largest drug trafficker. The general had indeed been tough on drug trafficking—tough, that is, on cartels that competed with Carrillo Fuentes's organization. The news that Mexico's drug czar had been on the take hit Washington hard. The drug warriors were not discouraged for long, though; soon McCaffrey and President Clinton were praising the Mexican government's efforts to root out corruption.

Police and military leaders in Mexico are not the only ones to have been seduced by the corruption flowing from the drug trade. High-level elected officials and other well-connected politicians also have been implicated in drug-related scandals. In 1997 American intelligence sources concluded that two Mexican state governors, Manlio Fabio Beltrones Rivera and Jorge Carrillo Olea, along with Raúl Salinas de Gortari, brother of former president Carlos Salinas de Gortari, had collaborated with various drug kingpins.[34] Two years later the Mexican government issued a warrant for the arrest of Mario Villanueva, former governor of Quintana Roo state (which includes Cancún), on 28 drug charges.[35] In April 2001 the government arrested Brigadier General Ricardo Martínez Perea and two other high-ranking officers for allegedly collaborating with one of Mexico's leading drug cartels.[36] A month later authorities apprehended Villanueva. (He had disappeared just days before leaving office in 1999 as U.S and Mexican law enforcement agencies investigated his involvement in the drug trade.) Among other allegations, a U.S. indictment unsealed in May 2001 charged that he had accepted $500,000 in payoffs for each of several cocaine shipments that came through his state between 1994 and early 1999. In all, the indictment charged, he had conspired to bring 200 tons of cocaine across the U.S.–Mexico border.[37]

But it is not just the high-profile cases that illustrate how extensively drug-related corruption has penetrated Mexican society. The extent of the corruption became evident in 2001 when the new attorney general fired more than 1,400 of the country's 3,500 federal police officers for that offense and criminally prosecuted 357 of them.[38] Jorge Chabat, a drug policy expert at Mexico City's Center for Economic Development Research, stated bluntly, "You need a professional and honest police force. These are different things, and we have neither."[39] Alejandro González Alcocér, the governor of Baja California, reached a similar conclusion. "The drugs are coming in by land, sea and air," he stated in an interview. "The federal authorities have jurisdiction. But frankly we don't have much confidence in them. We worry that if we try to coordinate operations with them, our plans will be communicated to the traffickers."[40]

One knowledgeable Mexican source estimates that at least 20 percent of agents supposedly fighting the drug trade are actually on the payroll of the drug gangs. That is depressing enough, but one former gang member puts the figure at 80 percent for state and federal police officers.[41] Even if the lower figure is accurate, it suggests such a degree of penetration of law enforcement by drug-trafficking organizations as to render supposed antidrug efforts in Mexico farcical.

In addition to fostering corruption throughout the Mexican government, the illicit drug trade has been associated with a rising tide of violence—some of it almost routine, some of it quite horrific. The assassination of the commander of investigative police and an assistant in the northern border state of Tamaulipas was so ordinary that it scarcely merited comment in the news media.[42] Other incidents, though, were more remarkable.

American drug warriors have been shocked at the brazenness of both the corruption and the violence. One especially revealing incident took place in November 1991, when U.S. radar tracked a suspicious plane flying north out of Colombia and U.S. authorities alerted their Mexican counterparts as the plane approached Veracruz. Mexican Federal Police closed in on the plane as soon as it landed, but they quickly came under fire and most were killed. Retired DEA agent John Hensley noted the surprising element of that episode: "There were army vehicles in the perimeter area around where this attack took place. We found out later [that] army troops had been paid to protect that airstrip and that load coming into Mexico. Of all the shocks I've had in my career, that was probably the biggest, that an entire military unit would be involved in protecting drug lords, and to the point that they would actually attack and murder Mexican federal drug police."[43]

The level of drug corruption and its related violence has only grown with the passage of time. In August 1997 gunmen walked into a restaurant near the border in Juárez and fired more than 100 rounds at a group gathered around a single large table. The incident left six people dead and three others wounded. Investigators speculated that the bloody incident was part of a war for control of the Juárez drug cartel.[44] In May 2001 Jesús Carrola (who had served briefly as head of the Mexico City judicial police in 1997) and his two brothers were found executed gangland style. Carrola had had a checkered past. The main reason for his abrupt departure as head of the judicial police was a flurry of media reports linking him to the Tijuana cartel.[45]

Struggle over drug-trade turf also has produced an epidemic of violence in other Mexican cities. "In Tijuana, these kinds of killings have become so frequent that it's almost a normal occurrence," admitted Teodoro González Luna, the spokesman for the Baja California state government.[46] That state's attorney general estimated that drug-related violence accounted for 40 percent of the homicides.[47] Another Tijuana official also emphasized the link between the illicit drug trade and the growing level of violence: "There are well-known public officials who are assassinated for doing their jobs. Other men are killed because they want easy money and turn to drug trafficking. This is definitely on the rise in Tijuana."[48]

The level of violence in Tijuana had become so bad by the spring of 2000 that the U.S. Drug Enforcement Administration seriously considered pulling all of its agents out of the city. "Tijuana's drug-related killings appear to be escalating in the last year and a half and have reached into Mexican government circles," Florida International University professor William Walker stated. "In a way, U.S. agents are in over their heads. They don't know who among their contacts they can trust."[49]

As Walker's comments suggest, in many cases the problems of corruption and violence appear to overlap. On February 27, 2000, Alfredo de la Torre Márquez became the second Tijuana police chief assassinated in less than six years. A week later seven men were arrested for his murder and confessed to working for Sinaloa-based drug kingpin Ismael "Mayo" Zambada. Two of the men were former members of de la Torres Márquez's own police force.[50] Those members of police forces who choose to get involved in the drug trade have highly marketable skills, including inside knowledge of police methods and crime-scene investigation techniques, weapons training, and insider connections to insulate themselves (and their kingpin employers) from prosecution.

One of the worst incidents of violence that implicated government agencies occurred in September 1998. A 38-year-old rancher, apparently the target of a drug-related killing, was tortured in his own living room before gunmen put him against a wall and shot him along with 18 relatives and neighbors. Investigators stated that men carrying assault rifles and dressed in the color of Federal Police uniforms carried out the shootings.[51]

Two years earlier the grotesquely tortured body of Rafael López Cruz was found dumped along the side of a road outside Tijuana. He had been killed by individuals who had first meticulously broken nearly every bone in his body. The episode might have been dismissed as just another drug-gang killing had López Cruz not been a state judicial police agent who had previously complained about narcotics-related corruption in the ranks of his agency.[52]

The Márquez assassination and the Cruz murder were not isolated incidents. In another episode, a bloody gun battle ensued when Mexican Federal Police tried to stop the Arellanos' armed motorcade in downtown Tijuana. The commander of the police unit and three other officers were killed by the Arellanos' bodyguards. Those bodyguards, it turned out, were local police officers.[53]

The drug-related violence in Tijuana has long intimidated the national government. After several special federal prosecutors sent to Tijuana from Mexico City were murdered, the attorney general said that he could not find anyone else willing to take the post.[54] Mexican leaders are not the only ones intimidated by the drug lords. Stan Pimental, an FBI agent stationed in Mexico during the early and mid-1990s, expressed sympathy for the plight of the special prosecutors: "I wouldn't go to Tijuana unless I had a battalion-size force that I knew were loyal to me to go after somebody like the Arellanos."[55]

Attempts at reforming corrupt police forces have fizzled. In Juárez, for example, the one-time mayor, Gustavo Elizondo, fired more than 300 corrupt policemen and substantially raised the salaries of the remaining officers in the hope of counterbalancing the financial inducements offered by the drug lords. Elizondo's plan was well motivated, but it failed to address another important reason why police personnel were willing to cooperate with drug-trafficking organizations: self-preservation. In a city such as Juárez, where the drug-trafficking organizations are clearly more powerful than the authorities, choosing to side with the rather hapless government poses a bigger threat to the safety of oneself and one's family.

Thus, the police in the city remain corrupt. As noted by Ignacio Alvarado, a journalist based in the city for many years, during the entire decade of the 1980s, the police "made only one seizure [of cocaine routed through the city], and that was by mistake." He adds: "The police are completely corrupted. They never investigate any murder by narco-traffickers. They only talk to the family of the victims, and they do that only so they can say that they did it. The police know exactly who the traffickers are, but they're either bought or threatened, so nothing happens."[56]

U.S. support for reform of Mexico's police forces has not changed the equation. In 1998 polygraph evidence indicated that most top investigators of an elite U.S.-trained police unit had ties to drug traffickers. Many of those investigators had been chosen for their posts after rigorous screening methods set up by American operatives. A high-level U.S. law enforcement official stated bluntly: "It's a disaster."[57] But it was a disaster that has become the norm in Mexico.

Washington has found that it cannot even be certain of Mexican officials who seem to be blowing the whistle on corrupt colleagues. In July 1996 Ricardo Cordero Ontiveros, who had resigned his post in the attorney general's office the previous November, charged at a news conference that Mexico's antidrug effort was "a joke." Brandishing official memos and tape recordings to prove his allegations, Cordero alleged that the attorney general had angrily cut him off when he tried to present evidence of official wrongdoing.[58] Ten days later Cordero himself was arrested on charges of bribery and narcotics trafficking.[59] Was the arrest merely retaliation for his public revelations of corruption in the attorney general's office? Or was Cordero as corrupt as many others in Mexico's law enforcement agencies? American officials have no way of knowing.

Even the most prominent Mexicans are not immune from the violence spawned by the drug-trafficking organizations. The assassinations of José Francisco Ruiz Massieu, head of the long-dominant Institutional Revolutionary Party (PRI), Luis Donaldo Colosio, the PRI's presidential candidate in the 1994 election, and Cardinal Juan Jesús Posadas Ocampo, are all widely believed to have been drug related.[60] Colosio's assassination was eerily reminiscent of the earlier assassination of presidential candidate Luis Carlos Galán in Colombia. Mike Gray expresses a cynical but perhaps appropriate conclusion: "If there was any doubt that Mexico was swirling down the same drainpipe as Colombia, the killing of Colosio—a reformer in the mold of Carlos Galan—should have put it to rest."[61] Associated Press correspondent Mark Stevenson reaches an equally pessimistic conclusion: "The violence of Mexico's drug trade is beginning to seep into all levels of society. No longer confined to high-rolling drug lords in rough border towns and addicts on the streets, it is striking at lawyers, judges, police, soldiers and even doctors."[62]

A prominent Mexico City newspaper editor, speaking off the record, claimed that the killing of Ruiz Massieu, who was a close friend of former president Carlos Salinas de Gortari and former agricultural minister Carlos Hank González , was part of a continuing feud between Mexico's largest drug cartels and their associates in the Salinas government. The editor charged further that "Carlos Hank is the biggest money launderer in Mexico. . . . This killing was a reprisal for the murder of Colosio, a tragic event that many people believe was engineered by Hank and other officials around

Salinas."[63] Whatever the truth of such allegations, the murky circumstances surrounding the assassinations of Colosio and Ruiz Massieu (as well as the murders of other prominent Mexicans) raise serious questions about the extent of high-level Mexican officials' involvement in the drug trade. It also raises questions about the extent to which a succession of Mexican governments have waged the war on drugs as opposed to merely maintaining the appearance of waging that battle in order to appease Washington.

The root problem in Mexico, as in Colombia and other drug-producing or drug-transshipment states, is that the narcotics trade has become an important part of the economy, and powerful constituencies have grown up around that trade. Shortly before he became foreign minister in the government of Vicente Fox, Jorge Castañeda bluntly admitted that reality: "It's a business. It has to be seen as a business. And there are regions of the country where the drug economy really is central to the local economy."[64] Former FBI agent Stan Pimental describes the pervasive economic role played by the drug-trafficking organizations: "Cartel leaders have built roads. They've built houses. They've built hospitals. They've built clinics, chapels, you name it, supporting teachers for the families that work for them. So it's a lot of money being expended by these cartels there. And if we, the U.S. government, could stop that, or the Mexican government could stop that, it would put a big crimp for a number of years in the economy of Mexico."[65] That is precisely why the prohibitionist strategy is an exercise in futility, not just in Mexico but in any country where the drug trade plays a significant economic role.

WILL VICENTE FOX'S ADMINISTRATION BE DIFFERENT?

U.S. officials remain optimistic that the administration of President Vicente Fox will be much more dedicated and effective than preceding governments in waging the war on drugs. Joe Keefe, special operations chief of the DEA, pronounced himself "cautiously optimistic." The new government, he said, was "showing us things early on. . . . I really think, honestly, that the Fox administration is dealing with the corruption that has been endemic for many moons."[66] Edward Jurith, acting director of the White House Office of National Drug Control Policy, seemed even more optimistic in November 2001, stating "President Fox has made a real commitment that I think is different from the past. Granted, there are some rough challenges ahead, corruption obviously, and the resistance of many Mexican institutions to move forward. But I think with leadership from the top and reform of the Mexican political system there's hope that I've not seen in years past."[67]

Washington has acted on its optimism about Fox's leadership in the Mexican component of the war on drugs by tripling the funding of force law enforcement assistance to the Mexican police.[68] For the first time in years, U.S. authorities seem willing to share intelligence on drug traffickers with their Mexican federal counterparts, especially the newly formed Federal Agency of Investigation, patterned after America's own FBI. (The greater U.S. confidence about sharing information has not yet made it down to the state and local levels of Mexican law enforcement.)

Thus far, the Fox administration does seem to be making a more serious effort than its predecessors to go after major drug traffickers. The most notable success to date was the dramatic weakening of the Arellano Félix organization. The death of Ramon Arellano Félix (the cartel's especially brutal enforcer) and the subsequent capture of his brother Benjamin (the head of the organization) astonished Mexicans and Americans alike. Previously, the Arellano Félix gang seemed invincible. (Even that achievement may be tainted, however. Evidence has emerged that the police who shot Ramon may have been working for a rival trafficker.)[69]

Besides striking a blow against Mexico's most violent drug-trafficking cartel, the Fox administration has made the extradition of accused drug traffickers a cornerstone of its new crime-fighting effort with the United States, and there were a number of high-profile extraditions during Fox's first year in office. That trend experienced a setback in October 2001, however, when the Mexican supreme court ruled that the government cannot extradite to the United States any suspect who might receive a sentence that exceeds Mexico's maximum punishment of 60 years in prison. U.S. officials expressed disappointment with the ruling, since the maximum penalty for convicted drug kingpins in the United States often exceeds 60 years. It remains to be seen whether the court's decision creates the conditions for a nasty fight on the extradition issue similar to those that have flared periodically between the United States and Colombia over the past three decades.

The upsurge in extraditions under the Fox administration also creates concerns about a potential increase in the level of violence. Some Mexicans worry that the policy could incite the wrath of the drug cartels. They point explicitly to Colombia, where the extradition of drug lords to the United States became a major factor triggering an epidemic of murders and terrorist bombings in the late 1980s. "We are about to enter into a serious crisis like Colombia if the government insists with [sic] this," warned a lawyer representing several cartel members. "The traffickers could create serious problems for the government. It will be like a bomb that explodes when you least expect it."[70]

Moreover, even if the campaign against the drug traffickers persists and other major cartels are weakened as the Arellano Félix organization has been, it may simply lead to a decentralization of the drug trade—much as the Colombian government's war against the Medellín and Cali cartels in the 1990s led to such decentralization. Adolfo Aguilar Zínser, Mexico's national security adviser, contends that the increasing government pressure has forced the cartels to split up different parts of their business. He also admits, though, that this fragmentation has led to the emergence of smaller drug gangs and independent operators. Moreover, he fears that there could be an increase in turf battles as a larger number of competitors battle over market share.[71] Indeed, that appears to have been a major initial effect of the weakening of the Arellano Félix cartel. Less than two weeks after authorities captured Benjamin Arellano Félix, three people were killed and two others wounded in what observers speculated was the opening round of a struggle for control of the Tijuana drug trade.[72] As those who have witnessed such turf battles in American cities can testify, a great many innocent victims can get caught in the crossfire.

Beyond those concerns, it is still not clear whether the Fox administration will stay the course in supporting Washington's war on drugs, especially if the adverse domestic consequences begin to mount. At the November 2001 Binational Conference on Reducing Drug Demand, Mexico's interior minister, Santiago Creel Miranda, conceded that, while the 2002 budget would emphasize public security and the war on drugs, the extent of his government's commitment would be constrained by "the limited resources we have," including an expected decline in tax revenues.[73] Creel Miranda also pointed to the assassination of two federal judges in Mazatlán during the week before the conference as another example of the difficulties his government faced.

Of greater concern to some U.S. policymakers are the views of President Fox and his foreign minister, Jorge Castañeda. On several occasions Fox has flirted rhetorically with the option of drug legalization. In one interview he indicated agreement with a police officer who had suggested that the only way to win the war on drugs, thus eliminating the profits and violence caused by drug trafficking, was legalization. Perhaps cognizant of the fate that befell Colombian president Ernesto Samper for similar rhetorical infractions, Fox quickly amended that statement to emphasize that he did not expect such a step to be taken anytime soon.[74] Castañeda has been even more negative toward the drug war. On one occasion he stated bluntly that the time had come for rethinking "this absurd war no one really wants to wage."[75]

A veteran observer of the Mexican drug scene, *Washington Times* correspondent Johanna Tuckman takes a more skeptical view than do U.S. officials of the Fox administration's commitment to the war on drugs. "After nearly six months in office, the Fox administration can boast of several high-profile arrests and a steady string of sizable drug seizures, but nothing spectacularly different from previous occasions when new Mexican governments sought to put their drug-fighting credentials on display."[76]

The historical record supports that skepticism. Even President Carlos Salinas de Gortari, whose brother was later implicated in the drug trade, took vigorous (and highly visible) actions during his initial year in office. Among other things, he stepped up crop eradication efforts, created a new post in the attorney general's office to coordinate antidrug activities, and pushed to amend the criminal legal code to increase the penalties for crimes linked to drug trafficking, especially actions involving public officials.[77] The campaign against drugs came to involve one-third of the nation's defense budget and 60 percent of the attorney general's budget.[78] None of those flamboyant gestures amounted to anything in the long run. Salinas's successor, Ernesto Zedillo, also charged that the drug trade posed a mortal threat to Mexico and pledged a vigorous campaign to eliminate that scourge.[79] But the trade, and the accompanying corruption, grew steadily worse during his presidency.

Given the ambivalence that both Fox and Castañeda have expressed about the prohibitionist strategy, there is legitimate reason to wonder whether the new government is not simply going through the motions to placate the United States. That would not be surprising. After all, previous Mexican governments experienced the consequences of seeming to be insufficiently cooperative in waging Washington's war on drugs. The Fox administration certainly has no desire to repeat their experience.

A few months before he became foreign minister, Castañeda himself related how the game is played. "It is said that each administration in Mexico . . . will pick and choose which cartel to go after, to sort of offer them up as a sacrificial lamb to the Americans and, in a way, at least tolerate the other cartels that they don't go after."[80]

WILL MEXICO GO THE WAY OF COLOMBIA?

In some ways Mexico has the potential to become even more corrupt than Colombia. Money laundering is an important part of the drug-trafficking network. In fact, then-secretary of the treasury Robert Rubin called it "the life-blood of organized crime" after the completion of Operation Casablanca in 1998. [81] That sting operation, which led to the arrest of 16 members of the Cali and Juárez drug cartels, also alleged that 12 of Mexico's 19 largest banks were involved in laundering activities.[82]

It appears that money laundering is quite lucrative in Mexico. For one thing, the impediments to money laundering are far less in Mexico than they are in Colombia and many other countries. Because U.S. dollars are not a negotiable currency in Colombia, drug traffickers must go through at times complex money laundering maneuvers to repatriate their profits. Mexican drug traffickers have no such problems. As one U.S. official put it, "[T]hey don't have to launder per se. To a Mexican, to launder means to put a million bucks in the trunk and drive across the border to Tijuana."[83] Of course, Mexican traffickers typically use more sophisticated techniques, but the underlying point remains valid: Money laundering in Mexico is tantalizingly easy.[84]

Those who would argue that there is almost no chance that Mexico will replicate Colombia's slide into chaos point to some crucial differences between the two societies. Mexico, they argue, has had an ultra-stable political system. That has been true historically—at least since the early years of the twentieth century. But that difference may be less dramatic than it might appear. Not long ago Colombia was widely hailed as the model of a stable democracy in Latin America, in marked contrast to many other hemispheric nations that seemed to oscillate between periods of civilian rule and authoritarian (usually military) regimes. Moreover, Mexico's political stability may no longer be quite the same as it was during the decades of one-party domination by the PRI. Competing political forces have emerged, and while thus far most of the competition has been expressed peacefully through other political parties, that may not always remain the case. The potential at least for greater political instability now exists.

The most obvious and significant difference between Colombia and Mexico is that Mexico does not face an armed insurgency remotely comparable to that afflicting Colombia. (Nor does the Mexican government face the challenge to its authority posed by armed, right-wing paramilitary organizations the way the Colombian government does.) True, Mexican officials have identified some 14 rebel groups operating in the country, but virtually all of them are small, prone to factionalism, and capable of only pinprick attacks.[85] One such attack occurred in early August 2001 when the small but noisy People's Armed Revolutionary Front (FARP) detonated bombs outside Mexico City branches of a leading Mexican bank. The bombs were crude and did little damage, but the incidents shook an already jittery public alarmed by the growing violence related to the drug trade.[86]

One rebel faction that does have significant capabilities is the Zapatista rebels in the southern province of Chiapas. A serious rebellion flared there in the 1990s, and despite talk of peace, reconciliation, and reform, there is little indication that the insurgents are about to disband. If that rebellion should reignite into full-scale warfare—much less if it should spread to other regions of Mexico with large indigenous Indian populations—Mexico could begin to face a threat comparable to that confronted by the Colombian government. For the moment, though, the government in Mexico City exercises a degree of territorial control that the Bogotá authorities can only dream about.

Another crucial difference is that there does not yet appear to be any significant linkage between insurgent groups and the drug-trafficking organizations. Nevertheless, the Fox government is sufficiently concerned about the upsurge of the drug trade in Chiapas and other portions of the southern border that it has ordered a reinforcement of both police and military units in the region.[87] That action suggests at least some concern on the part of Mexican authorities that the insurgents and the drug traffickers might eventually link up.

A less remarked on but significant potential for networks of organized violence and corruption exists with the *caciques*, or local political bosses. During the era of PRI political dominance, they acted as links between the party and their own private clientele, who wanted political favors. The *caciques* brought in votes for PRI candidates in exchange for those favors. The PRI has been badly weakened in recent elections—particularly with the victory of Fox, the candidate of the National Action Party. But the *caciques* remain, and with their sources of funding now greatly reduced, it would not be unthinkable for them to put their connections at the disposal of the drug cartels. Indeed, there was some evidence that this was already occurring during the administration of President Zedillo, Fox's predecessor.

U.S. policy seems to assume that if Mexico can capture the top drug lords, their organizations will fall apart, thereby greatly reducing the flow of illegal drugs to the United States. That is the same assumption that U.S. officials used with respect to the crackdown on the Medellín and Cali cartels in Colombia during the 1990s. But there is little evidence to support such an assumption. The arrests and killings of numerous top drug lords in both countries have yet to have a meaningful impact in terms of decreasing the quantity of drugs entering the United States. For example, the most wanted Mexican drug trafficker in the 1980s was Rafael Caro Quintero, who led a drug-smuggling organization based in Guadalajara. After Quintero's gang murdered a DEA agent, the DEA tracked him down in Costa Rica and arrested him. He eventually received a life sentence in a U.S. federal prison. But his drug organization did not die; rather, it was taken over by his brother, Miguel. Today the DEA still considers it to be one of Mexico's leading drug organizations.[88] As was the case in Colombia, cutting off one head of the drug-smuggling hydra merely results in more heads taking its place. U.S. drug policy in Mexico may simply serve to increase the number of drug-trafficking groups. It is likely to decentralize the problem, not solve it.

Of all the similarities between Colombia and Mexico, the most troubling may be the increasingly pervasive violence in the latter. No longer is just the cocaine and heroin trade characterized by violence. Today even the marijuana trade, which traditionally had generated little violence, is now accompanied by gruesome killings. Indeed, the biggest and bloodiest massacres over the past three years have involved marijuana trafficking.[89]

There is still time for Mexico to avoid going down the same tragic path as Colombia, but time is growing short. If Washington continues to pursue a prohibitionist strategy, the warfare that has convulsed Colombia will increasingly become a feature of Mexico's life as well. The illicit drug trade already has penetrated the country's economy and society to an unhealthy degree. U.S. officials need to ask whether they want to risk "another Colombia"—this time directly on America's southern border. If they do not want to deal with the turmoil such a development would create, the United States needs to change its policy on the drug issue and do so quickly.

Chapter Eight

Polluting the Republic:
The Drug War at Home

President Richard M. Nixon proclaimed a "war" on illegal drugs three decades ago. In 1986 President Ronald Reagan gave substance to that metaphor by issuing a presidential directive that drug trafficking constituted a national security threat. Reagan's directive thereby authorized the U.S. military and U.S. intelligence agencies to become involved in the effort to prevent drugs from entering the country. Advocates of the prohibitionist strategy now routinely refer to drug use, no matter how casual, mild, or infrequent, as a threat to national safety and well-being, akin to an armed menace posed by enemy states or terrorist movements. Given that mindset, it is perhaps appropriate symbolism that in the mid- and late 1990s the White House Office of National Drug Control Policy was directed by a general (albeit a retired one)—Barry McCaffrey.

The drive to make the notion of a drug "war" something more than a metaphor has been building for some time. Spurning suggestions for legalization, supporters of the war on drugs opt for stronger demand-reduction strategies, although they disagree about the relative emphasis that should be placed on the various components. Some stress educational programs that highlight the dangers of drug addiction and the other undesirable consequences of drug use. There is some evidence that such efforts are in fact producing a modest decline in drug use, especially among the young, just as similar efforts over the past three decades have helped reduce the percentage of the population that smokes cigarettes. But the effects of educational programs are notoriously slow, and such programs do not even promise to attain the chimera of the drug-free society sought by zealots. Impatience with the limited and gradual benefits of drug education has led many drug warriors to advocate ever-stronger steps to achieve demand reduction through force, along with tougher measures to interdict the supply.

Some of the strategies suggested in the 1980s and 1990s fell into one of two categories—the bizarre or the draconian. The former category included a $2.9 million federal grant to the Texas National Guard to have guard members disguise themselves as cactus plants to gather intelligence on drug-trafficking routes across the Rio Grande border.[1] Despite the egregious waste of taxpayers' money, such initiatives were more amusing than threatening, but the same could not be said of many other schemes.

Mandatory random drug-testing programs have become pervasive in the United States over the past decade and a half. Yet such measures—even though they wreak havoc on the constitutional right to privacy—actually are temperate in comparison with some ideas that have been advanced. Former New York mayor Ed Koch suggested establishing massive detention centers in the rural areas of western states so that authorities would have someplace to send large numbers of drug offenders. Several states experimented with military-style "boot camps" to re-educate young drug law violators, and former federal drug czar William Bennett (among others) suggested that the federal government consider establishing similar facilities.[2]

William von Raab, customs commissioner under the Reagan administration, became a prolific source of proposals for escalating the war on drugs. For example, he ordered his agency to confiscate the passports of U.S. citizens accused of attempting to bring drugs into the country—a move that was countermanded by the State Department.[3] On another occasion he suggested giving authority to military and law enforcement agencies to shoot down aircraft suspected of carrying drugs. The Reagan Justice Department—not generally considered an ardent defender of civil liberties—considered that proposal an "absolutely crazy" idea.[4]

It was a measure of how fast the drug war hysteria grew that Senator Mitch McConnell (R-KY) introduced von Raab's "crazy" idea as an amendment to the FY 1990 military spending bill. Moreover, over the vehement objections of Senator Sam Nunn (D-GA) and most other members of the Armed Services Committee, the Senate actually passed the McConnell amendment. That action was taken despite a General Accounting Office (GAO) study that underscored the danger of victimizing innocent parties. The GAO study found that of the 337 suspected drug-smuggling planes that the Customs Service forced to land over the previous two years, only 134 had drugs on board.[5] (McConnell's scheme was never adopted in the United States but it was—with U.S. help—in Peru, where American Roni Bowers met her tragic end.)

Such erosions of constitutional liberties are a direct product of viewing the drug problem as a "war." The extent of that hysteria at one point could be gauged by the results of a *Washington Post*/ABC News poll taken immediately after President Bush's address to the nation in early September 1989. The survey discovered that

- 62 percent of respondents were willing to give up "a few" freedoms in order to curb drug use
- 67 percent would allow police to stop cars at random to search for drugs
- 52 percent would allow the police to search without court order the homes of people suspected of selling drugs, even if some homes were searched by mistake
- 71 percent would make it against the law to show the use of illegal drugs in the movies.[6]

As the *Post* survey indicated, even the First Amendment's guarantees of freedom of expression were coming under siege. Lack of enthusiasm for the antidrug crusade, much less suggestions that the war is unwinnable or that the "drug problem" is largely the product of unrealistic drug laws that have created a flourishing black market, was denounced as "defeatism" or even "treason." That intolerance of dissent extended across the political spectrum. For example, Jesse Jackson charged that "treason abounds" in the war on drugs. "Drug pushers are terrorists, and those who consume drugs are engaged in treason," Jackson fumed.[7] Similar in tone was William Bennett's reaction to an article by Jefferson Morley in the *New Republic* that accused the government of overstating both the addictive properties and the unpleasant consequences of crack cocaine. Bennett's shrill attack on Morley impelled *New Republic* editor Michael Kinsley to observe that the drug czar's attitude was distressingly similar to the intolerance that had silenced critics of previous wars.[8]

Bennett and Jackson were hardly the only prominent figures to suggest that First Amendment freedoms should be curtailed in the name of war on drugs. Conservative activist Reed Irvine charged that drug war critics in the media were "a serious obstacle" to the adoption of the "harsh measures" needed to win that struggle.[9] Ronald Reagan once condemned the favorable portrayal of drugs in films and music and concluded with the ominous comment that no one "has a constitutional right to sell pro-drug propaganda to minors."[10] This statement was consistent with proposals that have surfaced periodically that would require movies portraying drug use as anything other than a menace to have an "adults-only" rating—something that would be a financial disaster for most mainstream films.

Such dangerously authoritarian schemes set the stage for the kinds of policies and court decisions that have become all to prevalent over the past decade. During the early stages of that trend *New York Times* columnist Tom Wicker warned prophetically:

"Like any other war, it's sure to produce a dangerous wartime mentality that 'anything' goes in pursuit of victory. . . . What will happen to public and Congressional attitudes if a supposed war—like the war in Vietnam—drags on endlessly with marginal achievements and no apparent hope of victory? Some will give up, no doubt; but many, perhaps more, will call for escalation, new weapons, more troops, tougher tactics—victory at any price."[11]

It might be tempting to sneer at the drug warriors' rhetorical overkill that drugs pose a threat to America's security and well-being comparable to that posed by a powerful armed adversary, but that reaction would be a serious mistake. The war mentality is not confined to the arenas of propaganda and personnel. Far more troubling is the mounting evidence about the way in which the prohibitionist strategy against drugs is being implemented. The tactics now in use suggest that the term "war" is no longer merely a metaphor.[12]

As in any war, there is an ever-growing roster of innocent victims: people who had the bad fortune to run afoul of warriors pursuing their objective with single-minded intensity, or who were simply in the wrong place at the wrong time. There are also the inevitable undesirable (albeit usually unintended) side effects. Periods of war are not known for fostering the health of civil liberties. The history of armed conflicts involving the United States demonstrates the truth of that observation. During the War Between the States, President Abraham Lincoln illegally suspended the writ of habeas corpus, and civilians were tried before military tribunals, among other abuses. America's entry into World War I impelled the administration of Woodrow Wilson to impose pervasive censorship, jail pacifists and other opponents of the war, and preside over a veritable reign of terror against German Americans. During World War II President Franklin Roosevelt ordered the detention of Japanese Americans in "relocation centers"—a euphemism for concentration camps. The Vietnam war saw the military, the CIA, and the FBI illegally conduct surveillance of antiwar groups—and attempt to discredit them through disinformation campaigns.[13] That historical record alone should give pause to those Americans who believe that it is proper for the U.S. government to wage a war against the decision of their fellow citizens to use certain mind-altering substances.

Only incurable optimists would argue that America's thirty-year war against drugs has been a success. Although the percentage of Americans using illegal drugs is down from the peak levels of the late 1970s and early 1980s, use is still widespread and, indeed, is significantly higher than it was when Nixon issued his declaration of war. Despite the expenditure of more than $300 billion by federal, state, and local governments over those three decades (the federal government alone proposed to spend $19 billion in FY 2001)[14] on efforts to stem the trade, drugs remain cheap and easily available throughout the United States. Prices of cocaine and other drugs have generally shown a downward trend—a reliable indicator of a plentiful supply.[15]

The original Thirty Years' War, which brought so much misery to the people of Central Europe, finally ended with the Treaty of Westphalia in 1648. Unfortunately, no comparable end to the current war is in sight. (Perhaps the drug warriors, with a nod to history, seek to replicate the Hundred-Years War between England and France.) As is so often the case with failing wars, fanatical proponents prefer escalation to surrender or even a compromise settlement. It is indicative of such a mentality that advocates of the drug war seek additional increases in an already bloated budget and wage campaigns of vilification against such modest proposals as legalizing the limited medical use of marijuana. Financier George Soros, one of the chief financial backers of various state medical marijuana initiatives, decried the vitriolic and personal nature of the attacks: "Our drug warriors have responded by pushing the panic button. Joseph Califano described me in the [Washington] Post as the 'Daddy Warbucks of drug legalization' and accused me of 'bamboozling' the voters with misleading advertisements. I was denigrated in congressional hearings chaired by Sen. Orrin Hatch (R-Utah), and in the *New York Times*, A. M. Rosenthal went so far as to imply that I represent a new kind of 'drug money.'"[16]

Calls to escalate the war on drugs must be firmly rebuffed. The current drug war has already caused major social disruptions and badly eroded important liberties guaranteed by the U.S. Constitution.[17] An escalation could pose a mortal threat to the remaining civil liberties of Americans—even in cases far removed from the drug issue.

SOME PROMINENT EXAMPLES OF COLLATERAL DAMAGE

Critics of the war on drugs have documented a variety of disastrous side effects of the prohibitionist strategy.[18] They have pointed out that more than 60 percent of the inmates in federal prisons and 25 percent of the inmates in state prisons are incarcerated for drug offenses. The trend is also getting worse; the total number of people in federal prison on drug charges in 2000 was 62 percent greater than in 1990.[19] Moreover, the explosion in the overall size of prison populations (increases of 160 percent at the federal level and 126 percent at the state level between the mid-1980s and mid-1990s alone)[20] has not only caused overcrowding but has led to the early release of prisoners—including some individuals convicted of violent crimes—to make cells available for drug offenders.

Books and studies by antiprohibitionists also have shown how the drug war has led to violent struggles between rival gangs over control of the black market in American cities, spawning a spiraling crime rate during the 1980s and early 1990s until most of the turf battles were sorted out.[21] Those conflicts not only destabilized entire neighborhoods but produced a tragically long list of unlucky victims caught in the crossfire. Other studies have noted that, given the economics of prohibition, such a result was inevitable—as should have been learned from the similar upsurge of violence in the 1920s, when the United States government attempted to outlaw the sale of alcoholic beverages.[22]

Still other analyses have provided compelling evidence that the war on drugs has led to the inexorable erosion of the protections against unreasonable searches and seizures provided by the Fourth Amendment.[23] Police have far greater latitude than they did a few decades ago to search automobiles (and sometimes the occupants) following routine traffic stops. Motorists who fit the "profile" of probable drug couriers developed by law enforcement bureaucracies are especially at risk for such stops and the subsequent searches.[24]

The situation is not yet as bad with regard to the searches of homes and businesses, but there are enough ominous trends. Search warrants often are issued on information provided by an informant that law enforcement authorities believe to be credible. In a distressing number of instances, that assumption of reliability proves to be unfounded—sometimes with tragic consequences. The preferred method of conducting raids in suspected narcotics violation cases: "no-knock" break-in-the-door searches of homes—often in the middle of the night—have compounded the danger. In August 1999 such a raid resulted in the death of a 64-year-old grandfather. He and his family were asleep in their beds when police searching for illegal drugs broke down the front door. The victim was shot in the back as he, apparently believing that a break-in by criminals was under way and his family was in danger, reached into a nightstand drawer for a gun. No drugs were found anywhere on the premises.[25] Typically, the drug warriors and their defenders dismissed this episode as a tragic accident. Unfortunately, such "accidents" are becoming all too common.[26]

The war on drugs has undermined the Fourth Amendment's protection against unreasonable seizures at least as badly as it has the protection against unreasonable searches. Representative Henry Hyde (R-IL) and others have documented how all levels of government have increasingly exploited the power to seize and keep property allegedly involved in the commission of a crime.[27] The abuses are legendary. Authorities have sought to have property worth tens of thousands of dollars forfeited even for minor drug offenses. They have seized valuable property on little more than their personal suspicion that an individual is involved in drug trafficking. Law enforcement agencies have refused to relinquish the confiscated items even when an accused party is not formally indicted for a crime and in some instances when a defendant has been acquitted of the alleged crime. Because such forfeiture proceedings can be considered civil rather than criminal trials, the burden of proof for the government is far lower than the requirement of "beyond a reasonable doubt" in criminal cases. Apparently reflecting the attitude that all is fair in war, prosecutors do not seem to mind that they are getting a second shot at an accused based on the absurd fiction that depriving someone of valuable property is not, in a strictly legal sense, "punishment" and, therefore, does not require conviction of a criminal offense. Passage of the Forfeiture Reform Act by Congress in early 2000 should help end the worst abuses by federal agencies, but it still gives them far too much latitude.[28] Moreover, the legislation will not curb the abuses perpetrated by state and local law enforcement agencies.

Even as Congress partially curtailed one repulsive practice in the arena of search and seizure, it sought to create a new one. A group of mainly conservative Republicans lawmakers introduced a proposed "Methamphetamine Anti-Proliferation Act" in early 2000. Under existing law, owners must be notified immediately if law enforcement personnel seize any portion of their property. The new legislation sought to rescind that requirement. Critics pointed out that such a change would have an especially insidious effect on the new information technology. The police could download computer files containing private records, correspondence, and the like without the target of the investigation even being aware of the seizure.

Such a mauling of Fourth Amendment protections was too much even for the staunchly conservative and pro-law enforcement Free Congress Foundation. Lisa Dean, the organization's vice president for technology policy, ripped the proposed act, saying "While the bill is designed to better equip law enforcement to stop drug trafficking and shut down methamphetamine labs, it does more. It shuts down the Fourth Amendment."[29]

As will be discussed, abuses of the government's seizure and forfeiture powers have moved far beyond the arena of drug cases. Nevertheless, the drug war has been the principal factor in the malignant expansion of that authority, just as it has been for the lowering of the barriers against arbitrary searches. One cannot look at the damage that has been done to the Fourth Amendment without recognizing that it has been a casualty of the war on drugs.

An especially worrisome trend, but an inevitable one, is the growing militarization of the drug war. Amendments passed in 1981 weakened the provisions of the Posse Comitatus Act that barred the military from involvement in domestic law enforcement. It was no coincidence that the amendments were approved specifically to enable the military to assist law enforcement agencies in the enforcement of the drug laws. In the intervening years, the definition of "assist" has grown ever more expansive and flexible.[30]

Proponents of the drug war have tried to draw the military into the struggle throughout the 1980s and 1990s. In 1988 Congress explicitly directed the National Guard to assist various law enforcement agencies in counternarcotics operations. The following year President George Bush created six regional joint task forces (JTFs) in the Department of Defense to coordinate the activities of the Pentagon and domestic police agencies in antidrug activities. Most ominously, the JTFs were authorized to respond to requests from law enforcement agencies for military reinforcement in drug cases.

To its credit, the military hierarchy generally has tried to resist the pressure for deeper involvement, even though in the immediate post–Cold War period it seemed that the drug war was one of the few missions that might prevent the downsizing of the Pentagon's budget and force structure.[31] Leaders of the uniformed services quite correctly fear that such quasi-police functions are a dangerous diversion from the military's primary role: protecting the American people from foreign military threats. Resistance to calls by the White House for a more extensive role in the fight against drugs led to a surprisingly public tiff between Barry McCaffrey and Secretary of Defense William Cohen in 1997.[32]

Nevertheless, the military has been drawn, however reluctantly, into the domestic as well as the international phase of the drug war. Units of the U.S. Marine Corps began patrolling the border with Mexico in a vain attempt to stem the flood of illegal drugs coming into the United States. The military's comparative advantage—described by one cynic as an unparalleled ability to smash things and kill people—was not well suited for such a delicate mission. The result was the death of 18-year-old goat herder Esequiel Hernández (described in the introduction).

The Hernández tragedy has done little to dissuade drug war advocates that the campaign against drugs should be conducted like a real war and that the military has a crucial role to play. Just weeks after the killing, the House of Representatives voted to station 10,000 troops along the Mexican border to combat drug trafficking.[33] Representative Charles Norwood (R-GA) remained equally militant a year later, stating "Put the 82nd Airborne on maneuvers down there [at the border] if you want to stop drugs."[34] In the years since the Hernández incident, National Guard units have been used to raze 42 alleged crack houses in Indiana and to drive drug dealers from open-air markets in Washington, D.C. As law enforcement analyst Diane Cecília Weber writes, National Guard units "in all 50 states fly across America's landscape in dark green helicopters, wearing camouflage uniforms and armed with machine guns, in search of marijuana fields."[35]

For a nation that once viewed even the concept of a standing army with suspicion, the spectacle of military forces—active duty or National Guard—having a significant domestic presence is more than a little unsettling. But the logic of waging a "war" against the production, sale, and use of certain substances inevitably led to an expanded role for the military in that struggle. Symptomatic of the danger inherent in viewing drug use as a national security threat was the comment by Attorney General Janet Reno on the occasion of a 1994 technology transfer agreement between the Pentagon and the Justice Department. Reno challenged the military to "turn your skills that served us so well in the Cold War to helping us with the war we're now fighting daily in the streets of our towns and cities across the Nation."[36] The point that apparently eluded Reno and others who advocate the militarization of the crusade against illegal drugs is that there is a vast difference between having the military confront enemy armed forces and using similar tactics against American civilians.

CALLS FOR YET MORE ESCALATION

As victory in the war against illegal drugs remains as elusive as ever, the level of frustration on the part of drug-war supporters has grown. That development, in turn, has led to accusations that the war has not been prosecuted with sufficient vigor and that an even more hard-line policy is needed. During the 1992 presidential campaign, Ross Perot contended that, if he were elected, the federal government would wage a "serious" war on drugs—implying that the ongoing campaign had been halfhearted and ineffectual.

Criticism of that sort burgeoned during the Clinton years. When the president initially sought to scale back the bloated personnel levels of the White House Office of National Drug Control Policy, congressional Republicans and other drug warriors reacted with howls of rage and vilification, accusing the president of pursuing a defeatist strategy. Even when Clinton reversed course and sought record funding levels for the federal government's portion of the drug war, the criticism did not abate. Indeed, it actually became more pervasive and vitriolic. In July 1999 GOP presidential candidate Steve Forbes excoriated Clinton: "In his first year, Bill Clinton reduced the staff at the Office of the 'Drug Czar' by 83%. He has never delivered an Oval Office address on the drug issue. He is now proposing to reduce prison sentences for possession of crack cocaine."[37] Three years earlier, during the 1996 presidential campaign, GOP nominee Bob Dole accused Clinton of having a "just say nothing" drug policy.[38]

Some critics blamed the Clinton administration for a modest rise in the percentage of American teens using drugs. Although the substantive features of any alternative strategy—other than a return to the fatuous just-say-no propaganda campaign championed by First Lady Nancy Reagan in the mid-1980s—remain vague, the critics' rhetoric implies even more dangers to the health of civil liberties in the United States. Bob Dole, for example, argued that U.S. leaders should "treat drugs for what they are, the moral equivalent of terrorism."[39] Equally troubling was then-Representative Bill McCollum's criticism of the Clinton administration's alleged unwillingness to wage "an all-out drug war."[40] If the annual expenditure of more than $20 billion for the federal government's antidrug campaign (plus billions of dollars at the state and local level), filling America's prisons with drug law offenders, and pressuring the governments of drug-producing countries to wage low-intensity conflicts against their own populations are not the characteristics of an "all-out" war, one shudders to contemplate what such hard-liners as Perot, Dole, and McCollum have in mind.

Unfortunately, we have glimpses of what they may be contemplating. Senator Orrin Hatch (R-UT) and other hard-liners have proposed inflicting capital punishment on drug traffickers—the same penalty imposed by such enlightened countries as Malaysia, Saudi Arabia, and China.[41] The opposition of uncompromising pro-drug-war forces to even the very modest legislation pushed by Henry Hyde to correct the worst perversions and abuses of the government's seizure and forfeiture powers is another example of their concept of a "real" war on drugs. For ardent supporters of the drug war, the injustice of innocent people being stripped of their property without conviction in a criminal trial is apparently an acceptable price to pay for the goal of victory.

But some drug warriors favor even more repressive measures. The most ominous proposal comes from the United Nations, where the 1997 report of the International Narcotics Control Board implicitly called on member states to criminalize opposition to the war on drugs. Citing the 1988 UN Convention Against Illicit Trafficking in Narcotic Drugs and Psychotropic Substances, the board asserted that all governments are obligated to enact laws that prohibit "inciting" or "inducing" people to use illegal drugs and to punish such violations as criminal offenses.[42] The report noted that "in some countries" criminalization of such incitement "may run counter to guarantees of freedom of expression" embodied in their constitutions. "It should, however, be the duty of States to find a practical way of conciliation between the contradictory exercise of rights. The freedom of expression cannot remain unrestricted when it conflicts with other values and rights. The Board notes that it has been possible in most countries to take measures against the . . . propagation of pornographic literature and material; it hopes that similar measures might be feasible with respect to the promotion of drug use."[43]

If such a vague and chilling restriction on freedom of expression were not odious enough, the board contends further that any portrayal that shows illicit drug use "in a favourable light" constitutes incitement and therefore should be banned as well.[44] Since the report also repeatedly denounces medical marijuana initiatives as well as decriminalization or legalization proposals, even the most sedate advocacy of changing prohibitionist drug laws might run afoul of the censorship regime being pushed by the United Nations.[45]

If enacted in the United States, such legislation would, of course, be a flagrant violation of the First Amendment. But it must be remembered that censorship measures—including the banning of opposition to administration policies—have on occasion been a feature of American life during wartime and have received the imprimatur of the courts. It is also not reassuring that the U.S. government has pledged to cooperate with the board's global antidrug efforts. Although the Clinton administration did not explicitly endorse the censorship recommendations, neither did it state explicitly that the United States rejected such proposals—even though it certainly could have added that caveat. Indeed, two years later, McCaffrey pledged "absolute cooperation" with the UN's drug control programs.[46]

Unfortunately, the UN bureaucracy is not the only source of intolerance regarding views critical of the war on drugs. Ardent drug warriors repeatedly have accused advocates of legalization as constituting a "fifth column" in the struggle against illicit substances and stated or implied that pro-legalization views are illegitimate. An article by Mary O'Grady, the Americas column editor at the *Wall Street Journal,* argued that "American cokeheads" were guilty of "underwriting" political turmoil and other societal misery in Colombia.[47] The White House Office of National Drug Control Policy (ONDCP) has updated that argument and linked the drug war to the war on terrorism. In a slick ad campaign launched during the 2002 Super Bowl, the ONDCP argues that anyone who purchases illegal drugs helps fund terrorist organizations around the world. Some of the accusations have difficulty passing the straight-face test. For example, two-time presidential candidate Steve Forbes and others have even argued that proponents of ballot initiatives legalizing the medical use of marijuana are serving the interests of the international drug cartels.[48] *New York Times* columnist A. M. Rosenthal likened the fortune of financier George Soros, one of the chief financial supporters of the medical marijuana initiatives, as similar to "the fortunes manipulated by drug criminals." He also accused Soros and his colleagues of "preaching the benefits of slavery."[49]

When a group of 500 luminaries from around the world—including Nobel Laureate Milton Friedman, former Secretary of State George Shultz, and former UN Secretary General Javier Perez de Cueller—signed a public letter arguing that the global war on drugs was causing more harm than good and urging that alternatives be considered, the editorial page of the *Wall Street Journal* impugned their motives: "It occurs to us to suggest that the future of the debate would profit if all of these people stated publicly whether they themselves use any of these drugs recreationally."[50]

Such tactics are clearly designed to silence opposition to the drug war and are unworthy of an honest debate on an important public policy issue. Ardent drug warriors occasionally have ventured beyond rhetorical vilification in an effort to silence their opponents . In the mid-1990s, Representative Gerald Solomon (R-NY) attempted to have the tax-exempt status of the Cato Institute revoked because the institute had the temerity to sponsor discussions of the legalization option. Unfortunately, such examples of intolerance are all too typical of a "wartime" mind-set in which opponents are seen not as people who hold a different point of view but as traitors to a noble cause.

Those who might be tempted to dismiss the dangers of efforts to gag proponents of drug legalization should be aware that government officials already have sought to implement censorship measures (albeit more limited ones than the comprehensive bans suggested by some drug warriors). For example, authorities in Maryland prosecuted an individual for publicly divulging the identity of two undercover narcotics officers. Attempting to prohibit such disclosures by charging the defendant with "obstructing and hindering a police officer," Maryland officials endeavored to give undercover narcotics officers the same protection that Congress afforded to CIA and other intelligence agents during the Cold War.[51]

Although the Maryland court of special appeals eventually overturned the conviction on the grounds that it violated the defendant's state and federal constitutional rights to freedom of speech, several aspects of the case remain troubling:

- The fact that Maryland authorities sought to impose such censorship in the first place is worrisome
- The defendant was convicted at the trial court level
- The Court of Appeals decision overturning the conviction was on a divided vote.

It is hardly reassuring that a minority of the justices were willing to allow such a violation of the First Amendment's guarantee of freedom of speech to pass constitutional muster.

The drug czar's office seems inclined to pursue a strategy that mixes censorship and propaganda. The latter component emerged with stunning clarity during the final year of the Clinton administration. Evidence came to light that the office reviewed the scripts of popular television programs to determine whether their anti-drug messages were strong enough to warrant giving the networks credit toward "public service" ads that stations are required to run to maintain their license to operate under the rules of the Federal Communications Commission. When the reports of script monitoring surfaced, the drug policy office initially denied doing anything improper; soon the office promised not to do it again.[52]

A few months later it became apparent that the drug czar and his subordinates had done more than dangle financial carrots to induce television networks to air programs with "drug-war-friendly scripts." They had offered similar rewards to at least a half dozen prominent magazines.[53] According to Daniel Forbes, a freelance writer who broke the story for online news magazine *Salon*, the six magazines were *U.S. News & World Report, Sporting News, Family Circle, Seventeen, Parade,* and *USA Today Weekend.*[54] That list represents a major portion of the mass-circulation magazines in the United States. The expanded revelation was troubling enough, but the Office of National Drug Control Policy's response was even worse. In a letter to the editor of *Salon,* assistant director for strategic planning Robert Housman demanded that the online magazine disclose Forbes's alleged bias against the drug war. It was clear, Housman asserted, "that Dan Forbes . . . is more than just a disinterested reporter in search of a story."[55] Housman's "evidence" was that Forbes had contributed articles to the Media Awareness Project's website, which frequently publishes pieces criticizing the war on drugs. The editor of *Salon* responded that the drug czar's office was "coming close to Nixonian behavior in trying to nail the messenger."[56]

Attempts to censor critics and propagandize the American public are not the only manifestations of a drive to escalate the war on drugs and use even more draconian measures than those pursued to this point. The drug czar's office came up with another odious initiative in 2000: Anyone making inquiries about the drug issue on several of the most prominent Internet search engines would encounter an ad banner from the Office of National Drug Control Policy. Clicking on that ad would send the user to an antidrug website, Freevibe.com, which was operated by the ONDCP. As that site was activated, a tracking "cookie" was then—unknown to user—inserted in the user's computer. The cookie could then secretly track the user's subsequent online activity—specifically, what other websites were visited.[57]

As with the script-monitoring scandal, the drug czar's staff professed innocent intent. The cookie was merely used to monitor how well the ONDCP's advertising campaign was going, a spokesman insisted. There was absolutely no goal of collecting personal information on visitors to the site; only aggregate data was collected. Civil libertarians were not entirely reassured, however, and some denounced the White House's "Big Brother" tactics. President Clinton responded to the crescendo of criticism by ordering the ONDCP to cease using the "web bug."[58] Once again the government's response to revelations of dubious conduct was to insist that it had done nothing wrong—and then promise never to do it again.

The whiff of police state tactics is not confined to the activities of the federal government. Local police officers and other members of outreach programs in the public schools now routinely suggest that students report illegal drug use—even by other family members—to their teachers or other authorities. Rarely do they bother to mention to impressionable youngsters that such revelations could subject parents, siblings, or other relatives to criminal prosecution and possible imprisonment.

Tragically, such incitements to snitch sometimes get the desired result. In September 1999 a 16-year-old Maryland girl turned in her parents to police for growing marijuana in their home. The police promptly arrested both parents and charged them with two felonies and two misdemeanors, and state child protective services officials stripped the couple of custody of their daughter.[59] Nor is this an isolated episode. The previous week an 11-year-old Jacksonville, Florida, boy saw his father and step-mother carted off to jail after he reported their indoor marijuana garden to authorities. Earlier in the year a 16-year-old boy, upset at his family's impending move from New York to Washington, tipped police off about the stash of marijuana in his parents' bedroom. Keith Stroup, executive director of the National Organization for the Reform of Marijuana Laws (NORML) states that his organization receives at least one call a month from an attorney or defendant whose child has turned in a parent for marijuana use or possession.[60] Since it is unlikely that NORML is informed of every incident—much less those instances in which a child snitches on a family member for using or possessing other drugs—the actual number of cases is undoubtedly larger.

Encouraging in any manner whatsoever children to turn in family members to the police for violating the drug laws has an ugly totalitarian aura. It is reminiscent of the similar campaigns in the name of ideological conformity in Nazi Germany, the Soviet Union, and Maoist China, which Americans once regarded as an odious practice unique to police states. That it occurs at all in the

United States is an alarming indicator of how the concept of a "war" on drugs is warping our society. It has no place in an America that values individual liberties—much less to the promotion of "family values."

THE EXPANDING SCOPE OF COLLATERAL DAMAGE

The corrosive consequences of the drug war are not confined to the crusade against narcotics. Perhaps the most insidious effect of the war on drugs is how it has conditioned the American people to think in prohibitionist terms generally. Francis X. Kinney, deputy director for strategy at the Office of National Drug Control Policy during the Clinton administration, stated simply, "Drugs are illegal because they are harmful."[61] But using that standard inevitably puts American policy on a very slippery slope. A good many things are—or at least may be—harmful to their users, including tobacco products, alcoholic beverages, and high-fat foods. If the government can ban certain drugs on that basis, what is the barrier to governmental action to criminalize those other products? The only barrier would seem to be strong political resistance. But depending on that for protection removes a whole range of behaviors from the arena of personal choice to the arena of political struggle in which the outcome is anything but certain. The rights that Americans enjoy today about what substances they put into their bodies could be far more limited in the future.

That is not an excessively alarmist conclusion. After all, most currently illegal drugs were legal earlier in the twentieth century. Conversely, America has already had one fling with an attempt by Congress to outlaw alcoholic beverages. No less a drug war luminary than Thomas Constantine, director of the Drug Enforcement Administration in the late 1990s, stated "When we look down the road, I would say 10, 15, 20 years from now, in a gradual fashion, smoking will probably be outlawed in the United States."[62]

The ever-tightening restrictions on the marketing of tobacco products—the banning of billboard advertising; the elimination of vending machine sales; the attempt to bar sales to anyone under 21 years of age; statutes and ordinances prohibiting smoking in restaurants, office buildings and other "public" locales—all point in that direction.

The situation with respect to alcoholic beverages is not yet as dire, but the assault on the legitimacy of drinking has taken on new vigor in the past six or seven years. (Indeed, one might argue that the alcohol beverage industry is about where the tobacco industry was some two decades ago: beset by annoying but not yet life-threatening restrictions.) The trend, though, is troubling enough. Under the guise of a campaign against drunken driving, all 18- to 21-year-old Americans have been stripped of their legal right to drink. Anti-alcohol crusaders are now mounting offensives on several fronts. One of the most significant was the effort to have Congress mandate a nationwide standard declaring that any driver with a blood alcohol level of 0.08 or higher be considered legally drunk. Such a measure passed Congress, and President Clinton signed it into law in October 2000.[63]

Aside from the fact that the standard itself is draconian (a 100-pound woman consuming one drink on an empty stomach could find herself perilously close to the limit), proponents candidly admit that the 0.08 mandate is merely an interim measure. Their ultimate goal is to ban anyone who has consumed *any* amount of alcohol from driving. Ominously, Karolyn V. Nunnallee, national president of Mothers Against Drunk Driving, notes that "studies show that many people are dangerously impaired at lower levels."[64]

There are indications that the focus on the (admittedly very real) menace of drunken driving is largely a pretext for a much broader attack on the alcohol industry—and even more fundamentally on the legitimacy of drinking such beverages at all. Some of the "anti–drunk driving" measures stretch credulity to the breaking point. For example, the U.S. Senate passed a bill in March 1998 banning *passengers* in a car from drinking. The same measure sought to ban sales entirely from drive-through liquor windows, although senators rejected that provision by a vote of 56 to 43.[65] Similar campaigns are under way at the state and local levels to ban not only such drive-through sales but even the right of convenience stores and gas stations to sell alcohol. Reminiscent of the campaigns against tobacco advertising, the advertising of alcoholic beverages has come under increasing fire as well. Some of the criticism is transparently silly—for example, the allegation that the Budweiser frogs were a nefarious attempt by Anheuser-Busch to target children as potential consumers. (One wonders what such critics thought of the subsequent ad campaign featuring Louie the lizard and his friend; perhaps lizards inherently have less appeal to children.) Given the tobacco precedent, however, the tendency to smirk at such excesses should be resisted. Once again, there is a broad-range attack under way on the right to market an ostensibly legal product.

True, there is no imminent prospect of national legislation outlawing tobacco products and alcoholic beverages. But the same result can be achieved incrementally as well as in a legislative blitzkrieg; it merely takes longer. After all, the great experiment in Prohibition during the 1920s did not occur out of the blue. Indeed, as scholars have shown, the roots of national Prohibition went back more than half a century before the ratification of the Eighteenth Amendment and the enactment of the Volstead Act. And it began innocuously enough, with temperance campaigns to encourage more responsible drinking or, preferably, voluntary declarations of abstinence. The campaign gradually escalated to the passage of local prohibition ordinances, followed by the enactment of similar laws on the state level in more and more states. Only then was there a drive to enact a comprehensive national ban. The tobacco and alcohol industries today face a similar "death by a thousand cuts."

The key point is that the prohibitionist mentality is insatiable by nature. Once the public accepts the logic that it is appropriate to outlaw the sale and possession of certain substances (marijuana, cocaine, and other drugs) because they are "harmful," other substances are vulnerable to attack on that same basis. And who can dispute the argument that tobacco products and alcoholic beverages are often harmful to their users? A mountain of scientific evidence has implicated cigarette smoking as a cause of numerous health maladies. Similarly, millions of Americans battle alcoholism, and the effects of that condition impact family members and other innocent parties. Excessive alcohol consumption is a factor in numerous cases of violence as well as other antisocial acts—in addition to the problem of drunken driving. Indeed, one can make the argument that alcohol and tobacco cause as many or more societal problems than do currently illegal drugs. For example, a 1998 study by Columbia University's National Center on Substance Abuse found that alcohol, more than *any* illegal drug, was closely associated with violent crimes, including murder, rape, assault, and child and spousal abuse. Twenty-one percent of state inmates convicted of violent crimes committed them under the influence of alcohol alone, according to the report. Only 3 percent were high on crack or powder cocaine, and just 1 percent were under the influence of heroin.[66]

Proponents of drug legalization often invoke precisely such points to expose the hypocrisy of the drug war and to call for treating illegal drugs the same as tobacco and alcohol. It is right to point out the flagrant inconsistency of treating various mind-altering substances in such widely different fashions. But drug-war opponents should perhaps be more sensitive to the reality that the inconsistency can be resolved in two ways. One solution would be to apply the alcohol and tobacco model to illegal drugs. But the other possibility would be to apply the drug-war model to alcohol and tobacco.[67] The chances of the second scenario are now nearly as great as prospects for the first.[68] Indeed, Gro Harlem Brundtland, the head of the World Health Organization (WHO), virtually declared war on tobacco, calling for a worldwide ban on all tobacco advertising and for a package of other international controls, including very high levels of taxation.[69] That approach is little more than prohibition on the installment plan. Equally ominous, some school districts in the United States are now testing students for alcohol and nicotine, just as they do for illegal drugs.[70]

If anyone doubts that the antidrug crusading mentality is fast moving into the arenas of policymaking regarding tobacco and even alcohol, consider the comments of Brundtland and her colleague Marc Danzon, a regional director at WHO. At a global conference on youth and alcohol, Brundtland asserted: "Young people are vulnerable. They need to be protected. They need to grow up without being drawn into something that can ruin their life, change their future and lead to alcohol dependence." Where Brundtland implicitly drew a parallel between alcohol consumption and drug abuse, Danzon was explicit. "We need to raise understanding among young people that consuming alcohol is no different to consuming a drug," he stated. "More and more it is seeming that as a product alcohol is being used like a drug."[71]

Just as the drug warriors habitually do, the two officials ignore the reality that most consumers of alcohol are adults. And in the name of "protecting the children" they would ban virtually all alcohol advertising. If they have their way, alcoholic beverages (along with tobacco) would slip into a societal gray area—technically legal for adults but subject to a growing array of restrictions designed to thwart marketing and convey the message that it is a damaging, immoral, and antisocial product that should not be used by *anyone*. One wonders how long it would remain legal under such a barrage. And Brundtland and Danzon are not alone in equating alcohol consumption and the use of illegal drugs. A comment by Barry McCaffrey is most revealing. Referring to the problem of "poly-drug abuse," McCaffrey explained, "It's booze and pot and other things, and it causes $100 billion in damages a year. It's outrageous."[72]

The conditioning of the American people to accept whatever is necessary to prosecute the war on drugs creates other dangers in addition to the possibility that a prohibitionist strategy might someday be applied to alcohol and tobacco. The erosion of fundamental civil liberties that began with the drug war is rapidly expanding into other arenas.

For example, just as the courts have lowered the barriers to automobile searches to facilitate police antidrug efforts, they also countenanced "sobriety checkpoints" (roadblocks) to combat drunken driving and Immigration and Naturalization Service (INS) checkpoints to apprehend illegal aliens. A colleague of mine encountered such an INS checkpoint on the main highway between San Diego and Los Angeles—some 50 miles from the U.S.-Mexico border—while on his way to a speaking engagement. INS agents (together with members of the California Highway Patrol) pulled cars over—whether randomly or based on some mysterious "profile" was not clear—and interrogated the unlucky motorists. My colleague (who is not Hispanic) was one of those detained. He was asked where he was coming from, what his destination was, if he traveled that route frequently, and what his business was in Los Angeles—as if any of that information was properly the business of INS bureaucrats.

One can hope that the decision of the U.S. Supreme Court in November 2000 striking down checkpoints for the enforcement of drug laws will slow the proliferation of that tactic.[73] But the Court's decision was a narrow one. The justices had the opportunity to reverse earlier decisions allowing such stops for drunken driving and immigration matters, but instead chose to make a tortured distinction between such checkpoints and those for the enforcement of criminal statutes against the possession or trafficking of illegal drugs. Moreover, proponents of the checkpoints will try every means to skirt the strictures of the latest decision.

Some Americans (and unfortunately most state and federal courts) have rationalized intrusions such as highway checkpoints as a "minor inconvenience" that enables law enforcement personnel to pursue a greater good. But it was not that many decades ago that Americans assumed they had a right to drive down the nation's highways and not be molested by authorities conducting investigative fishing expeditions. It would have been considered a revolutionary (and odious) notion that a motorist could be stopped when there was no reasonable cause to believe that he had violated any law. Checkpoints to conduct even cursory interrogations, examine one's papers, or otherwise interfere with one's freedom to travel from place to place were considered the features of dictatorial societies, not an America that regarded itself as the citadel of freedom.

Abuses of the government's seizure and forfeiture powers, which had become a hallmark of the drug war, have also expanded into other areas. Authorities in several cities have begun to seize the automobiles of individuals accused of soliciting sex from prostitutes. In early 1999 New York City mayor Rudolph Giuliani expanded the concept still further by ordering the seizure of automobiles of people arrested for drunken driving.

As in the cases of drug-war property seizures, valuable property is taken by the authorities upon arrest—before the accused party has been convicted of any crime. The Alice in Wonderland concept of "punishment first, verdict later" seems now to be the operating doctrine of U.S. law enforcement. And as in the drug-war cases, there is no guarantee that even a not-guilty verdict will result in the return of property. Mayor Giuliani, in fact, explicitly stated that the city might retain seized property in cases where an acquittal did not seem (to whom?) warranted by the facts.[74] Nor is there any greater protection for the rights of innocent third parties in the new nondrug seizure and forfeiture cases. One key case that went to the U.S. Supreme Court involved a woman who jointly owned an automobile with her husband, who had been arrested for soliciting sex from a prostitute. Although no one disputed the fact that she was in no way involved in the alleged violation of the law (indeed, she was mightily annoyed at her husband), the Court nevertheless upheld the government's seizure and forfeiture actions depriving her of her share (50 percent) of the auto's value.

The drug war has produced other more subtle but equally dangerous trends. It has led to the militarization of police departments and an increase in the level of force used by those departments in situations that have little or nothing to do with illegal drugs.[75] It has emboldened federal authorities to pursue measures that would further dilute the expectation of privacy that customers have when doing business with their bank.[76] Such efforts include the aborted know-your-customer rule proposed by the Federal Deposit Insurance Corporation in 1999 that would have required banks to know where there customers got their money, how they got it, and monitor accounts to determine whether transactions were "normal." The proposed rule—withdrawn at least temporarily after a storm of public protest—would have greatly expanded the already disturbing requirements that banks spy and report on their own customers.[77]

Although it is possible that such an array of abuses of government power might have become the norm even in the absence of a war on drugs, that is most unlikely. The erosion of key civil liberties coincides with the onset or the incremental escalation of the drug war. Many of the practices that are now becoming pervasive in various areas of law enforcement either began as features of the drug war or received a huge boost from that struggle. The crusade against drugs has conditioned the American people to listen to the siren song that it is necessary for them to give up a few of their freedoms for the greater good of ridding the nation of the scourge of drugs. Once that rationale is accepted, it becomes ever easier for authorities to use the same argument in the name of combating other "scourges"—such as drunken driving, prostitution, illegal immigration, and the alleged conspiracy by tobacco companies to snare American children.

Adopting a prohibitionist strategy against certain drugs was a bad enough course of action. But using the metaphor of "war" for such a campaign has created an assortment of disasters. Americans now face a fundamental choice: They can end the failed crusade against drugs or they can watch as those disasters burgeon in size and multiply in number.

CHAPTER NINE

A BLUEPRINT FOR PEACE:
ENDING THE WAR ON DRUGS

The United States has waged an intense war on drugs both at home and abroad for more than three decades. Throughout that period, domestic support for the effort has been consistent and strong. Although there have been a few prominent critics in the United States, their voices usually have been drowned out by calls for the expenditure of more funds and the adoption of ever-harsher measures to overcome the scourge of drugs. Latin American critics have been even rarer and quieter. Few wanted to incur Washington's wrath by criticizing the drug war, and the fate of the handful of individuals who dared to do so did not encourage emulation.

There are signs, though, that the strategy of intimidation used by drug warriors is beginning to lose its effect. For the first time since the late 1970s, there appears to be a reasonable chance that the prohibitionist strategy eventually could be overturned. Such prominent businessmen as financier George Soros, Peter Lewis, the chairman of Progressive Insurance, Inc. (the nation's fifth largest auto insurer), and John Sperling, a wealthy entrepreneur, have funded a variety of initiatives that challenge the sacred cows of the drug war. They have promoted various measures that embody a strategy of "harm reduction" and treatment, not jail. As the *Wall Street Journal* noted, since 1996 the three men have spent more than $20 million "on a state-by-state campaign to chip away at the hard-line policies" of the war on drugs.[1] Most of their efforts have focused on two issues: allowing the medical use of marijuana and curbing the authority of law enforcement agencies to seize property from accused drug law violators without a conviction for that crime.

Their financial support has enabled opponents of the drug war to put referenda on the ballots in various states permitting the use of marijuana (and in some cases other now-illegal drugs) for medical purposes. Indeed, by the end of 2000, nine states—Alaska, Arizona, California, Colorado, Hawaii, Maine, Oregon, Nevada, and Washington—had adopted such measures. One of the more revealing pieces of evidence of waning public enthusiasm for an across-the-board prohibitionist strategy is that initiatives on making medical exceptions to the drug laws were approved by voters—and usually adopted by wide margins—in state after state. Another indicator was the approval by California voters in the November 2000 elections of Proposition 36, an even more ambitious proposal that sought to bar state judges from sending people to prison after their first or second conviction for drug use or possession. Instead, such nonviolent offenders would be directed into treatment programs.

Signs of change are surfacing elsewhere as well. At the beginning of 2001, the government of Jamaica appointed a commission to examine the possible legalization of marijuana. Interestingly, a majority of people appearing before the commission favored legalization. Among those who testified were representatives of the Medical Association of Jamaica, the Scientific Research Council, the Jamaica Manufacturers Association, and the National Democratic Movement, the country's third largest political party.[2] In September 2001 the commission issued a report recommending the decriminalization of marijuana, despite U.S. warnings that passage of such a measure by Jamaica's parliament could lead to the country's decertification under the 1988 Drug Abuse Act and the imposition of economic sanctions.[3]

In addition to the growing roster of domestic critics in the United States, some Latin American officials are beginning to advocate an end to the drug war, even though they risk denunciation and harassment from Washington for doing so. One prominent convert is Uruguayan president Jorge Batlle. "During the past 30 years [the drug war] has grown, grown, grown, every day more problems, every day more violence, every day more militarization," Batlle told a nationwide radio audience in February 2001. "This has not gotten people off drugs. And what's more, if you remove the economic incentive of [the drug trade] it loses strength, it loses size, it loses people who participate."[4] Although the president pledged continued cooperation with antidrug efforts until the laws are changed, having a head of state condemn the logic of the drug war caused Washington no small amount of concern.

Although few other Latin American officials are as bold as Batlle, several have dared to criticize the drug war as a failure and hint at their support for legalization. A little more than a year before he became Mexico's foreign minister, Jorge Castañeda wrote a scathing commentary in *Newsweek* proclaiming the war a failure. "It's hard to find a place where the war on drugs is being won," Castañeda concluded. "Indeed, the time is uniquely propitious for a wide-ranging debate between North and Latin Americans on this absurd war that no one really wants to wage." Moreover, "In the end, legalization of certain substances may be the only way to bring prices down, and doing so may be the only remedy to some of the worst aspects of the drug plague: violence, corruption, and the collapse of the rule of law."[5]

Perhaps the most surprising critique came from Castañeda's boss, Mexican president Vicente Fox, in a March 2001 interview in the newspaper *Unomásuno*. Alluding to the violence and corruption that drug trafficking has spawned, Fox stated that the solution might be eventually to legalize drugs. He added an important caveat, however. "When the day comes that it is time to adopt the alternative of lifting punishment for consumption of drugs, it would have to come from all over the world because we would gain nothing if Mexico did it but the production and traffic of drugs . . . continued here" for lucrative markets where the substances remained illegal.[6] Even with that caveat, Fox's comments caused more than a little consternation in official Washington.

Perhaps most significant, at "ground zero" in the war on drugs (Colombia), criticism of the prohibitionist strategy is mounting. Some of the critics are now openly advocating the legalization of drugs. In the summer of 2001 Liberal Party senator Viviane Morales submitted a bill to the Colombian congress calling for legalization. "The main ally of narcotrafficking is prohibition," Morales states bluntly. Another influential Colombian politician, Guillermo Gavíria, governor of powerful Antioquia province, insists that his country should lead an international debate on legalization. Although there is little chance that Morales's legislation will pass in the near future, the fact that a serious legalization campaign in Colombia surfaced at all in the face of vehement opposition from the United States and the Pastrana government is remarkable.

A few countries are abandoning the prohibitionist strategy, despite pressure from Washington not to do so. The Netherlands has had de facto decriminalization of marijuana for years, even though that policy has been a frequent target of wrath from U.S. officials.[7] Indeed, Dutch authorities in one town now plan to open "drive-through" drug shops to better accommodate the drug tourists who flock to that country from jurisdictions (especially Germany) with far more restrictive drug laws.[8] Recently the government of Belgium decided to legalize the possession of small quantities of marijuana for personal consumption. Growing marijuana plants for personal use also would be permitted.[9] The government of Canada is seriously considering the decriminalization of marijuana, making possession a civil rather than a criminal offense. In May 2001 the House of Commons established a committee to examine the merits of decriminalization, and Justice Minister Anne McLellan is openly encouraging the debate. Advocates of decriminalization include members of the principal conservative political party, the Canadian Alliance, as well as the Royal Canadian Mounted Police.[10] Two months later the Canadian government made it legal for terminally ill patients, as well as some patients with chronically debilitating conditions such as multiple sclerosis, to use marijuana to alleviate their symptoms.[11]

Even Portugal, not known as a bastion of radical libertarian thinking on law enforcement issues, is rethinking its position on the drug war. Although the government maintains a harsh policy toward traffickers, it has adopted a far less punitive approach to drug users. A new law that went into effect in July 2001 eliminates the threat of prison for possession of small quantities of any drug, not merely marijuana. Punishment is confined to fines or mandatory community service. While the Portuguese law does not constitute legalization or even true decriminalization, it is a major step for a socially conservative country.

Potentially as significant as the episodes of reform overseas and the adoption of medical marijuana initiatives in the United States is the evidence of growing ambivalence about the drug war itself on the part of the American people. Underlying that ambivalence is the widespread belief that the drug war has been a failure. A detailed public opinion survey conducted by the Pew Research Center in February 2001 confirmed that point. Not only did 74 percent of respondents agree that the drug war is being lost, but the same percentage agreed with the statement that "demand is so high we will never stop drug use."[12] Equally revealing, only 6 percent considered illegal drug use to be the nation's most pressing problem. That compared to 37 percent in a similar survey conducted in 1990.[13]

Respondents also were less than enthusiastic about the supply-side campaign. Some 68 percent believed that Latin

America would never be able to control the outflow of drugs. When asked whether the U.S. government should provide more, less, or about the same amount of financial assistance to help drug-producing countries stem the flow, only 11 percent wanted to give more aid; 42 percent advocated giving less aid. Their response was only slightly more favorable when queried specifically about military aid: 23 percent favored giving more aid; 28 percent wanted to reduce the level of assistance.[14]

Although despondency about the drug war did not necessarily translate into a surge of support for outright legalization, there were also signs of softening public attitudes about criminalizing drug use. As many respondents (47 percent) agreed with the statement that "too many people are put in jail for drug offenses" as disagreed. And by a narrow plurality (47 percent to 45 percent) respondents thought that eliminating mandatory jail sentences would be "a good thing."[15] In addition, only 49 percent favored retaining criminal penalties for possessing small quantities of marijuana, and by better than a three-to-one margin (73 percent to 21 percent), respondents supported permitting doctors to prescribe marijuana to their patients.[16] That result suggests that the victory of medical marijuana initiatives in several states was not a fluke.

Although such survey data hardly reveal a popular mandate for drug legalization, they do reveal the profile of a public that is war weary, pessimistic about the efficacy of drug-war tactics in the future, and supportive of a limited legalization of some drugs under some conditions—especially medical marijuana. That is not the profile of American public opinion likely to gladden the hearts of committed drug warriors. It suggests a public that is gradually becoming receptive to alternative policies.

An admission by former DEA chief Jack Lawn underscores one reason why the drug war should be ended: "With all of our efforts, with the military in their aircraft and Coast Guard cutters and helicopters, traffickers will just move to a third country to get things done. They don't lose money. They don't lose hours. I don't think they have lost anything substantial in the last 20 years."[17]

Laws and other policy initiatives must be judged by their consequences, not their intentions. By that measure, the war on drugs over the past three decades has been a colossal failure. The international drug traffickers have been barely inconvenienced while societies in drug-producing and drug-transiting countries have experienced a massive upsurge in corruption and violence. In at least one drug-source country (Colombia), the entire social and political system is in peril. On the domestic front, the sole achievement has been a decline in recreational use of illegal drugs by casual, occasional users. Even assuming that the decline is the result of the prohibitionist strategy and not the effect of educational campaigns about the health consequences of drug abuse, the benefit has been achieved at enormous cost. We have filled our prisons with drug offenders, diverted criminal justice resources and personnel away from serious crimes to wage the drug war, and badly damaged the Fourth Amendment and other portions of the Bill of Rights.[18]

The only realistic way out of this policy morass is to adopt a regime of drug legalization. And contrary to the alarmists in the prohibitionist camp, that option is not a venture into terra incognita, replete with unimaginable horrors. Although the fact is largely forgotten, now-illicit drugs were once legal in America. At the beginning of the twentieth century, there were virtually no restrictions on opiates, cocaine, or marijuana.

Even the first "antidrug measure" approved by Congress was quite modest and reasonable. In 1906 Congress enacted the Pure Food and Drug Act, which required that labels on medicine list any narcotic content. (Some American consumers had unwittingly become dependent on patent medicines containing opiates or cocaine.) It was not until the adoption of the Harrison Narcotic Act in 1914 that the United States took a major step toward drug prohibition. (It may be more than coincidental that it was about this same time that the movement for a national prohibition of alcoholic beverages also began to gather steam.) Yet although the Harrison Act outlawed normal commerce in opiates and cocaine, even that legislation permitted medically prescribed uses of those drugs, and addicts were still able to obtain drugs legally from physicians and clinics. Only after a dubious decision by the U.S. Supreme Court in 1919, ruling that providing morphine to an addict with no intention to cure him violated the Harrison Act, and the passage of subsequent amendments to the law by Congress, did prohibition become complete with regard to opiates and cocaine.[19]

Marijuana remained legal even longer. Not until the passage of the Marijuana Tax Act in 1937 did that drug join the rank of banned substances.

Granted, America was not free of drug-related problems under a regime of legalization. For example, in the early years of the twentieth century there were an estimated 300,000 opiate addicts—often individuals who had become dependent on patent medicines.[20] Yet that was still a relatively small portion of the population. And America was certainly not plagued with the violence, corruption, economic distortions, and abasement of the Bill of Rights that have accompanied the prohibitionist regime. Legalization may not be a panacea, but it certainly beats the alternative.

It is time to terminate the prohibitionist strategy. We need an entirely new policy, not merely an effort to repackage the war on drugs as a "compassionate crusade," as Asa Hutchinson, the new head of the Drug Enforcement Administration, seeks to do. The first step ought to be to end the browbeating of our neighbors in the Western Hemisphere to take actions that create massive problems for their societies and undermine the stability of democratic institutions. It is bad enough if we inflict the many follies of prohibition on ourselves; we should at least have the decency not to inflict them on others.

Washington's supply-side campaign against drugs has not worked, is not working, and, given economic realities, will not work. That is not to suggest that the influence of the drug trade is a benign one or that Latin American countries would not be better off if the trafficking organizations were less powerful. The exaggerated importance that the drug trade has acquired is an economic distortion caused by foolish policies adopted in Washington and the drug-source countries themselves. Immediate steps can and should be taken to eliminate that distortion.

Latin American governments should move more aggressively to deregulate their economies and spur economic growth, thereby creating new opportunities for those people who are now involved in the lower echelons of the drug trade. Although some governments took promising steps in that direction during the 1990s, the trend has stalled and in some places (e.g., Venezuela, Peru, and Argentina) even reversed. Adopting policies that promoted real growth in the private sector of the economy (as opposed to sterile government-directed economic development programs funded by U.S. aid dollars) would give new options to those who now see drug trafficking as the only path to prosperity.

The United States also can take steps to reinforce the benefits of such reforms. The adoption of the North American Free Trade Agreement provided important new economic opportunities for Mexico. Creating a hemispheric free trade agreement would extend such opportunities to other societies. Latin American representatives have long complained that U.S. import quotas on sugar, textiles, and an array of other products have retarded the development of their economies. Although those officials often ignore the fact that many of the problems with their economies are self-inflicted, their complaints have some validity. U.S. import restrictions needlessly injure Latin American business enterprises as well as U.S. consumers, and a hemispheric free trade zone would be an important step toward eliminating such inequities. More than a decade ago economist Scott MacDonald aptly observed, "Protectionism, in itself, is a dangerous force, but in the drug trade, it is negative reinforcement in the movement from legal products to illicit products."[21]

Certainly Latin American leaders recognize the importance of more open access to the U.S. market for their legal products. In arguing for renewal and expansion of the Andean Trade Preferences Act, Peru's vice president, Raúl Diez Canseco, told a forum in Colombia that such a deal could lift his country's exports to the United States to some $2.5 billion within five years. That growth in turn would create 140,000 jobs in Peru's apparel industry and up to 400,000 new jobs in the agricultural sector. Foreign Minister Diego García Sayán added that it was absolutely essential that textiles be included in the renewed pact, arguing that in many former drug-producing areas, textiles were becoming an alternate economic way of life.[22]

Yet even if the governments of drug-source countries enact the most comprehensive and worthwhile economic reforms and Washington adopts unusually enlightened trade policies, drug commerce will continue to play a disproportionate role in many Latin American countries unless the United States ends its futile experiment in drug prohibition. Without that action, drug trafficking still will carry a risk premium that drives up the price and the profit margin. Traffickers still will be able to pay farmers more than they can make from alternative crops or alternative occupations. Because ruthless individuals who do not fear the law tend to dominate black markets, the drug trade, in both its international and domestic incarnations, will remain largely the domain of violence-prone criminal organizations. Without legalization in the United States, the threat that such organizations pose to the governments and societies of source countries will abate only marginally, even if other reforms are enacted.

Drug legalization—treating currently illicit drugs as alcohol and tobacco are now treated—would provide important benefits to the United States: It would eliminate a significant portion of the crime and violence that plagues the streets of our major cities. It would halt the clogging of the court system with charges against nonviolent drug offenders and the clogging of our prisons with such inmates. Most important, abandoning the drug war would stop the alarming erosion of civil liberties.

Ending the war on drugs also would aid the effort against a real threat to America's security and well-being: the threat posed by international terrorism. Terminating the prohibitionist strategy would deprive terrorist organizations of an important source of revenue. (As mentioned earlier, the Taliban regime in Afghanistan, for example, derived a substantial portion of its income from narcotics trafficking.) Equally important, ending our latest fling with prohibition would free up thousands of personnel and billions of dollars for waging the war against terrorism. Imagine if all the well-trained personnel working for the DEA (to say nothing of the talent being wasted in state and local antidrug units) could be reassigned to antiterrorism missions.

The long-term benefits to Latin American societies from abandoning a prohibitionist strategy also would be substantial, although the short-term economic effects of a price decline might be adverse. No longer would Latin American nations suffer the massive distortions to their economies, the political corruption, and the escalating violence that accompany the lucrative black market in drugs. No longer would the governments of those countries have to dissemble in a futile attempt to satisfy the conflicting demands of the United States and their own citizens. No longer would Washington engage in the demeaning spectacle of alternately bribing and threatening its neighbors to get them to do the impossible.

NOTES

INTRODUCTION

1. "Missionary Group Releases Peru Flight Plan," Reuters, April 23, 2001.
2. See Craig Mauro, "Key Facts Disputed in Plane Downing," Associated Press, April 23, 2001; and Jude Webber, "Peru Says Went by the Book in U.S. Plane Tragedy," Reuters, April 24, 2001.
3. Karen DeYoung, "U.S. Shares Fault in Peru Incident," *Washington Post*, July 31, 2001, p. A1.
4. Twenty people were killed as a result of airplanes being shot down by the Peruvian air force. All twenty were confirmed to be drug smugglers—according to Peruvian authorities who conducted the investigations. It should be noted, though, that those investigations were conducted without any participation by U.S. officials, much less by independent observers. Ibid.
5. Quoted in Mike Gray, *Drug Crazy: How We Got into This Mess and How We Can Get Out* (New York: Random House, 1998), p. 104.
6. For a discussion of the Hernández incident, see William Branigin, "Questions on Military Role in Fighting Drugs Ricochet from a Deadly Shot," *Washington Post*, June 22, 1997, p. A1.
7. Gary E. Johnson, "It's Time to Legalize Drugs," in *After Prohibition: An Adult Approach to Drug Policies in the 21st Century,* ed. Timothy Lynch (Washington, DC: Cato Institute, 2000), pp. 14-15. See also Gary E. Johnson, "Another Prohibition, Another Failure," *New York Times*, December 30, 2000, p. A31.
8. Quoted in Jared Kotler, "Colombian Candidate Questions Plan," Associated Press, August 26, 2001.
9. Quoted in "Drug Wars: Part 1," PBS, *Frontline*, October 9, 2000, transcript, p. 24.
10. Dennis Jett, "Remember the Drug War?" *Washington Post*, January 13, 2002, p. B4.
11. "Stopping It: How Governments Try—and Fail—to Stem the Flow of Drugs," *The Economist*, July 28, 2001, p. 11.
12. Quoted in "Drug Wars: Part 2," PBS, *Frontline*, October 10, 2000, transcript, p. 33.
13. Ibid.
14. For an early account of the growth in the European market, see Patrick L. Clawson and Rensselaer W. Lee III, *The Andean Cocaine Industry* (New York: St. Martin's Press, 1996), pp. 62-89.
15. Paul B. Stares, *Global Habit: The Drug Problem in a Borderless World* (Washington, DC: Brookings Institution Press, 1996), p. 1.
16. Mathea Falco, *The Making of a Drug-Free America: Programs That Work* (New York: Times Books, 1992), p. 8.

17. Eva Bertram and Kenneth Sharpe, "The Unwinnable Drug War: What Clausewitz Would Tell Us," *World Policy Journal* 13, no. 4 (Winter 1996-1997): 41-51.

CHAPTER ONE

1. "Remarks About an Intensified Program for Drug Abuse Prevention and Control," document 202, *Public Papers of the Presidents of the United States, Richard Nixon, 1971* (Washington, DC: Government Printing Office, 1972), pp. 738-39. See also Special Message to Congress on Drug Abuse Prevention and Control, June 17, 1971, document 203, ibid., pp. 739-49.

2. Quoted in Edward J. Epstein, *Agency of Fear: Opiates and Political Power in America* (New York: Putnam, 1977), p. 61.

3. For discussions of those earlier measures, see William O. Walker, ed., *Drugs in the Western Hemisphere: An Odyssey of Cultures in Conflict* (Wilmington, DE: Scholarly Resources, 1996.)

4. Epstein, *Agency of Fear*, p. 82. See also Lawrence A. Gooberman, *Operation Intercept: The Multiple Consequences of Public Policy*, http//:druglibrary.org/ schaffer/history/e1960/ intercept/chapter1.htm.

5. Gordon Liddy, *Will: The Autobiography of G. Gordon Liddy* (New York: St. Martin's Press, 1980), p.134.

6. Ibid.

7. Epstein, *Agency of Fear*, p. 84.

8. Liddy, *Will*, p. 135.

9. Quoted in Epstein, *Agency of Fear*, p. 84.

10. Miguel Ruiz-Cabañas I, "Mexico's Permanent Campaign: Costs, Benefits, Implications," in *Drug Policy in the Americas*, ed. Peter H. Smith (Boulder, CO: Westview, 1992), p. 155.

11. "Drug Wars: Part 1," PBS *Frontline*, October 9, 2000, transcript, p. 5.

12. Ibid., p. 8.

13. Quoted in Austin Scott, "Ford Urges Jailing of Drug Dealers," *Washington Post*, April 28, 1976, p. A1.

14. DuPont describes his experiences with Nixon and Ford on the marijuana issue. "When I came to the White House, Richard Nixon said, 'You're the drug expert, not me, on every issue but one, and that's the decriminalization of marijuana. If you make any hint of supporting decriminalization, you are history.' Later on, I of course grew restless under that restriction. And when Gerald Ford was president, the first thing I did as White House drug czar was come out for decriminalization of marijuana." "Drug Wars: Part 1," p. 13.

15. Leslie Maitland, "Heroin Trade Rising Despite U.S. Efforts," *New York Times*, February 15, 1981, p. A1.

16. Quoted in ibid.

17. Martin Schram, "TV Coverage of Jordan Drug Charge Adds to Carter's Political Problems," *Washington Post*, September 21, 1979, p. A14.

18. For a concise account of Bourne's rise and fall in the administration, see Mike Gray, *Drug Crazy: How We Got into This Mess and How We Can Get Out* (New York: Random House, 1998), pp. 98-100.

19. Quoted in Fred Barbash, "President Warns Staff Against Use of Illegal Drugs," *Washington Post*, July 28,1978, p. A1.

20. Quoted in Gray, *Drug Crazy*, p.98.

21. Comments of Hon. Gerald B. H. Solomon, March 2, 1995, *Congressional Record*, 104th Cong., 1st Sess., p. E499.

22. Even some political leaders who took a hard-line position on hard drugs seemed to view marijuana differently. For example, Senator Joseph Biden (D., DE) urged more vigorous action to stem the tide of heroin imports but also advocated amending the law to eliminate all federal criminal penalties for up to one ounce of marijuana. Charles R. Babcock, "Biden Urges U.S. to Step Up War on Drug Traffic," *Washington Post*, July 18, 1980, p. A21.

23. "California Awaits the Signature of Governor on Marijuana Bill," *New York Times*, June 30, 1975, p A8.

24. "Marijuana Use Legalized by Alaska Court," *New York Times*, May 27, 1975, p. A12.

25. See "Drugs and Public Policy," editorial, *Washington Post*, December 6, 1976, p. A21; and Lesley Oelsner, "In a Sometimes Bitter Fight, States and Cities Are Easing Marijuana Laws," *New York Times*, July 13, 1975, p. A13.

26. Paul B. Stares, *Global Habit: The Drug Problem in a Borderless World* (Washington, DC: Brookings Institution Press, 1996), p. 79.

27. *Monitoring the Future: Questionnaire Responses from the Nation's High School Seniors, 1975-1980* (Ann Arbor, MI: Institute for Social Research, 1981), pp. 1-7.

28. Richard Craig, "La Campaña Permanente: Mexico's Antidrug Campaign," *Journal of Interamerican Studies and World Affairs* 20, no. 2 (May 1978): 110-121.

29. For an account by the deputy chief of mission at the U.S. embassy in Colombia describing the antinarcotics efforts in that country during the late 1970s, see Robert W. Drexler, *Colombia and the United States: Narcotics Traffic and a Failed Foreign Policy* (London: McFarland and Company, 1997).

30. "Drug Wars: Part 1," p. 20.

31. *Public Papers of the Presidents of the United States: Ronald Reagan, 1981* (Washington, DC: Government Printing Office, 1982), p. 842.

32. Quoted in Gray, *Drug Crazy*, p. 100.

33. George Shultz, "The Campaign Against Drugs: The International Dimension," *Department of State Bulletin* (November 1984): 29. In retrospect, it appears that much of the strident rhetoric may have been political posturing. It is instructive that in their respective memoirs, Reagan, Shultz, and Secretary of Defense Caspar Weinberger do not even mention the international drug war. Indeed, for all of the emphasis he placed when he was president on the need to eliminate the scourge of illegal drugs, Reagan's memoirs contain only three brief references to the issue—and all of them in connection to Nancy Reagan's "Just Say No" campaign.

34. Joseph H. Linnemann, "International Narcotics Control Strategy," *Department of State Bulletin* (February 1982): 46.

35. For a typical example, see the comments of Senator Jeremiah Denton (R-AL) in Senate Committee on the Judiciary, Subcommittee on Security and Terrorism, *DEA Oversight and Budget Authorization, Hearing*, 95th Cong, 2d sess., March 9, 1984, p. 6.

36. Shultz, "The Campaign Against Drugs," p. 29.

37. Quoted in Suzanna McBee, "Flood of Drugs—A Losing Battle," *U.S. News + World Report,* March 25, 1985, p. 57.

38. William O. Walker III, *Drug Control in the Americas* (Albuquerque: University of New Mexico Press, 1981), pp. 2-3, 9-11.

39. Bruce Michael Bagley, "The New Hundred Years War?: U.S. National Security and the War on Drugs in Latin America," in *The Latin American Narcotics Trade and U.S. National Security,* ed. Donald J. Mabry (New York: Greenwood, 1989), p. 46.

40. Kevin Jack Riley, *Snow Job? The War Against International Cocaine Trafficking,* (New Brunswick, NJ: Transaction, 1996), pp. 102-3. See also LaMond Tullis, *Unintended Consequences: Illegal Drugs and Drug Policies in Nine Countries* (Boulder, CO: Lynne Rienner, 1995), p. 205.

41. Francisco E. Thoumi, *Political Economy and Illegal Drugs in Colombia* (Boulder, CO: Lynne Rienner, 1995), p. 205.

42. Quoted in "Fighting the Cocaine Wars," *Time,* February 25, 1985, p. 31.

43. Walker, *Drug Control in the Americas,* pp. 21, 75-97, 153-79.

44. U.S. Department of State, *The Global Legal Framework for Narcotics and Prohibitive Substances,* June 29, 1979, pp. 7-8, 10-13.

45. "Fighting the Cocaine Wars," pp. 30, 33; McBee, "Flood of Drugs," pp. 54-55; and "The Bahamas—Pot Shots," *Time,* February 13, 1984.

46. For a discussion of the "cocaine coup" and its aftermath, see Clare Hargreaves, *Snowfields: The War on Cocaine in the Andes* (New York: Holmes and Meier, 1992), pp. 102-25.

47. Senate Committee on Labor and Human Resources, Subcommittee on Alcoholism and Drug Abuse, *Drugs and Terrorism, 1984, Hearing,* 98th Cong., 2d sess, August 2, 1984, p. 10; and "Fighting the Cocaine Wars," p. 31.

48. For a comprehensive account of the Bolivian drug trade in the 1980s and the growing U.S. pressure on Bolivian officials, see Jaime Malamud-Goti, *Smoke and Mirrors: The Paradox of the Drug Wars* (Boulder, CO: Westview, 1992).

49. Such desultory cooperation in U.S. antidrug initiatives was hardly a new phenomenon. Washington's pressure on Latin American drug-source countries in the 1920s and 1930s often produced a strikingly similar response. Walker, *Drug Control in the Americas,* pp. 35-36, 45-46, 57, 92-93.

50. Ted Galen Carpenter, "Foreign Anti-Drug Wars Carry a Hefty Tab," *Wall Street Journal,* October 31, 1985, p. A18.

51. Riley, *Snow Job?* p.114.

52. Ibid., pp. 114-115. For a discussion of Ley 1008 and its provisions, see Robert Painter, *Bolivia and Coca: A Study in Dependency* (Boulder, CO: Lynne Rienner, 1994), pp.79-80.

53. Charles B. Rangel, "Latin America Needs Anti-Drug Aid," letter to the editor, *Wall Street Journal,* December 6, 1985, p. A21.

54. Ibid.

55. For discussions of the 1986 and 1988 drug abuse acts and their international policy implications, see Bagley, " The New Hundred Years War?" pp. 43-58; and Raphael Perl, "International Narcopolicy and the Role of the U.S. Congress," in

The Latin American Narcotics Trade and U.S. National Security, ed. Mabry, pp. 89-102.

56. "Drugs Wars: Part 2," PBS, *Frontline*, October 10, 2000, transcript, p. 13.

57. National Security Decision Directive (NSDD) 221, Narcotics and National Security, April 8, 1986, Ronald Reagan Presidential Library. See also Keith B. Richburg, "Reagan Order Defines Drug Trade as Security Threat," *Washington Post*, June 8, 1986, p. A28.

58. NSDD 221, p. 1.

59. Ibid.

60. Ibid., p. 2.

61. Ibid.

62. Ibid., p. 3.

63. Ibid.

64. James J. Kilpatrick, "It's a Matter of National Security: Use Every Weapon," *Baltimore Sun*, May 18, 1988, p. A14.

65. Rensselaer W. Lee III, *The White Labyrinth: Cocaine and Political Power* (New Brunswick, NJ: Transaction, 1989), pp. 72, 196; and Carla Ann Robbins, "U.S. Mission: Cut Off Drugs at the Source," *U.S. News & World Report*, July 28, 1986, p. 55.

66. Gerald M. Boyd, "Drug Talks Begun with Latin Lands," *New York Times*, September 26, 1986, p. A1.

67. Peter B. Bensinger, " An Inadequate War Against Drugs," *Newsweek*, July 28, 1986, p. 8.

68. Poll results in *New York Times*, April 10, 1988, p. A10.

69. See Donald J. Mabry, "Narcotics and National Security," in *The Latin American Narcotics Trade and National Security*, ed. Mabry, pp. 3-10.

CHAPTER TWO

1. LaMond Tullis, *Unintended Consequences: Illegal Drugs and Drug Policies in Nine Countries* (Boulder, CO: Lynne Rienner, 1995), p. 102.

2. General Accounting Office, *Controlling Drug Abuse: A Status Report, 1988* (Washington, D.C. Government Printing Office, 1989). For a discussion of those trends, see James Ostrowski, "Thinking about Drug Legalization," Cato Institute Policy Analysis, no. 121, May 25, 1989, pp. 28-29.

3. U.S. Congress, House, Committee on the Judiciary, *Posse Comitatus Act, Hearing*, 97th Cong., 1st sess., June 3, 1981. For a discussion of that step and those that followed in getting the military involved in the domestic phase of the drug war, see David B. Kopel, "Militarized Law Enforcement: The Drug War's Deadly Fruit," in *After Prohibition: An Adult Approach to Drug Policies in the 21st Century*, ed. Timothy Lynch, (Washington, DC: Cato Institute, 2000), pp. 61-88.

4. Quoted in Arnold S. Trebach, *The Great Drug War* (New York: Macmillan, 1987), p. 167.

5. Linda Wheeler, "A Drug War with Real Troops," *Washington Post*, February 14, 1988, p. C5.

6. Keith B. Richburg, "Reagan Order Defines Drug Trade as Security Threat," *Washington Post*, June 8, 1986, p. A28.

7. Susan F. Rasky, "Facing a Rising Clamor to Fight Drugs, Congress Crosses a Long-Held Line," *New York Times*, May 16, 1988, p. B5.

8. James Longo, "Tempers Rise During Face-off over Initiatives," *Army Times*, May 23, 1988, p. 3.

9. Peter Reuter et al., "Sealing the Borders: The Effects of Increased Military Participation in Drug Interdiction," RAND Report R-3594-USDP (Santa Monica, CA: RAND Corporation, January 1988).

10. Jonathan Marshall, "A New Scare, a New Assault on Liberties," *Baltimore Sun*, May 18, 1988, p. A14.

11. Longo, "Tempers Rise During Face-off." For a discussion of efforts to involve the military more extensively in the drug war, see Donald J. Mabry, "The Role of the Military in the War on Drugs," in *The Latin American Narcotics Trade and U.S. National Security*, ed. Donald J. Mabry (New York: Greenwood, 1989), pp. 75-88.

12. Text of the address by President Bush, White House Press Office, press release, September 5, 1989, p. 3.

13. Quoted in Elaine Shannon, "Attacking the Source," *Time*, August 28, 1989, p. 10.

14. Michael Isikoff, "Drug Plan Allows Use of Military," *Washington Post*, September 10, 1989, p. A1.

15. Ann Devroy, "Bush Insists U.S. Troops Have Minimal Drug Role," *Washington Post*, September 12, 1989, p. A28.

16. Paul Bedard, "Bush to Widen Military Role in Drug War," *Washington Times*, August 15, 1989, p. A3.

17. Washington's failure to even consult the Colombian government produced a furious reaction in that country and throughout Latin America, eventually compelling the Bush administration to postpone implementation. See Bernard E. Trainor, "Colombians Balk at a Crucial Part of U.S. Drug Plans," *New York Times*, January 7, 1990, p. A1. and Michael Isikoff, "U.S. Defers Antidrug Naval Plan," *Washington Post*, January 9, 1990, p. A1. For a discussion of the growing sensitivity of Latin Americans to a U.S. military role in the drug war, see Eugene Robinson, "Latins Leery of Any U.S. Military," *Washington Post*, January 9, 1990, p. A16.

18. Michael Isikoff and Patrick E. Tyler, "U.S. Military Given Foreign Arrest Powers," *Washington Post*, December 16, 1989, p. A1.

19. George C. Wilson, "Experts Doubt Military Can Stop Flow of Drugs," *Washington Post*, September 6, 1989, p. A19.

20. Michael Isikoff, "More Military, Economic Aid for Drug Source Nations Urged," *Washington Post*, June 8, 1989, p. A4.

21. Paula Yost, "Role for GIs in Colombian Drug War?" *Washington Post*, August 21, 1989, p. A16; and Helen Dewar, "Sununu Indicates U.S. Would Send GIs to Colombia," *Washington Post*, September 4, 1989, p. A11.

22. For a general discussion of the issues involved in militarizing the international component of the drug war, see Bruce M. Bagley, "Myths of Militarization: Enlisting the Military in the War on Drugs," in *Drug Policy in the Americas*, ed. Peter H. Smith (Boulder, CO: Westview, 1992), pp. 129-150.

23. Ibid., pp. 214-221.

24. David Hoffman, "U.S. Aid to Colombians Expands in Drug War," *Washington Post*, August 26, 1989, p. A1.

25. David Hoffman and Bob Woodward, "President Launched Invasion with Little View to Aftermath," *Washington Post*, December 24, 1989, p. A1.

26. "U.S. Invades Panama; Bush Orders Troops to Capture Noriega," *Orange County Register*, December 20, 1989, p. A1.

27. Quoted in David Adams, "Drug Cartels Reported Flourishing in Panama; U.S. Called Its Invasion a 'Drug Bust,'" *San Francisco Chronicle*, July 16, 1991, p. A9.

28. Quoted in David Johnston, "No Victory for Panama," *New York Times*, April 10, 1992, p. A1. For a discussion of how important the drug war was as a motive for the invasion of Panama, see David Harris, *Shooting the Moon: The True Story of an American Manhunt Unlike Any Other, Ever* (Boston: Little, Brown, 2001).

29. Quoted in Wilson, "Experts Doubt Military Can Stop Flow of Drugs."

30. Caspar W. Weinberger, "Our Troops Shouldn't Be Drug Cops," *Washington Post*, May 22, 1988, p. C2.

31. Howard quote in Ed Magnuson, "A New Mission Impossible, Seal the Border in 45 Days," *Time*, May 30, 1988, p. 19.

32. Quoted in George C. Wilson, "Cheney Pledges Wider War on Drugs," *Washington Post*, September 19, 1989, p. A 16.

33. Crowe's remarks in "Americans Urged to Sacrifice," *Washington Post*, September 22, 1989, p. A22. Crowe did caution, however: "Perhaps the expectations are a little too high as to what we [the military] will achieve" in South America. Bob Woodward, "The Admiral of Washington," *Washington Post Magazine*, September 24, 1989, pp. 18-26, 42-47, describes Crowe's political acumen.

34. Dov S. Zakheim, "Let the Osprey Fly," *Washington Post*, October 19, 1989, p. A22.

35. For a discussion of the intense rivalry that often exists between the police forces and military establishments in Latin American drug-producing countries, see Rensselaer W. Lee, *The White Labyrinth: Cocaine and Political Power* (New Brunswick, NJ: Transaction, 1989), pp. 221-224.

36. Quoted in U.S. Congress, House, Committee on Armed Services, Defense Policy Panel and Investigations Subcommittee, "Narcotics Interdiction and the Use of the Military: Issues for Congress," 100th Cong., 2d sess., August 24, 1988, pp. 12-13.

37. Irving Kristol, "War on Drugs? Then Get Serious and Use the Military," *Washington Post*, March 28, 1988, p. A15.

38. Charles B. Rangel, "We *Can* Do Something for Colombia," *Washington Post*, August 24, 1989, p. A23.

39. MacNeil/Lehrer Newshour, PBS, transcript of the August 28, 1989, telecast, p. 7.

40. Jim Hoagland, "It's a Crisis of Drugs—And Guns," *Washington Post*, September 5, 1989, p. A19.

41. Stephen S. Rosenfeld, "Our Ossified National Security Budget," *Washington Post*, September 8, 1989, p. A23.

42. For examples, see Michael Ledeen, "K.G.B. Connections: Guns and Terrorists," *New Republic*, February 23, 1989, pp. 9-10; and Rachel Ehrenfeld, "Narco-Terrorism: The Kremlin Connection," Heritage Foundation Lecture no. 89, December 4, 1986.

43. James A. Michel, "Cuban Involvement in Narcotics Trafficking," *U.S. Department of State Bulletin* 83 (August 1989): 86; see also Brian Crozier, "Terror, New Style," *National Review*, August 9, 1985, p. 24; and Scott B. MacDonald, *Dancing on a Volcano: The Latin American Drug Trade* (New York: Praeger, 1988). For a critique of such conspiratorial theories, see Lee, *White Labyrinth*, pp. 178-184.

44. The trial and confession of General Arnaldo Ochoa in the summer of 1989 provided some evidence of high-level Cuban governmental involvement in the drug trade. Robert Pear, "Cuba Arrests Top General on Corruption Charges," *New York Times*, June 16, 1989, p. A7; and Mark A. Uhlig, "Cuban General Fully Confesses and Declares 'I Deserve to Die,'" *New York Times*, June 28, 1989, p. A1. It is entirely possible, however, that Ochoa's real crime was being perceived as a potential rival to Fidel Castro.

45. See, for example, John Kerry, "Fighting Drug Lords Is Not Imperialism," *Washington Post*, March 19, 1988, p. A21.

46. Bruce Bagley, *MacNeil/Lehrer Newshour*, p. 7. Bagley, however, was skeptical about a purely military approach. He presented a detailed discussion of his strategy for fighting the international phase of the drug war—including an extensive U.S. developmental aid program for the Andean region—in "Colombia: The Wrong Strategy," *Foreign Policy* 77 (Winter 1989-90): 154-171.

47. The Declaration of Cartageña, White House Press Office, press release, February 15, 1990.

48. Figures for all three Andean countries are included in "One Year Later: Update on Andean Drug Strategy," Department of State *Dispatch*, October 29, 1990, pp. 220-221.

49. Mark R. May, "Peru Balks at U.S. Military Aid Offer," *Christian Science Monitor*, May 3, 1990, p. 3.

50. Guy Gugliotta, "The Colombian Cartels and How to Stop Them," in *Drug Policy in the Americas*, ed. Smith, pp. 111-128.

51. Kevin Jack Riley, *Snow Job?: The War Against International Cocaine Trafficking* (New Brunswick, NJ: Transactions, 1996), pp. 178-179. On the Colombian government's war against the Medellín cartel, see Mark Bowden, *Killing Pablo: The Hunt for the World's Greatest Outlaw* (New York: Atlantic Monthly Press, 2000).

52. Riley, *Snow Job*, pp. 179-182.

53. James Brooke, "U.S. Halts Flights in Andes Drug War Despite Protests," *New York Times*, June 4, 1994, p. A1.

54. Karen DeYoung, "Behind U.S.-Peru Pact, a History of Division," *Washington Post*, April 25, 2001, p. A28.

55. Mark Matthews, "U.S. Arms Colombia in Drug Fight," *Baltimore Sun*, October 10, 1996, p. A1.

56. "Officials Reassess Using U.S. Pilots in Colombia Drug Fields," *Dallas Morning News*, December 4, 1996, p. A20.

57. Douglas Farah, "A Tutor to Every Army in Latin America," *Washington Post*, July 13, 1998, p. A1.

58. Quoted in Don Podesta and Douglas Farah, "Drug Policy in Andes Called Failure," *Washington Post*, March 27, 1993, p. A1. See also Carla Anne Robbins,

"Drug War Tactic Shifts as Clinton Aims to Curb U.S. Demand Instead of Supply," *Wall Street Journal,* February 22, 1993, p. A6.

59. Quoted in Podesta and Farah, "Drug Policy in Andes."

60. Office of National Drug Control Policy, *National Drug Control Strategy Budget Summary* (Washington, DC: White House, 1996), p. 3.

61. A. M. Rosenthal, "Dismantling the War," *New York Times,* May 18, 1993, p. A21.

62. Podesta and Farah, "Drug Policy in Andes."

CHAPTER THREE

1. For a concise discussion of Plan Colombia and its rationale, see Gabriel Marcella, "Plan Colombia: The Strategic and Operational Imperatives," *Implementing Plan Colombia, Special Series,* Strategic Studies Institute, U.S. Army War College and The Dante B. Fascell North-South Center, University of Miami, April 2001. For a skeptical assessment of the plan, see Edgardo Buscaglia and William Ratliff, "War and Lack of Governance in Colombia: Narcos, Guerrillas, and U.S. Policy," Hoover Institution Essays in Public Policy, no. 107 (2001).

2. For a discussion of the U.S. role in Plan Colombia, see Russell Crandall, "Clinton, Bush and Plan Colombia, " *Survival* 44, no. 1 (Spring 2002): 159-170.

3. Jason Webb, "U.S. Helicopters Land to Bolster 'Plan Colombia,'" Reuters, July 27, 2001.

4. Margarita Martinez, "Colombia Drug Crop Fumigation Resumes," Associated Press, July 31, 2001.

5. Juan Forero, "Ranchers in Colombia Bankroll Their Own Militia," *New York Times,* August 8, 2001, p. A1.

6. For a discussion of the connection between drug traffickers and the rebels, see Alejandro Reyes, "Drug Trafficking and the Guerrilla Movement in Colombia," in *Drug Trafficking in the Americas,* ed. Bruce M. Bagley and William O. Walker III (Miami: North-South Center Press, 1996), pp. 121-130.

7. "Colombia's War Displaced 126,000 in 2000—Report," Reuters, January 24, 2001.

8. Arnaud de Borchgrave, "Four-Way Civil War Makes Colombia a Nightmare," *Washington Times*, February 13, 2001, p. A12.

9. Ibid.

10. Juan Pablo Toro, "Rebels Cripple Colombia Oil Industry," Associated Press, August 10, 2001.

11. Quoted in George Gedda, "Bush Mulls Activist Colombia Stance," Associated Press, December 27, 2000.

12. Quoted in ibid., emphasis added.

13. Quoted in Alan Sipress, "U.S. Reassesses Colombia Aid," *Washington Post,* September 10, 2001, p. A1.

14. Angel Rabasa and Peter Chalk, *Colombian Labyrinth: The Synergy of Drugs and Insurgency and Its Implications for Regional Stability* (Santa Monica, CA: RAND Corporation, 2001), p. xviii.

15. Quoted in Ken Guggenheim, "Terror Fight Changes Colombia Angle," Associated Press, October 16, 2001.

16. Ibid.

17. Quoted in Jared Kotler, "U.S. Sees Role in Colombia on Terror," Associated Press, October 26, 2001.

18. Anthony Boadle, "U.S. Hardens View on Colombian Rebels after Sept. 11," Reuters, October 26, 2001.

19. Quoted in Anthony Boadle, "Pastrana Seeks U.S. Aid to Fight 'Narco-Terrorism,'" Reuters, November 8, 2001.

20. Quoted in Deborah Charles, "Pastrana to U.S.: Fight Drug Traffickers, Terrorists," Reuters, November 9, 2001. For a well-argued case by one of Colombia's opinion leaders linking the rebels and drug traffickers to terrorism, see Miguel Posada, "Terrorism in Colombia," Foreign Policy Research Institute E-Note, January 21, 2002. Posada is the director of the Centro de Analisis Sociopoliticos in Bogotá and a leading member of Colombia's business community.

21. Quoted in Boadle, "Pastrana Seeks U.S. Aid to Fight 'Narco-Terrorism.'"

22. Ibid.

23. Quoted in Charles, "Pastrana to U.S."

24. Phil Stewart, "U.S.-Trained Colombian Troops Kill Nine FARC Rebels," Reuters, April 24, 2001.

25. For its part, the Colombian government wants to triple the number of jungle bases devoted to antinarcotics efforts. "Colombia Proposes to U.S. Tripling Anti-Drug Bases," Reuters, October 4, 2001.

26. Quoted in T. Christian Miller, "U.S. May Broaden Its Role in Colombia," *Los Angeles Times,* July 26, 2001, p. A1.

27. Karen DeYoung, "U.S. May End Curbs on U.S. Aid to Colombia," *Washington Post,* March 15, 2002, p. A1.

28. Karen DeYoung, "Pastrana Pledges Colombia Won't Be Like Vietnam," *Washington Post,* February 26, 2001, p. A12.

29. Quoted in Will Weissert, "Leaders Debate Colombia Aid," Associated Press, August 14, 2000.

30. Quoted in Harold Olmos, "Chavez: Colombia May Mirror Vietnam," Associated Press, August 30, 2000.

31. Karen DeYoung, "House Rejects Bush Request on Colombia," *Washington Post,* July 25, 2001, p. A17.

32. T. Christian Miller, "U.S. Employs Foreign Pilots in Drug War," *Los Angeles Times,* August 18, 2001, p. A1.

33. Norman Kempster, "Colombia Want U.S. as Peace Talks Partner," *Los Angeles Times,* February 27, 2001, p. A5.

34. Tom Carter, "Bush Declines Role in Talks with Rebels," *Washington Times,* February 28, 2001, p. A13.

35. Karen DeYoung, "U.S. Now Sees Possible Role in Colombian Peace Talks," *Washington Post,* March 9, 2001, p. A21.

36. For a discussion of the many economic, social, and political pathologies in Colombia, see Francisco E. Thoumi, *Political Economy and Illegal Drugs in Colombia* (Boulder, CO: Lynne Rienner, 1995).

37. "The Threat Posed by the Convergence of Organized Crime, Drug Trafficking, and Terrorism," Written Testimony of Ralf Mutschke, Assistant Director, Criminal Intelligence Directorate, International Criminal Police Organization, General Secretariat, before a hearing of the Committee on the Judiciary,

Subcommittee on Crime, U.S. House of Representatives, 106th Cong., 2d sess., December 30, 2000, p. 10.

38. Steve Salisbury, "Raid Shows Colombian Rebels Are Also Drug Lords," *Washington Times*, March 20, 2001, p. A1.

39. Ibon Villelabeitia, "Colombian Peasants Block Road to Protest Enclave," Reuters, February 16, 2001. There were some legitimate reasons to be skeptical about Pastrana's approach. Among other things, the FARC apparently exploited the use of its sanctuary to expand its area of control. Colombian military officials in one region estimated that the FARC had pushed out the boundaries of its enclave by at least another 100 miles. Scott Wilson, "Colombian Rebels Use Refuge to Expand Their Power Base," *Washington Post,* October 3, 2001, p. A25.

40. Quoted in "Colombian Paramilitaries Oppose Rebel Enclave," Reuters, March 5, 2001.

41. Phil Stewart, "Far Right Fighters Storm Colombia Rebel Stronghold," Reuters, April 9, 2001; and Scott Wilson, "Colombia Right's 'Cleaning' Campaign," *Washington Post*, April 17, 2001, p. A1.

42. Scott Wilson, "Rightist Forces Seize Key Area in Colombia," *Washington Post*, April 19, 2001, p. A13.

43. Michael Radu, "Chaos in the Andes," Foreign Policy Research Institute E-Note, March 20, 2001, pp. 2-3.

44. Will Weissert, "Colombian Guerrilla Groups Allying," Associated Press, April 23, 2001.

45. T. Christian Miller, "Pastrana Signs Law Widening Military's Role," *Los Angeles Times*, August 17, 2001, p. A3.

46. Scott Wilson, "Colombia Ends Talks with Rebels," *Washington Post,* January 10, 2002, p. A-14; T. Christian Miller, "Colombia Peace Talks Fail Amid Fears of War," *Los Angeles Times*, January 10, 2002, p. A3; and T. Christian Miller, "Bogotá Moves Closer to War," *Los Angeles Times*, January 14, 2002, p. A1.

47. Scott Wilson, "Colombian Soldiers Move into Rebel Zone," *Washington Post*, February 23, 2002, p. A12.

48. Quoted in Frances Kerry, "Proponents Defend U.S. Aid to Plan Colombia," Reuters, February 2, 2001.

49. Jason Webb, "Colombian Rebel Group Grew from Attack on Commune," Reuters, February 8, 2001; and Ralf Mutschke, "The Threat Posed by the Convergence of Organized Crime, Drug Trafficking and Terrorism," p. 10. Mutschke placed the revenue figure for the ELN at approximately $380 million.

50. Juan Pablo Toro, "U.S. Envoy Criticizes Colombian Rebels," Associated Press, October 25, 2001.

51. For a concise history of the Medellín and Cali cartels and their methods, see Patrick L. Clawson and Rensselaer W. Lee III, *The Andean Cocaine Industry* (New York: St. Martin's Press, 1996), pp. 37-61.

52. de Borchgrave, "Four-Way Civil War."

53. Karen DeYoung, "U.S.: Colombia Abuses Continue," *Washington Post*, January 20, 2001, p. A21.

54. For the Colombian government's own assessment of the human rights situation, see Republic of Colombia, Ministry of National Defense, *Annual Human Rights*

and International Humanitarian Law Report, 2000 (Bogotá, Colombia, Ministry of National Defense, 2001).

55. Quoted in Jude Webber, "Colombia Charges 26 Army, Police in Rights Probe," Reuters, December 21, 2000.

56. Miller, "Pastrana Signs Law Widening Military's Role."

57. Quoted in Arnaud de Borchgrave, "Pastrana Calls Paramilitaries in Colombia a 'Cancer,'" *Washington Times*, January 10, 2001, p. A1. See also Ministry of National Defense, *Annual Human Rights and Humanitarian Law Report, 2000*, pp. 104-128.

58. For a profile of the AUC and its tactics, see Scott Wilson, "Colombia's Other Army," *Washington Post*, March 12, 2001, p. A1.

59. T. Christian Miller, "They Took No Prisoners on the Banks of the Naya," *Los Angeles Times*, May 20, 2001, p. A1.

60. Quoted in Jared Kotler, "Colombia Massacre Warnings Unheeded," Associated Press, April 21, 2001.

61. Miller, "They Took No Prisoners."

62. Scott Wilson, "Rampage by Colombian Rebels Marks New Level of Brutality," *Washington Post*, June 3, 2001, p. A 14.

63. Anthony Boadle, "Colombian Governors Slam U.S.-Backed Coca Spraying," Reuters, March 13, 2001.

64. Quoted in Ibon Villelabeitia, "Colombian Governors Slam U.S. Drug Offensive," Reuters, January 15, 2001.

65. Scott Wilson, "Battles Deferred: Colombia's Aerial Drug Campaign Showing Its Limits," *Washington Post*, March 6, 2001, p. A18.

66. "El Gran Fracaso," *Revista Cambio.com*, May 13, 2001. Also see Jason Webb, "Colombia Produces More Cocaine Than Thought—Source," Reuters, May 15, 2001.

67. Miller, "U.S. May Broaden Role in Colombia."

68. Quoted in Webb, "Colombia Produces More Cocaine than Thought—Source."

69. Quoted in Miller, "U.S. May Broaden Role in Colombia."

70. Quoted in Jared Kotler, "Colombian Candidate Questions Plan," Associated Press, August 26, 2001.

71. Phil Stewart, "Plan Colombia Not Shifting Cocaine Prices—DEA," Reuters, May 23, 2001.

72. Clawson and Lee, *Andean Cocaine Industry*, p. 219.

73. Jared Kotler, "Americans Work in Colombia War Zone," Associated Press, February 25, 2001; and Juan O. Tamayo, "U.S. Civilians Face Peril in Colombian Drug War," *Miami Herald*, February 23, 2001, p. A1.

74. For a discussion of the risks to planes and pilots, see Juan Forero, "U.S. Pilots Fight Coca in Colombia," *New York Times*, August 17, 2001, p. A8.

75. Juan O. Tamayo, "American Rescue Team Fired on in Colombia," *Miami Herald*, February 22, 2001, p. A1.

76. For general discussions, see Jonathan Wright, "Analysis—Latin Countries Wary of U.S. Role in Colombia," Reuters, August 23, 2000; Andrew Selsky, "Drug War Worries Colombia Neighbors," Associated Press, August 28, 2000; and Anthony Faiola, "Colombia's Creeping War," *Washington Post*, October 1, 2000, p. A1.

77. Quoted in Olmos, "Chavez: Colombia May Mirror Vietnam."

78. Quoted in Marco Sibaja, "Brazil Says 'Plan Colombia' Biggest Security Risk," *Reuters*, August 29, 2000.

79. Ibid.

80. Quoted in "Venezuela, Panama Voice Fears on Plan Colombia," *Reuters*, October 19, 2000.

81. Quoted in Larry Rohter, "Latin Leaders Rebuff Call by Clinton on Colombia," *New York Times*, September 2, 2000, p. A3.

82. Quoted in Peter Muello, "Colombia's Neighbors Bristle at Rebuke by U.S.," *Washington Times*, October 20, 2000, p. A17.

83. Gary Crosse, "Ecuador Official Warns U.S. of Colombia War Spillover," *Reuters*, March 2, 2001; and Eun-Kyung Kim, "Ecuador Seeks U.S. Aid in Drug War," *Associated Press*, March 2, 2001.

84. Quoted in Javier Mozzo Peña, "Venezuela's Chavez Changes, Backs Plan Colombia," *Reuters*, April 18, 2001.

85. Jared Kotler, "Colombia's Neighbors Seek U.S. Aid," *Associated Press*, April 19, 2001.

86. Quoted in ibid.

87. Quoted in "Peru's Toledo Sees Drugs Key Issue in Ties with U.S.," *Reuters*, June 7, 2001.

88. Quoted in Kotler, "Colombia's Neighbors Seek U.S. Aid."

89. Quoted in Anthony Faiola, "U.S. Flights Sow Discord in Ecuador," *Washington Post*, January 25, 2001, p. A1.

90. Ibid.

91. "Ecuadoreans Flee Colombian Armed Groups' Threats," *Reuters*, February 8, 2001; and "U.S. Senators to Visit Ecuador to Talk Plan Colombia," *Reuters*, February 19, 2001.

92. Quoted in "Official Blames Plan Colombia for Rebels in Ecuador," *Reuters*, June 8, 2001.

93. "Hundreds of Colombians Flee into Venezuela," *Reuters*, February 4, 2001.

94. "Panama Shelters Colombia Refugees after Mayor Shot," *Reuters*, January 26, 2001.

95. Lisa J. Adams, "Increase in Panama Drug Traffic," *Associated Press*, April 26, 2000; and Larry Rohter, "Latest Battleground in Latin Drug War: The Brazilian Amazon," *New York Times*, October 30, 2000, p. A1.

96. Stephen Buckley, "Brazil Fears Fallout of Drug Crackdown," *Washington Post*, October 1, 2000, p. A28.

97. Juanita Darling, "A New Battlefront Forms for the U.S. in Central America," *Los Angeles Times*, July 9, 2000, p. A1.

98. Anthony Boadle, "Colombia, U.S. Look at Andean Drug Plan," *Reuters*, February 13, 2001.

99. Quoted in Jonathan Wright, "U.S. Will Seek More South American Anti-Drug Aid," *Reuters*, November 27, 2000.

100. Will Weissert, "Cocaine War Weakens Heroin's," *Associated Press*, March 9, 2001; and Ken Guggenheim, "Less Opium Eradicated in Colombia," *Associated Press*, November 15, 2001.

101. Quoted in Wright, "U.S. Will Seek More South American Anti-Drug Aid."

102. "U.S. Increases Anti-Drug Aid to Colombia's Neighbors," *Reuters*, March 14, 2001.

103. David Rogers, "Committee Approves Foreign Aid Budget, Shifts Funds to Disease from Drug War," *Wall Street Journal*, July 27, 2001, p. A10.

104. Quoted in Scott Wilson, "Colombia to Ask Bush for Additional Funds," *Washington Post*, February 16, 2001, p. A18.

105. Quoted in Sipress, "U.S. Reassesses Colombia Aid."

106. Ibid.

107. Christopher Marquis, "America Gets Candid About What Colombia Needs," *New York Times*, February 25, 2001, p. WK1.

108. Quoted in ibid.

109. For a detailed analysis of post–Cold War nation-building failures, see Gary Dempsey (with Roger Fontaine), *Fool's Errands: Washington's Recent Encounters with Nation Building* (Washington, DC: Cato Institute, 2001).

110. Scott Wilson, "Pastrana Takes to the Road to Sell the Softer Side of Plan Colombia," *Washington Post*, May 22, 2001, p. A13.

111. Quoted in Andrew Selsky, "Colombian Chief Sells Cocaine Plan," Associated Press, May 19, 2001.

112. Quoted in Michael Easterbrook, "Drug Crop Spraying Debate Heats Up," Associated Press, August 6, 2001.

113. Rabasa and Chalk, *Colombian Labyrinth*, p. 94.

114. Scott Wilson, "Wider War in Colombia," *Washington Post*, September 6, 2001, p. A1.

115. Letter from Edward R. Harshbarger, June 5, 2001.

CHAPTER FOUR

1. Ricardo Rocha, "The Colombian Economy after 25 Years of Drug Trafficking," www.undcp.org/colombia/rocha.html.

2. Patrick L. Clawson and Rensselaer W. Lee III, *The Andean Cocaine Industry* (New York: St. Martin's Press, 1996), p. 33.

3. Paul B. Stares, *Global Habit: The Drug Problem in a Borderless World* (Washington, DC: Brookings Institution Press, 1996), p. 84.

4. Eugene E. Bouley Jr., "The Drug War in Latin America: Ten Years in a Quagmire," in *Drug War American Style: The Internationalization of Failed Policies and Its Alternatives,* ed. Jurg Gerber and Eric L. Jensen (New York: Garland, 2001), p. 183.

5. Larry Rohter, "Colombia Adjusts Economic Figures to Include Its Drug Crops," *New York Times,* June 27, 1999, p. A3.

6. For some earlier estimates, see James Painter, *Bolivia and Coca: A Study in Dependency* (Boulder, CO: Lynne Rienner, 1994), pp. 53-63; Francisco E. Thoumi, "The Economic Impact of Narcotics in Colombia," in *Drug Policy in the Americas,* ed. Peter H. Smith (Boulder, CO: Westview, 1992), pp. 57-71; Elena Álvarez, "Coca Production in Peru," in ibid., pp. 72-87; and Flavio Machicado, "Coca Production in Bolivia," in ibid., pp. 88-98.

7. Mary Jordan, "Drug Trafficking Declines on U.S-Mexico Border," *Washington Post*, September 29, 2001, p. A17.

8. Quoted in ibid.

9. Kevin Jack Riley, *Snow Job? The War Against International Cocaine Trafficking* (New Brunswick, NJ: Transaction, 1996), p. 187; and Dan Gardner, "Why Borders Don't Stop Illegal Drugs," *Ottawa Citizen,* September 5, 2000, p. A1.

10. For a good discussion of the different zones and the challenges to interdiction in each, see Riley, *Snow Job?* pp. 209-235.

11. Ibid., p. 209.

12. Ibid., pp. 215, 218-219.

13. Quoted in James Kitfield, "The Anti-Smugglers' Blues," *National Journal,* August 18, 2001, p. 2608.

14. Stares, *Global Habit,* p. 69.

15. Riley, *Snow Job?* p. 47.

16. Ibid., p. 208.

17. Ibid., p. 101.

18. Painter, *Bolivia and Coca,* p. 85.

19. Quoted in María Celia Toro, *Mexico's "War" on Drugs: Causes and Consequences* (Boulder, CO: Lynne Rienner, 1995), p. 17.

20. Clawson and Lee, *Andean Cocaine Industry,* pp. 146-147.

21. U.S. Department of State, *International Narcotics Control Strategy Report* (hereinafter *INCS Report*), March 1992, p. 1.

22. *INCS Report* , March 1991, p. 23.

23. *INCS Report,* March 1992, p. 1.

24. Ibid., p. 3.

25. *INCS Report,* March 2001, electronic version, "Overview for 2000," p. 1, www.state.gov/g/inl/rls/nrcpt/2000/index.cfm?docid=886.

26. Ibid.

27. The most recent report by the Organization of American States (OAS) gives slightly different figures for coca cultivation but shows a similar pattern. According to the OAS, the coca crop was 206,200 hectares in 1991 and 212,000 hectares in 2000. As in the State Department reports, the data indicate that cultivation went down in Peru and Bolivia over the decade but was sharply higher in Colombia. Organization of American States, *Statistical Summary on Drugs, 2001* (Washington, DC: Organization of American States, 2002), p. 21.

28. Ken Guggenheim, "U.S. Braces for Rise in Peru Coca," Associated Press, December 22, 2000.

29. *INCS Report,* March 2002, "South America," pp. IV-10, IV-44.

30. Ibid., "Canada, Mexico and Central America," pp. V-36.

31. Ibid., "South America," p. IV-29.

32. "U.S. Sees 25 Percent Surge in Coca Crops in Colombia," Reuters, March 7, 2002.

33. Ibid.

34. Quoted in George Gedda, "Bush Dismayed by Coca Production," Associated Press, March 8, 2002.

35. Clawson and Lee, *Andean Cocaine Industry,* p. 216.

36. Ibid.

37. Ibid., p. 217.

38. Riley, *Snow Job?* pp. 116-117.

39. Rensselaer W. Lee III, *The White Labyrinth: Cocaine and Political Power* (New Brunswick, NJ: Transaction, 1989), pp. 26-27.

40. LaMond Tullis, *Unintended Consequences: Illegal Drugs and Drug Policies in Nine Countries* (Boulder, CO: Lynne Rienner, 1995), p. 19.

41. Clawson and Lee, *Andean Cocaine Industry*, pp. 143-144.

42. Ibid., p. 131.

43. Ibid., p.132.

44. Riley, *Snow Job?* p. 104.

45. Ibid.

46. Quoted in Clawson and Lee, *Andean Cocaine Industry*, p. 151.

47. Mike Gray, *Drug Crazy: How We Got Into This Mess and How We Can Get Out* (New York: Random House, 1998), p. 115.

48. Clawson and Lee, *Andean Cocaine Industry*, p. 148.

49. U.S. Agency for International Development, *A Review of AID's Narcotic Control Development Assistance Program* (Washington, DC: USAID, 1996), pp. 38-39.

50. Stares, *Global Habit*, p. 66.

51. Clawson and Lee, *Andean Cocaine Industry*, p. 151.

52. Gray, *Drug Crazy*, p. 116.

53. Painter, *Bolivia and Coca*, p. 13.

54. Stares, *Global Habit*, pp. 64-65.

55. For a discussion of alternative development projects in Bolivia, see Painter, *Bolivia and Coca,* pp. 105-136.

56. Ibid., pp. 107-108.

57. Riley, *Snow Job?* pp. 140-141.

58. Quoted in "Peru's Toledo Sees Drugs Key Issue in Ties with U.S.," Reuters, June 7, 2001.

59. Ibid.

60. Jason Webb, "Colombian Peasants Not Yet Weaned from Coca," Reuters, May 30, 2001.

61. James Wilson, "Concern as Plan Colombia Fails to Cut the Supply of Illegal Drugs," *Financial Times*, January 2, 2002, p. 8.

62. Webb, "Colombian Peasants Not Yet Weaned from Coca."

63. Ibid.

64. Scott Wilson, "Coca Invades Colombia's Coffee Fields," *Washington Post*, October 30, 2001, p. A17.

65. T. Christian Miller, "In Colombia, Anti-Drug Plan Has Come a Cropper," *Los Angeles Times,* March 29, 2002, p. A1.

66. María Celia Toro, "Unilateralism and Bilateralism," in *Drug Policy in the Americas*, ed. Smith, p. 325.

67. Riley, *Snow Job?* pp. 75-76.

68. Ibid., p. 86.

69. Ibid., p. 90. Because the price markup for marijuana is not as great, marijuana retail markets are somewhat more price sensitive to the effects of source country control programs. Ibid., p. 249.

70. James A. Inciardi, *The War on Drugs: Heroin, Cocaine, Crime and Public Policy* (Palo Alto, CA: Mayfield, 1986).

71. Tullis, *Unintended Consequences*, p. 139.

72. Miguel Ruiz-Cabañas I, "Mexico's Permanent Campaign: Costs, Benefits, Implications," in *Drug Policy in the Americas*, ed.. Smith, p. 155.

73. Riley, *Snow Job?* p. 132.

74. Richard Craig, "Operation Condor: Mexico's Antidrug Campaign Enters a New Era," *Journal of Interamerican Studies and World Affairs* 22, no. 3 (August 1980): 345-363.

75. Ruiz-Cabañas I, "Mexico's Permanent Campaign," p. 155.

76. Quoted in Juan Forero, "Farmers in Peru Are Turning Again to Coca Crop," *New York Times*, February 14, 2002, p. A3.

77. Riley, *Snow Job?* p. 45. See also Richard Cowan, "How the Narcs Created Crack," *National Review*, December 5, 1986, pp. 30-31.

78. Riley, *Snow Job?* p. 45.

79. Gray, *Drug Crazy*, p. 107.

80. Juan Forero, "Europe Expands as Market for Colombia Cocaine," *New York Times*, May 29, 2001, p. A1.

81. Neil MacFarquhar, "Iran Shifts War Against Drugs, Admitting It Has Huge Problem," *New York Times*, August 18, 2001, p. A1.

82. Stares, *Global Habit*, p. 6. On the potential effect of economic globalization on narcotics trafficking, see also Tullis, *Unintended Consequences*, pp. 17-18.

83. Deborah Tedford, "Mexico Manufacturers Fight Piggyback Drug Loads," Reuters, October 4, 2001.

84. Stares, *Global Habit*, pp. 6-8, 80-84.

85. Jerry Seper, "Mexicans, Russian Mob New Partners in Crime," *Washington Times*, May 28, 2001, p. A1. Evidence of connections between Latin American drug traffickers and the Russian mob was already beginning to surface in the mid-1990s. See Douglas Farah, "Russian Mob, Drug Cartels Joining Forces," *Washington Post*, September 29, 1997, p. A1.

86. Stares, *Global Habit*, p. 13.

87. Ibid., p. 71.

88. For a detailed discussion of the importance of money laundering to the Latin American drug trade, see Robert E. Grosse, *Drugs and Money: Laundering Latin America's Cocaine Dollars* (Westport, CT: Praeger, 2001). See also David C. Jordan, *Drug Politics: Dirty Money and Democracies* (Norman: University of Oklahoma Press, 1999), pp. 99-116.

89. Stares, *Global Habit*, p. 6.

CHAPTER FIVE

1. For a discussion of the certification process and the range of sanctions, see Raphael Francis Perl, "Congress, International Narcotics, and the Anti-Drug Abuse Act of 1988," *Journal of Inter-American Studies and World Affairs* 30 (Summer-Fall 1988): 19-52.

2. Inter-American Development Bank, *Exports by Principal Markets*, www.iadb.org/int/sta/ENGLISH/staweb/index.htm#tiprof.passim.

3. Tom Carter, "Drug War Partners 'Certified' by U.S.," *Washington Times*, March 2, 2001, p. A13; and Norman Kempster, "U.S. Names 20 Nations as Its Anti-Drug Allies," *Los Angeles Times*, March 2, 2001, p. A4.

4. For a good overview of the U.S.-Samper confrontation, see Bert Ruiz, *The Colombian Civil War* (London: McFarland and Company, 2001), pp. 207-222.

5. For a discussion of the U.S. campaign of isolation, see Russell Crandall, "Explicit Narcotization: U.S. Policy Toward Colombia During the Samper Administration," *Latin American Politics and Society* 43, no. 3 (Fall 2001): 95-118.

6. For accounts of Samper's cautious embrace of the legalization option in the 1980s, see "Colombian Sees Possible Legalization of Drugs," *Chicago Tribune*, September 26, 1989, p. A10; James F. Smith, "A Bullet-Riddled Candidate Defies Fears, Seeks Colombia Presidency," *Los Angeles Times,* September 15, 1989, p. A12, and Francisco E. Thoumi, *Political Economy and Illegal Drugs in Colombia* (Boulder, CO: Lynne Rienner, 1995), p. 209.

7. Quoted in Mike Gray, *Drug Crazy: How We Got Into This Mess and How We Can Get Out* (New York: Random House, 1998), p. 125. On some of the evidence against Samper in the 1994 campaign, see ibid., p. 129.

8. Quoted in James Brooke, "Bogotá Journal: A Captain in the Drug War Wants to Call It Off," *New York Times*, July 8, 1994, p. A4.

9. Ibid.

10. Quoted in Douglas Farah, "U.S.-Bogotá: What Went Wrong?" *Washington Post*, March 3, 1996, p. A24.

11. Frank Bajak, "Colombian Leader Says Killing of Drug Boss Proves Resolve," *Chicago Sun-Times*, March 7, 1996, p. A23.

12. Quoted in Farah, "U.S.-Bogotá: What Went Wrong?"

13. Ruiz, *The Colombian Civil War*, p. 218.

14. Quoted in ibid.

15. "Samper's Clearing Prompts Questions: Action Puts Pressure on U.S. Drug Policy," *Dallas Morning News*, June 14, 1996, p. A26.

16. Mary Matheson, "Colombia Leader Tries to Please U.S. on Drugs, But Ignites Peasant Revolt," *Christian Science Monitor*, August 12, 1996, p. 7.

17. Quoted in ibid.

18. Ruiz, *The Colombian Civil War*, p. 222.

19. Quoted in Tom Brown, "Samper Tries to Cool Rhetoric on Narcotics, Then Heats It Up," *Washington Times*, March 12, 1997, p. A16.

20. Quoted in Kempster, "U.S. Names 20 Nations."

21. "Presidential Certification of Narcotics Source Countries," *Department of State Bulletin*, June 1988, p. 48.

22. Michael Isikoff, "U.S. Postponing Some Aid to Peru," *Washington Post*, March 2, 1991, p. A8. The United States employed a similar tactic—"freezing" $84 million in aid funds—to coerce Panama to amend its banking statutes. As part of Washington's ongoing campaign against money laundering and drug crimes, U.S. officials specifically sought the elimination of various laws protecting the secrecy of accounts. See Clifford Lewis, "Panama-U.S. Accord Set on Bank Records," *New York Times*, April 4, 1991, p. D1.

23. This was not the first time that U.S. officials apparently used the lure of antidrug aid to pressure Lima for policy concessions. In 1985 the Peruvian government complained bitterly that Washington was trying to link aid offers to concessions by Peru on the issue of foreign debt service payments. Bradley Graham, "Peru Complains of Strings on U.S. Aid," *Washington Post*, October 31, 1985, p. A21.

24. Quoted in Tom Carter, "OAS Pushes Own Drug War Approach," *Washington Times*, February 2, 2001, p. A11. For an earlier brief to have the OAS become more deeply involved in dealing with the drug issue instead of relying on purely U.S. initiatives, see Abraham F. Lowenthal, "The Organization of American States and Control of Dangerous Drugs," in *Drug Policy in the Americas*, ed. Peter H. Smith (Boulder, CO: Westview, 1992), pp. 305-313.

25. Quoted in Carter, "OAS Pushes Own Drug War Approach."

26. Audrey Hudson, "Senators Consider Drug-War Reprieve," *Washington Times*, February 16, 2001, p. A9.

27. See U.S. Department of State, *Peru: Country Reports on Human Rights Practices for 1993* (Washington, DC: Government Printing Office, 1994), p. 530; and U.S. Department of Justice, *Peru: Human Rights and Political Developments Through December 1994*, June 1995, www.umm.edu/humarts/ins/peru95.pdf.

28. Laurie Goering, "Production of Coca Goes Down in Peru; Nation May be Key to Andes Region," *Chicago Tribune*, February 13, 1998, p. A6; and David LaGesse, "Cocaine Plant Cultivation Goes Down in Peru and Bolivia, Up in Colombia," *Dallas Morning News*, January 7, 1998, p. 9A.

29. John J. Fialka, "U.S. Military Fights Drug War in Peru," *Wall Street Journal*, July 5, 1996, p. A4.

30. Laurie Goering, "In Peru, Battle Against Flow of Drugs Moves to Amazon River Maze," *Chicago Tribune*, June 30, 1998, p. A6.

31. See, for example, "Marco Aquino, "Drug Lord Says Montesinos Tipped Him Off on U.S. Raid," Reuters, February 2, 2001.

32. "Peru Spy Chief Tied to Mexican Drug Cartel?" Reuters, May 1, 2001.

33. "CIA Paid Millions to Montesinos Organization—Report," Reuters, August 3, 2001.

34. Quoted in Goering, "In Peru, Battle Against Flow of Drugs."

35. Patrick L. Clawson and Rensselaer W. Lee III, *The Andean Cocaine Industry* (New York: St. Martin's Press, 1996), p. 22.

36. Jacqueline Sharkey, "Noriega: How Bush Gave and Took Away," *Sunday Telegraph* (London), December 24, 1989, p. 13.

37. Robert Scheer, "Bush's Faustian Bargain with the Taliban," *Los Angeles Times*, May 22, 2001, p. A15. The Taliban's much-touted crackdown on opium poppy cultivation appears to have been little more than an illusion. Despite U.S. and UN reports that the Taliban had virtually wiped out the poppy crop in 2000-1, authorities in neighboring Tajikistan reported that the amounts coming across the border were actually increasing. Robyn Dixon, "Opium Trail Has New Stop," *Los Angeles Times* July 25, 2001, p. A1.

38. Richard Wollfe, "U.S. Prepares for Long Battle Against Heroin," *Financial Times*, January 10, 2002, p. 4.

39. Jerry Seper, "DEA Says Taliban Reaps Drug Profits," *Washington Times*, October 4, 2001, p. A4; and Betsy Pisik, "Taliban Opens Opium Floodgates Again," *Washington Times*, October 6, 2001, p. A7.

40. *U.S.-Cuban Relations in the 21st Century*, report of an Independent Task Force Sponsored by the Council on Foreign Relations, Bernard W. Aronson and William D. Rogers, co-chairs (New York: Council on Foreign Relations, 1999), pp. 26-27; and *U.S.-Cuban Relations in the 21st Century: A Follow-on Report*,

report of an Independent Task Force Sponsored by the Council on Foreign Relations, Bernard W. Aronson and William D. Rogers, co-chairs (New York: Council on Foreign Relations, 2001), pp. 25-26.

41. Anne Usher, "Bush Urged on Drug Efforts with Cuba," Associated Press, August 28, 2001.

42. Quoted in Clare Hargreaves, *Snowfields: The War on Cocaine in the Andes* (New York: Holmes and Meier, 1992) , p. 41.

43. Quoted in ibid., p. 149.

44. James Painter, *Bolivia and Coca: A Study in Dependency* (Boulder, CO: Lynne Rienner, 1994), p. 81.

45. For discussions of the connections between the drug issue and leftist insurgencies, see Alejandro Reyes, "Drug Trafficking and the Guerrilla Movement in Colombia," in Bruce M. Bagley and William O. Walker III, eds., *Drug Trafficking in the Americas* (Miami: North-South Center Press, 1996), pp. 121-130; and David Scott Palmer, "Peru, Drugs, and the Shining Path," in ibid., pp. 179-197.

46. Quoted in Alan Riding, "Colombians Grow Weary of Waging the War on Drugs," *New York Times*, February 1, 1988, p. A1.

47. Michael Gettler and Eugene Robinson, "Peru's Rebels Muddy Drug Drive," *Washington Post*, November 3, 1989, p. A31. See also Cynthia McClintock, "The War on Drugs: The Peruvian Case," *Journal of Interamerican Studies and World Affairs* 30 (Summer-Fall 1988): 127-142.

48. White House, Office of the Press Secretary, "Memorandum for the Secretary of State," Presidential Determination no. 95-15, February 28, 1995, http://clinton6.nara.gov/1995/02/1995-02-28-certification-for-major-narcotics-countries.html.

49. For a detailed discussion of that complex relationship, see Renssalaer W. Lee III, *White Labyrinth: Cocaine and Political Power* (New Brunswick, NJ: Transaction, 1989), pp. 155-184.

50. "Peter Jennings Reporting: The Cocaine War, Lost in Bolivia," *ABC News*, December 28, 1992, transcript, p. 10.

51. Michael Isikoff, "U.S. Protests Bolivia's Pick for Drug Unit," *Washington Post*, March 4, 1991, p. A8; Michael Isikoff, "Bolivian Aides Resign after Drug Charges," *Washington Post*, March 14, 1991, p. A32. For discussions of the Rico Toro episode and the intrusive role played by U.S. ambassador Robert Gelbard, see Painter, *Bolivia and Coca*, pp. 72-73; and Hargreaves, *Snowfields*, pp. 163-167. Two years later the U.S. embassy sought to force a prominent parliamentary candidate from Paz Zamora's party to quit because of alleged ties to drug traffickers. "U.S. Hand Stirs Controversy in Bolivian Election Campaign," *Financial Times*, June 4, 1993, p. 4.

52. Isikoff, "Bolivian Aides Resign After Drug Charges."

53. Quoted in Michael Easterbrook, "Drug Crop Spraying Debate Heats Up," Associated Press, August 6, 2001.

54. Quoted in Anthony Faiola, "U.S. Flights Sow Discord in Ecuador," *Washington Post*, January 25, 2001, p. A1.

55. For a discussion of Operation Leyenda, see María Celia Toro, *Mexico's 'War' on Drugs: Causes and Consequences* (Boulder, CO: Lynne Rienner, 1995), pp. 31, 64-65.

56. For a discussion of that trend, see Ethan Nadelman, *Cops Across Borders: The Internationalization of U.S. Criminal Law Enforcement* (University Park, PA: Pennsylvania State University Press, 1993).

57. U.S. Congress, "Anti-Drug Abuse Act of 1986," Public Law 99-570, HR 5484, 99th Cong., 2d sess., October 1986.

58. Toro, *Mexico's 'War' on Drugs,* p. 65.

59. Carlos Manuel Vasquez, "Misreading High Court's *Alvarez* Ruling," *Legal Times,* October 5, 1992, pp. 29-30.

60. Robert E. Grosse, *Drugs and Money: Laundering Latin America's Cocaine Dollars* (Westport, CT: Praeger, 2001), p. 141.

61. Nancy E. Roman, "House Vote Allows Mexico 90 Days to Clean Up Drug Act," *Washington Times,* March 14, 1997, p. A6.

62. Quoted in Dan Trotta, "Zedillo Calls U.S. House Vote Point 'Where We Draw the Line,' " *Washington Times,* March 15, 1997, p. A6.

63. Quoted in Sam Dillon, "U.S. Drug Agents Want Mexico to Ease 'Rules of the Game,'" *New York Times,* March 16, 1997, p. A8.

64. Quoted in Canute James, "U.S. Worried as Jamaica Rethinks Marijuana Stance," *Financial Times,* September 4, 2001, p. 3.

65. Quoted in ibid.

CHAPTER SIX

1. Quoted in Randall Mikkelsen, "Clinton Sees Drug Threat to Latin American States," Reuters, June 3, 2000.

2. Quoted in Anne Gearan, "Clinton: Colombia Aid Helps Others," Associated Press, May 2, 2000.

3. For a searing description of the violence, see María Jimena Duzán, *Death Beat: A Colombian Journalist's Life Inside the Cocaine Wars* (New York: HarperCollins, 1994).

4. Mike Gray, *Drug Crazy: How We Got into This Mess and How We Can Get Out* (New York: Random House, 1998), p. 125.

5. Ibid., p. 129.

6. Adalid Cabrera Lemuz, "Bolivia Pledges Coca Destruction," Associated Press, May 22, 2000.

7. U.S. Department of State, *International Narcotics Control Strategy Report,* March 2001, "South America," p. 6, www.state.gov/g/inl/rls/nrcpt/2000/index.cfm?docid=884.

8. U.S. Department of State, *International Narcotics Control Strategy Report,* March 2002, "South America," p. IV-10.

9. Lemuz, "Bolivia Pledges Coca Destruction."

10. This charge has been made by other officials in connection with other demonstrations as well. See Peter McFarren, "Bolivia Blames Traffickers," *Washington Times,* April 11, 2000, p. A14.

11. Lemuz, "Bolivia Pledges Coca Destruction."

12. Quoted in "Bolivia Drug Farmers Demand End to Crop Eradication," Reuters, May 21, 2000.

13. Alvaro Zuazo, "Bolivia Coca Growers Protest Gov't," Associated Press, October 7, 2000.

14. Quoted in Jonathan Wright, "U.S. Prods Bolivia to Pursue Coca Eradication," Reuters, August 18, 2000.

15. Wright, "U.S. Prods Bolivia to Pursue Coca Eradication."

16. "Cocaine Villagers Drive Out U.S.-Bolivian Raid," Washington Post, October 11, 1986, p. A18. For a discussion of episodes of resistance on the part of Bolivia coca farmers in the 1980s and 1990s, see LaMond Tullis, Unintended Consequences: Illegal Drugs and Drug Policies in Nine Countries (Boulder, CO: Lynne Rienner, 1995), pp. 99-104.

17. Clare Hargreaves, Snowfields: The War on Cocaine in the Andes (New York: Holmes and Meier, 1992), pp. 156-157.

18. Juan Bustamante, "Coca Leaf, Caught Between Custom and Crime," Reuters, July 17, 2000.

19. Patrick L. Clawson and Rensselaer W. Lee III, The Andean Cocaine Industry (New York: St. Martin's Press, 1996), p. 217.

20. Quoted in ibid., p. 218.

21. Scott Wilson, "Peru Fears Reemergence of Violent Rebels," Washington Post, December 12, 2001, p. A18.

22. Kevin Jack Riley, Snow Job? The War Against International Cocaine Trafficking (New Brunswick, NJ: Transaction, 1996), p. 155.

23. Frances Kerry, "Proponents Defend U.S. Aid to Plan Colombia," Reuters, February 2, 2001.

24. Scott Wilson, "Aerial Attack Killing More than Coca," Washington Post, January 7, 2001, p. A1. See also Juan Forero, "No Crops Spared in Colombia's Coca War," New York Times, January 31, 2001, p. A1.

25. Quoted in Anthony Boadle, "Colombian Governors Slam U.S.-Backed Coca Spraying," Reuters, March 13, 2001.

26. Wilson, "Aerial Attack Killing More than Coca." For a discussion of possible effects of the aerial spraying campaign on the public and the environment, see Sarah Peterson, "People and Ecosystems in Colombia: Casualties of the Drug War," Independent Review 6, no. 3 (Winter 2002): 427-439.

27. It is also creating tensions between Colombia and one of its neighbors. In July 2001 Ecuador formally asked Colombia to cease its aerial spraying operations along the border between the two countries. Ecuadorean officials specifically cited health concerns as the reason for the request. "Ecuador Asks Colombia to Halt Aerial Coca Fumigation," Reuters, July 19, 2001.

28. Andrew Selsky, "U.S.-Trained Colombians Destroy Labs," Associated Press, February 13, 2001.

29. Quoted in Jason Webb, "Villagers Face Ruin after Plan Colombia Kills Food," Reuters, March 9, 2001.

30. Ibid.

31. Diana Jean Schemo, "Coca Farmers in Colombia in Revolt Against Government," New York Times, August 5, 1996, p. A6.

32. Quoted in Christopher Torchia, "Colombian Coca Farmers Vent Rage," Washington Times, September 3, 1996, p. A10.

33. Quoted in Michael Easterbrook, "Drug Crop Spraying Debate Heats Up," Associated Press, August 6, 2001.

34. Jared Kotler, "Colombia Drug Policy Questioned," Associated Press, July 20, 2001.

35. Quoted in ibid.

36. Ibid.

37. Quoted in Karen DeYoung, "Colombians Protest Fumigation," *Washington Post*, August 1, 2001, p. A13.

38. Juan Forero, "Judge in Colombia Halts Spraying of Drug Crops," *New York Times*, July 30, 2001, p. A4.

39. Margarita Martinez, "Colombia Drug Crop Fumigation Resumes," Associated Press, July 31, 2001.

40. Miguel Ruiz-Cabañas I, "Mexico's Permanent Campaign: Costs, Benefits, Implications," in *Drug Policy in the Americas*, ed. Peter H. Smith (Boulder, CO: Westview, 1992), p. 158.

41. Anthony Faiola, "U.S. Allies In Drug War In Disgrace," *Washington Post*, May 9, 2001, p. A1.

42. Tullis, *Unintended Consequences,* p. 5.

CHAPTER SEVEN

1. Douglas Farah and Molly Moore, "Mexican Drug Traffickers Eclipse Colombian Cartels," *Washington Post,* March 30, 1997, p. A1.

2. Quoted in Jerry Seper, "Mexico Doubted as Drug Fighter," *Washington Times*, March 9, 1999, p. A4.

3. "U.S. Adds 12 to World Drug Kingpin Suspect List," Reuters, June 1, 2001.

4. The similarities between Colombia and Mexico were drawing comments already in the mid-1990s. See Dudley Althaus, " Drug-Trade Shift to Mexico Stirs Worry," *Washington Times*, November 11, 1997, p. A16; and John Ward Anderson, "Mexico Drug Crisis Echoes Bloody Colombia Pattern," *Washington Post*, August 11, 1997, p. A1.

5. Dan Gardner, "Drug Trade 'Rots' Away Mexican Society," *Ottawa Citizen*, September 8, 2000, p. A1. For a comparison of drug-related corruption in Colombia and Mexico, see David C. Jordan, *Drug Politics: Dirty Money and Democracies* (Norman, OK: University of Oklahoma Press, 1999), pp. 142-170.

6. For a discussion of that "permanent campaign" (as opposed to antidrug efforts confined to harvest season), see Miguel Ruiz-Cabañas I, "Mexico's Permanent Campaign: Costs, Benefits, Implications," in *Drug Policy in the Americas*, ed. Peter H. Smith (Boulder, CO: Westview, 1992), pp. 151-162.

7. Kevin Jack Riley, *Snow Job? The War Against International Cocaine Trafficking* (New Brunswick, NJ: Transaction, 1996), pp. 130-31.

8. Ibid., p. 132; Peter Reuter, "The Limits and Consequences of U.S. Foreign Drug Control Efforts," *The Annals* 521 (1992): 151-162; and Peter Reuter and David Ronfeld, *Quest for Integrity: The Mexican-U.S. Drug Issue in the 1980s* (Santa Monica, CA: RAND Corporation, 1992).

9. Riley, *Snow Job?* p. 132.

10. Ibid., pp. 182-83, 230-32.

11. Quoted in Simon Davis, "FBI Hunt for 100 Victims in Drug Gang Killing Fields," *Daily Telegraph* (London), December 1, 1999, p. 7.

12. Quoted in Mary Beth Sheridan, "Mexico Denounces U.S. Ambassador Over Drug Remarks," *Los Angeles Times*, February 26, 2000, p. A4.

13. "Mexico's Certifiable Corruption," editorial, *Washington Times*, April 12, 1998, p. B2.

14. Quoted in Tom Carter, "Helms: Certification of Drug War a 'Sham,'" *Washington Times*, February 29, 2000, p. A13.

15. John Ward Anderson, "Mexico Risks Decertification," *Washington Post*, February 10, 1999, p. A1; and Jerry Seper, "Mexico Doubted as Drug Fighter."

16. John E. Yang and Helen Dewar, "House Backs Conditional Decertification of Mexico," *Washington Post*, March 13, 1997, p. A4.

17. Peter Bate, "Clinton Urged to Decertify Mexico in Drug War," *Washington Times*, February 27, 1997, p. A11; and Nancy E. Roman, "House Vote Allows Mexico 90 Days to Clean Up Drug Act," *Washington Times*, March 14, 1997, p. A6.

18. Michael Massing, "Mexico: The Narco-State," *New York Review of Books*, June 15, 2000, p. 24.

19. Ibid.

20. Chris Kraul, "Tijuana Cartel's Kingpin Arrested," *Los Angeles Times*, March 10, 2002, p. A1; Chris Kraul, "The Collapse of Mexico's 'Invincible' Drug Cartel," *Los Angeles Times*, March 16, 2002, p. A1; and Chris Kraul, "Coastal Drug Kingpin Eyes Tijuana Turf," *Los Angeles Times*, March 19, 2002, p. A3.

21. "More Violence in Store for Mexico and Colombia," Stratfor Commentary, May 15, 2001. www.stratfor.com/latinamerica/commentary/0105142045.htm.

22. Amparo Trejo, "Mexican Drug Lords Seeking New Cartel," *Washington Post*, April 9, 2001, p. A12; and David Adams, "Mexican Drug Lords End Feud to Form Cartel," *The Times* (London), April 10, 2001, p. 19.

23. Mike Gray, *Drug Crazy: How We Got Into This Mess and How We Can Get Out* (New York: Random House, 1998), p. 134.

24. Richard B. Craig, "Mexican Narcotics Traffic: Binational Security Implications," in *The Latin American Narcotics Trade and U.S. National Security*, ed. Donald J. Mabry (New York: Greenwood, 1989), pp. 27-41.

25. Quoted in "Drug Wars: Part 2," PBS, *Frontline*, October 10, 2000, transcript, p. 6.

26. Ibid., p. 7.

27. Ibid., p. 8.

28. Ibid., p. 9.

29. "Mexico Arrests Four for Alleged Drug Cartel Ties," Reuters, September 1, 2001.

30. Silvana Paternostro, "Mexico as a Narco-Democracy," *World Policy Journal* 12, no. 1 (Spring 1995): 41-47.

31. Julia Preston, "A General in Mexico's Drug War Is Dismissed on Narcotics Charges," *New York Times*, February 19, 1997, p. A1; and John Ward Anderson, "Mexico Fires Anti-Drug Czar in Bribe Probe," *Washington Post*, February 19, 1997, p. A1.

32. Gray, *Drug Crazy*, p. 141.

33. Quoted in ibid., p. 141.

34. Sam Dillon and Craig Pyes, "Drug Ties Taint 2 Mexican Governors," *New York Times*, February 23, 1997, p. A1.

35. Testimony of Donnie R. Marshall, Acting Administrator, DEA, before the Senate Caucus on International Narcotics Control, 106th Cong., 2d sess., March 21, 2000, *drugcaucus.senate.gov/marshalltest.htm.*

36. James F. Smith, "General Accused of Aiding Drug Traffic," *Los Angeles Times,* April 6, 2001, p. A4.

37. James F. Smith, "U.S. Charges Former Mexican Governor as Cocaine Smuggler," *Los Angeles Times,* May 26, 2001, p. A16; and Tim Weiner, "U.S. Drug Indictment Chronicles King of Cancun's Fall," *New York Times,* June 11, 2001, p. A4.

38. Tim Weiner, "Mexican Jail Easy to Flee: Just Pay Up," *New York Times,* January 29, 2001, p. A7.

39. Quoted in Johanna Tuckman, "Ashcroft Praises Anti-Drug Efforts," *Washington Times,* May 22, 2001, p. A13.

40. Quoted in Sam Dillon, "Tijuana Governor Says Slaying Shows Drug Traffickers' Power," *New York Times,* February 29, 2000, p. A10.

41. "Stopping It: How Governments Try—and Fail—to Stem the Flow of Drugs," *The Economist,* July 28, 2001, p. 11.

42. "Mexican Police Official Killed," Associated Press, July 10, 2001.

43. Quoted in "Drug Wars: Part 2," p. 19.

44. "Gunmen Kill 6 People at Ciudad Juárez Restaurant," *Los Angeles Times,* August 5, 1997, p. A4.

45. "Former Senior Mexico City Cop, Brothers Executed," Reuters, May 29, 2001.

46. Quoted in Anne-Marie O'Connor, "Epidemic of Drug-Related Murders Plagues Tijuana," *Los Angeles Times,* September 10, 1996, p. A1.

47. Ibid.

48. Quoted in ibid. See also Molly Moore, "Drug Gang's Long Arm Grips Mexico," *Washington Post,* February 2, 1997, p. A1.

49. Quoted in Marisa Taylor, "DEA Ponders Pullout of Agents in Tijuana," *San Diego Union-Tribune,* April 19, 2000, p. A1.

50. Ibid.

51. Sam Dillon, "Mexico Rancher Tortured Before Mass Killing," *New York Times,* September 19, 1998, p. A6.

52. O'Connor, "Epidemic of Drug-Related Murders Plagues Tijuana."

53. "Drug Wars: Part 2," p. 32.

54. Ibid.

55. Quoted in ibid.

56. Quoted in Massing, "Mexico: The Narco-State," p. 25.

57. Quoted in Tim Golden, "Elite Mexican Drug Officers Said to Be Tied to Traffickers," *New York Times,* September 16, 1998, p. A1.

58. "Mexican Ex-Official Excoriates Anti-Drug Program as Corrupt," *Washington Post,* July 24, 1996, p. A26.

59. Sam Dillon, "Mexican Whistle-Blower Held on Drug Charge," *New York Times,* August 3, 1996, p. A5.

60. Paul B. Stares, *Global Habit: The Drug Problem in a Borderless World* (Washington, DC: Brookings Institution Press, 1996), pp. 98-99. For graphic accounts of the assassinations of Colosio and Ocampo as well as the suspicious aftermaths of

those events, see Gray, *Drug Crazy*, pp. 135-138. See also Jordan, *Drug Politics*, pp. 145-156.

61. Gray, *Drug Crazy*, p. 138.
62. Mark Stevenson, "Mexican Drug Killings Spread," *Washington Times*, December 18, 2001, p. A12.
63. Quoted in Christopher Whalen, *The Mexican Report* 3, no. 20, October 7, 1994, p. 2.
64. Quoted in "Drug Wars: Part 2," p. 32.
65. Ibid.
66. Quoted in James F. Smith, "Mexico Steps Up Its Battle on Drugs," *Los Angeles Times*, August 5, 2001, p. A1.
67. Quoted in Lorraine Orlandi, "Interview—Acting U.S. Drug Czar Lauds Mexico's Fight," Reuters, November 15, 2001.
68. Smith, "Mexico Steps Up Its Battle on Drugs."
69. Mark Stevenson, "Mexico Drug Lord Believed Executed," Associated Press, April 6, 2002.
70. Quoted in Andrea Mandel-Campbell, "Mexico Drug Barons Get a One-Way Ticket North of the Border," *Financial Times*, July 24, 2001, p. 5. Other aspects of the antidrug campaigns can produce a similar result. An upsurge of killings in Ciudad Juárez in early March 2002 appeared to be a response to increased seizures of cocaine and marijuana shipments by U.S. and Mexican authorities. See Deborah Tedford, "Spate of Mexico Slayings Seen Linked to Drug Trade," Reuters, March 11, 2002.
71. Kieran Murray, "Interview—Mexico Says Drug Trade Changing, Warns of Violence," Reuters, July 5, 2001.
72. Chris Kraul, "3 Killings May Signal Battle for Drug Trade," *Los Angeles Times*, March 20, 2002, p. A4.
73. "Mexican Official Denounces Legalization, Acting U.S. Drug Czar Cheers," "The Week Online with DRCNet," November 23, 2001, p. 13.
74. "Mexico: Legalizing Drugs Possible, Fox Says," *San Diego Union*, March 20, 2001.
75. Jorge G. Castañeda, "How We Fight a Losing War," *Newsweek*, September 6, 1999, electronic version.
76. Tuckman, "Ashcroft Praises Anti-Drug Efforts."
77. Ruiz-Cabañas I, "Mexico's Permanent Campaign," p. 160.
78. María Celia Toro, "Unilateralism and Bilateralism," in *Drug Policy in the Americas*, ed. Smith, p. 316.
79. See, for example, Molly Moore and John Ward Anderson, "Drug Trade Called Greatest Threat to Mexico," *Washington Post*, October 23, 2001, p. A1.
80. "Drug Wars: Part 2," p. 20.
81. Quoted in "U.S. Success in War Against Drugs," BBC News, May 19, 1998, transcript www.bbc.com.
82. Ibid.
83. Quoted in "Drug Wars: Part 2," p. 30.
84. For a discussion of money laundering in Mexico and its relationship to corruption in that country, see Robert E. Grosse, *Drugs and Money: Laundering Latin America's Cocaine Dollars* (Westport, CT: Praeger, 2001), pp. 136-170.

85. George W. Grayson, "Mexico: Guerrillas, Protestors Bedevil President Fox," Foreign Policy Research Institute E-Note, August 17, 2001, p. 1.

86. Lorraine Orlandi, "Analysis—Mexico Bank Explosions Raise Fear of Armed Uprising," Reuters, August 17, 2001.

87. Kieran Murray, "Mexico Targets Traffic of Drugs, Migrants in South," Reuters, July 5, 2001.

88. Massing, "Mexico: The Narco-State."

89. Mark Stevenson, "Mexican Drug Killings Spread."

CHAPTER EIGHT

1. "Pete Stark's Drug Test," *Washington Post*, October 4, 1989, p. A25.

2. "The Boot Camp Alternative," *Washington Post*, May 10, 1989, p. A20. For a withering critique of that panacea, see Tom Wicker, "Bennett Boots It," *New York Times*, May 12, 1989, p. A31.

3. Neil A. Lewis, "Passport Seizures Ordered by U.S. for Illicit Drugs," *New York Times*, March 3, 1988, p. A1.

4. Quoted in Michael Isikoff, "Suspect Planes May Become Targets," *Washington Post*, September 17, 1989, p. A12.

5. Ibid. McConnell conceded that mistakes might be made but added, "Mistakes are a part of living." More accurately, for the victims of McConnell's scheme, mistakes would have been a part of dying.

6. Richard Morin, "Many in Poll Say Bush Plan Is Not Stringent Enough; Mandatory Drug Tests, Searches Backed," *Washington Post*, September 8, 1989, p. A1.

7. Quoted in William Raspberry, "And Don't Play at War," *Washington Post*, September 8, 1989, p. A23.

8. Michael Kinsley, "Lying about Crack: Bennett's Call for Self-Censorship on Drugs," *Washington Post*, September 21, 1989, p. A25.

9. Reed Irvine, "Comfort for the Cartel?" *Washington Times*, September 21, 1989, p. F3.

10. Quoted in Steven B. Roberts, "Reagan Says Films and Music Must Stop Glorifying Drugs," *New York Times*, May 20, 1987, p. A22.

11. Tom Wicker, "The Wartime Spirit," *New York Times*, October 3, 1989, p. A23.

12. The war on drugs even includes a full-blown propaganda campaign featuring a $195 million media blitz on the evils of drug use. That figure makes the government's antidrug advertising campaign larger than the campaigns of such companies as American Express, Nike, and Sprint. Roberto Suro, "Government Blankets Media with Anti-Drug Message for Youth," *Washington Post*, July 9, 1998, p. A9

13. For a discussion of the destructive effect of wartime policies on the First Amendment and other constitutional protections of civil liberties, see Ted Galen Carpenter, *The Captive Press: Foreign Policy Crises and the First Amendment* (Washington, DC: Cato Institute, 1995), pp. 13-44, 107-119, 125-131, 141-150.

14. Budget of the United States Government, Fiscal Year 2001, "Reducing Drug Use, Trafficking, Drug-Related Crime, and Its Consequences," *frwebgate1.access.gpo.gov/cgi-bin/waisgate.cgi?WAISdocID+6088321202+1+0+0&W,6/19/01.*

15. "Stopping It: How Governments Try—and Fail—to Stem the Flow of Drugs," *The Economist*, July 28, 2001, p.11.

16. George Soros, "The Drug War Cannot be Won," *Washington Post*, February 2, 1997, p. B2.

17. Peter Andreas aptly describes these tendencies as signaling the rise of the "crimefare state," which has supplanted the Cold War–era specter of a "national security state." Peter Andreas, "The Rise of the American Crimefare State," *World Policy Journal* (Fall 1997): 38-45.

18. For good overviews, see the various chapters in *After Prohibition: An Adult Approach to Drug Policies in the 21st Century*, ed. Timothy Lynch (Washington, DC: Cato Institute, 2000); and Steven Wisotsky, *Beyond the War on Drugs: Overcoming a Failed Public Policy* (Buffalo, NY: Prometheus, 1990). Also see James Bovard, *Lost Rights: The Destruction of American Liberty* (New York: St. Martin's Press, 1994), pp. 199-257.

19. Greg Krikorian, "More Imprisoned Under Clinton," *Los Angeles Times*, February 19, 2001, p. A3.

20. Glen Frankel, "U.S. War on Drugs Yields Few Victories," *Washington Post*, June 8, 1997, p. A 1.

21. Sam Staley, *Drug Policy and the Decline of American Cities* (New Brunswick, NJ: Transaction, 1992).

22. Mark Thornton, *The Economics of Prohibition* (Salt Lake City: University of Utah Press, 1991).

23. Even some early analyses warned of the trend and noted that the war on drugs was the principal factor in the narrowing of Fourth Amendment protections. See Silas J. Wasserstrom, "The Incredible Shrinking Fourth Amendment," *American Criminal Law Review* 21, no. 3 (Winter 1984): 257-401.

24. Advocates of the drug war defend profiling even though they admit the process snares a disproportionate number of young minority males. See Clayton Searle, "Profiling in Law Enforcement," *Washington Times*, September 9, 1999, p. A 21. Searle is the president of the International Narcotics Interdiction Association.

25. Barbara Whitaker, "A Father Is Fatally Shot By the Police in His Home, and His Family Is Asking Why," *New York Times*, August 28, 1999, p. A7.

26. For some earlier examples, see Michael Cooper, "Family Says Police Raided Wrong Home," *New York Times*, May 8, 1998, p. A23; Kit R. Roane, "Again, Police in Search of Drugs Raid the Wrong Home," *New York Times*, March 21, 1998, p. B1; and Timothy Lynch, "Drug War Is Slowly Diluting Constitutional Safeguards," *Los Angeles Daily Journal*, December 2, 1998, p. A10.

27. Henry Hyde, *Forfeiting Our Property Rights: Is Your Property Safe from Seizure?* (Washington, DC: Cato Institute, 1995). See also Terrance G. Reed, "American Forfeiture Law: Property Owners Meet the Prosecutor," Cato Institute Policy Analysis no. 179, September 29, 1992; and Steven Duke, "The Drug War and the Constitution," in *After Prohibition*, ed. Lynch, pp. 51-57.

28. Stephen Labaton, "Congress Raises Burden of Proof on Asset Forfeitures," *New York Times*, April 12, 2000, p. A1.

29. Lisa S. Dean, "Deadbeat Privacy Rights," *Washington Times*, May 28, 2000, p. B5.

30. Diane Cecilia Weber, "Warrior Cops: The Ominous Growth of Paramilitarism in American Police Departments," Cato Institute Briefing Paper no. 50, August 26,

1999, pp. 3-5; and David B. Kopel, "Militarized Law Enforcement: The Drug War's Deadly Fruit," in *After Prohibition*, ed. Lynch, pp. 61-88.

31. For a discussion of the attempts during the 1980s to enlist the military as a major participant in both the foreign and domestic phases of the war on drugs, see Ted Galen Carpenter and R. Channing Rouse, "Perilous Panacea: The Military in the Drug War," Cato Institute Policy Analysis no. 128, February 15, 1990.

32. Bradley Graham, "Drug Control Chief Won't Let Pentagon Just Say No," *Washington Post*, November 24, 1997, p. A17.

33. Stephen Chapman, "When the War on Drugs Comes Home," *Washington Times*, August 26, 1997, p. A13.

34. Quoted in "Some Lawmakers Clueless About Life on the Border," *San Antonio Express-News*, May 25, 1998, p. B4.

35. Weber, "Warrior Cops," p. 5. See also John Johnson, "Weeding Out Pot Farms from Aloft," *Los Angeles Times*, September 6, 2000, p. A1.

36. Quoted in "Technology Transfer From Defense: Concealed Weapon Detection," *National Institute of Justice Journal*, no. 229 (August 1995): 35.

37. "Steve Forbes on Drugs," Issues 2000, www.*issues2000.org/ Steve_Forbes_Drugs.htm.*

38. Quoted in E. Michael Myers, "Dole Calls Clinton Soft on Drugs," *Washington Times*, August 26, 1996, p. A1.

39. Ibid.

40. Bill McCollum, "Waving the White Flag in Drug War?" *Washington Times*, March 10, 1998, p. A1. Also see "A Timid War on Drugs," editorial, *Washington Times*, December 29, 1997, p. A14.

41. "Orrin Hatch on Drugs," Issues 2000, www.issues2000.org/Orrin-Hatch-Drugs.htm.

42. *Report of the International Narcotics Control Board for 1997*, Chapter 1, Section B, paragraph 8, www.incb.org/e/ar/1997/chpt1.h.

43. Ibid., paragraph 10.

44. Ibid., paragraph 13.

45. For a discussion of the censorship agenda in the INCB report, see Phillip O. Coffin, "A Duty to Censor: UN Officials Want to Crack Down on Drug War Protestors," *Reason*, (August-September 1998): 54. For examples of the Report's hostility toward even mild advocacy of liberalizing the drug laws, see *Report of the International Narcotics Control Board for 1997*, Chapter 1, Section B, paragraphs 16, 18, 20, 21, 22, 25 and 26.

46. Quoted in "U.S. Drug Czar Takes Campaign to the United Nations," Reuters, May 26, 2000.

47. Mary Anastasia O'Grady, "American Coke-Heads Underwrite Colombia's Misery," *Wall Street Journal*, August 20, 1999, p. A11.

48. In opposing medical marijuana, Forbes insisted, "America must not be made safe for Colombian-style drug cartels." "Steve Forbes on Drugs." For an excellent discussion of the medical marijuana initiatives and their critics, see Alan Bock, *Waiting to Inhale: The Politics of Medical Marijuana* (Washington, DC: Seven Locks Press, 2000).

49. Quoted in Hendrik Hertzberg, "The Pot Perplex," *The New Yorker*, January 76, 1997, p. 4.

50. "500 Drug Geniuses," editorial, *Wall Street Journal*, June 10, 1998, p. A18.

51. That measure was the Agents Identities Protection Act, passed in 1982 following the "outing" of several agents by former CIA agent Philip Agee and the death of one of those agents. For a discussion, see Carpenter, *The Captive Press*, p. 128.

52. Don Van Natta, "Drug Office Will End Scrutiny of TV Scripts," *New York Times*, January 20, 2000, p. A11.

53. "U.S. Drug Office Gives 6 Magazines Anti-Drug Discounts," *Los Angeles Times*, April 2, 2000, p. A7.

54. Mark Jurkowitz, "Online Journalist Tangles with Feds over Antidrug Ad Policy," *Boston Globe*, April 7, 2000, p. D12.

55. Quoted in ibid.

56. Ibid.

57. Lance Gray, "White House Uses Drug-Message Site to Track Inquiries," *Washington Times*, June 21, 2000, p. A3.

58. Ted Bridis, "Clinton Tells Drug Office to Stop Using 'Web Bug,'" *Wall Street Journal*, June 22, 2000, p. B13.

59. Melissa Healy, "Parents Reach Out to Informant Daughter," *Los Angeles Times*, September 9, 1999, p. A3.

60. Ibid.

61. "It's Time to Rally the Troops in Our War on Drugs," letter to the editor, *Washington Times*, June 20, 1998, p. A14.

62. Quoted in "Sex, Drugs and Consenting Adults" with John Stossel, *ABC News Special Report*, May 26, 1998, transcript #98052601-j13, p. 14.

63. Terrence Hunt, "Clinton Signs National Drunk-Driving Bill," Associated Press, October 23, 2000.

64. "Americans Are Fed Up with Drunken Drivers," letter to the editor, *Washington Times*, February 5, 1998, p. A14.

65. Lance Gay, "Drinking Passengers Hit by Senate Vote," *Washington Times*, March 6, 1998, p. A6.

66. Christopher S. Wren, "Alcohol or Drug Link Seen in 80% of Jailings," *New York Times*, January 9, 1998, p. A11.

67. Critics have correctly pointed out that a prohibitionist strategy—or even a "prohibition-lite" approach of very high taxes on tobacco products—would create (and in some foreign countries already have created) a lucrative black market. See Bruce Bartlett, "Hiking Cigarette Taxes Is Good for (Illegal) Business," *Wall Street Journal*, May 12, 1998, p. A22; Nick Brookes, "Black-Market Bonanza," *Washington Post*, May 20, 1998, p. A25; and Robert Levy, "High Taxes Fuel Black Market," *USA Today*, January 5, 1999, p. A16. Reminiscent of tactics in the war on drugs, federal authorities have now established a cigarette smuggling "war room" in the U.S. Federal Building in Raleigh, North Carolina. Walter E. Williams, "Smuggling Smokes," *Washington Times*, August 5, 2000, p. A12.

68. An especially worrisome development is the growing tendency of prominent drug warriors to link illegal drugs and the two legal products. In a *Washington Post* op-ed arguing that marijuana is a hard drug, former Health, Education, and Welfare secretary Joseph Califano makes that linkage on several occasions. For instance, in a passage arguing that marijuana was a "gateway" to harder drugs,

he nevertheless adds the observation that "virtually all teens who smoke marijuana also smoke nicotine cigarettes and drink alcohol." Later he argues that marijuana affects the level of dopamine in the brain and "may prime the brain to seek substances such as heroin and cocaine that act in a similar way." But then he adds a comment that undermines his ostensible argument, noting that studies have found that nicotine also affects dopamine levels. One must at least consider the possibility that Califano is building the foundation for the case that not only is marijuana a dangerous drug that must remain outlawed but that alcohol—and especially cigarettes—must logically be treated the same way. Joseph A. Califano, "Marijuana: It's a Hard Drug," *Washington Post*, September 30, 1997, p. A21. See also Mathea Falco, "Alcohol: Kids' Drug of Choice," *Washington Post*, May 27, 2000, p. A27.

69. Betsy Pisik, "WHO Leader Seeks Treaty in Tobacco Fight," *Washington Times*, October 21, 1998, p. A11.

70. Sue Anne Pressley, "High School Smokes Out Tobacco Users," *Washington Post*, September 25, 2000, p. A3.

71. Quoted in Will Hardie, "WHO Warns of Youth Alcohol Danger in Internet Age," Reuters, February 19, 2001.

72. Quoted in "Drug Wars: Part 2," PBS, *Frontline*, October 10, 2000, transcript, p. 33.

73. Peter Slavin, "Drug Roadblocks Struck Down," *Washington Post*, November 29, 2000, p. A4.

74. For a blistering critique of Giuliani's initiative, see Stephen Chapman, "Exceeding Reasonable Limits," *Washington Times*, February 27, 1999, p. D8. See also Alan Finder, "Questions Over City's Plan Against Drunk Drivers," *New York Times*, January 23, 1999, p. A16.

75. See Weber, "Warrior Cops"; and Timothy Egan, "Soldiers of the Drug War Remain on Duty," *New York Times*, March 1, 1999, p. A1.

76. Joe Davidson, "U.S., in Anti-Drug Move, Plans to Lower Threshold for Money-Transfer Reports," *Wall Street Journal*, May 20, 1997, p. A4; and Richard Rahn, "Treasury's Newest Assault on Privacy," *Investor's Business Daily*, August 12, 1997, p. A28.

77. Solveig Singleton, "Let Federal Eyes Ogle Your Account?" *Washington Times*, February 10, 1999, p. A15.

CHAPTER NINE

1. David Bank, "Counterattack: Soros, Two Rich Allies Fund a Growing War on the War on Drugs," *Wall Street Journal*, May 30, 2001, p. A1.

2. "Jamaica Looks at Crime of Marijuana Use," Reuters, May 23, 2001.

3. Canute James, "U.S. Worried as Jamaica Rethinks Marijuana Stance," *Financial Times*, September 4, 2001, p. 3; and David Gonzalez, "Panel Urges Legalization of Marijuana in Jamaica," *New York Times*, September 30, 2001, p. A9.

4. Quoted in Sebastian Rotella, "Uruguayan Leader Urges Legalizing Drugs," *Philadelphia Inquirer*, February 11, 2001, online edition.

5. Jorge G. Castañeda, "How We Fight a Losing War," *Newsweek*, September 6, 1999, electronic version.

6. Quoted in John Rice, "Mexican President Vicente Fox Discusses Drug Legalization in Newspaper Interview," Associated Press, March 19, 2001.

7. For a discussion of the Netherlands policy and U.S. hostility toward it, see Ineke Haen Marshall and Henk Van De Bunt, "Exporting the Drug War to the Netherlands and Dutch Alternatives," in Jurg Gerber and Eric L. Jensen, eds., *Drug War American Style: The Internationalization of Failed Policies and Its Alternatives* (New York: Gardner, 2001), pp. 197-217; and Robert J. MacCoun and Peter Reuter, *Drug War Heresies: Learning from Other Vices, Times, and Places* (Cambridge: Cambridge University Press, 2001), pp. 238-264.

8. "Dutch to Open Drug Drive-Thru Shops," Associated Press, May 1, 2001; "Dutch Approve Coffee and Pot for German Tourists," Reuters, May 31, 2001; and Suzanne Daley, "The New Reefer Madness: Drive-Through Shops," *New York Times*, May 28, 2001, p. A4.

9. "Belgium Agrees to Legalize Cannabis," Associated Press, January 19, 2001.

10. Joel Baglole, "O Cannabis: Ottawa May Soon Ease Up on Its Marijuana Laws," *Wall Street Journal*, June 5, 2001, p. A18.

11. Jim Burns, "Canada Legalizes Marijuana for Medicinal Purposes," CNS News.Com, July 30, 2001, E-Brief@topica.email-publisher.com.

12. Pew Research Center for the People and the Press, "74% Say Drug War Being Lost," February 2001, part 1, p. 1.

13. Ibid., p. 3.

14. Ibid., part 2, p. 4.

15. Ibid., p. 1.

16. Ibid., part 1, pp. 2-3.

17. "Drug Wars: Part 2," PBS, *Frontline*, October 10, 2000, transcript, p. 35.

18. For a good, concise discussion, see "Collateral Damage: The Drug War Has Many Casualties," *The Economist*, July 28, 2001, pp. 12-13.

19. The definitive accounts of early twentieth century drug policies are David T. Courtwright, *Dark Paradise: Opiate Addiction in America Before 1940* (Cambridge, MA: Harvard University Press, 1982); and David F. Musto, *The American Disease: Origins of Narcotics Control*, expanded edition (New York: Oxford University Press, 1987).

20. Mathea Falco, *The Making of a Drug-Free America: Programs That Work* (New York: Times Books, 1992), p. 17.

21. Scott MacDonald, *Dancing on a Volcano: The Latin American Drug Trade* (New York: Praeger, 1988), p. 150.

22. Jude Webber, "Peru to Push Powell for New Anti-Drug Flights," Reuters, August 21, 2001; see also George Gedda, "Colombia Chief Seeks Trade Benefits," Associated Press, November 8, 2001.

Index

Page references in italic refer to tables.